CHOCLATIQUE®

150 Simply Elegant Desserts

Ed Engoron

with Mary Goodbody

Photography by Jason Varney

RUNNING PRESS
PHILADELPHIA · LONDON

In
honor
of

JDV'S
FIFTIETH

Thanks for twenty-seven years of inspiration, innovation,
dedication, perspiration, and demanding expectations.

Acknowledgments

A cookbook is a difficult task to undertake. Thank you, Joan, Dave, Karen, Wayne, Iisha, Erin, and Victor,
for patiently testing, tasting, documenting, and proofing the many rounds of food and copy.
Special thanks to Jane, Mary, and Geoff for supporting my world of chocolate.

Printed in China

Books published by Running Press are available at special discounts for bulk purchases in the United States by corporations, institutions,
and other organizations. For more information, please contact the Special Markets Department at the Perseus Books Group, 2300 Chestnut
Street, Suite 200, Philadelphia, PA 19103, or call (800) 810-4145, ext. 5000, or e-mail special.markets@perseusbooks.com.

ISBN 978-0-7624-3964-5
Library of Congress Control Number: 2011929082

E-book ISBN 978-0-7624-4360-4

9 8 7 6 5 4 3 2 1
Digit on the right indicates the number of this printing

Cover design and interior design by Frances J Soo Ping Chow
Food Stylist: Carrie Purcell
Assistant Food Stylist: Sarah Abrams
Typography: Fairfield, Helvetica, and Memoir

Additional photo credits: p11 © Tom Grundy/iStock Photos,
p32 © Brasil2/iStock Photos, p125 © Gene Krebs/iStock Photos

Running Press Book Publishers
2300 Chestnut Street
Philadelphia, PA 19103-4371

Visit us on the web!
www.runningpresscooks.com

CONTENTS

Acknowledgments 2

Foreword 5

Introduction 6

Chapter 1: All About Chocolate 9

Chapter 2: The Choclatique Method 15

Chapter 3: The Five Basic Ganaches 25

Chapter 4: Chocolates Out of the Box! 35

Chapter 5: Let Them Eat Chocolate Cake and Cupcakes 49

Chapter 6: Smooth and Creamy Chocolate Cheesecakes 83

Chapter 7: Chocolate Cookies, Brownies, and Bars—Oh My 103

Chapter 8: Chocolate Pies and Tarts 131

Chapter 9: Chocolate Puddings, Custards, Mousses, and Trifles 153

Chapter 10: Chocolate Drinks 177

Chapter 11: Chocolate Ice Creams 191

Chapter 12: Chocolate Candies 203

Chapter 13: Morning Chocolate 215

Chapter 14: Essentials 227

Timeline of Chocolate Innovation 250

Where Can I Find That Keon Stuff? 252

Chocolate Glossary 262

Conversion Charts 264

Index 266

FOREWORD

Ed Engoron is fearless in his pursuit of chocolate flavor thrills. His spirit of adventure

infuses his inventiveness when it comes to building a dessert, whether it's an American

classic or a French delicacy.

The combination of flavors he uses to take chocolate to a new level seems endless.

In his book *Choclatique*, he takes us on a culinary roller coaster ride around the world of

desserts from San Francisco, Rio, and Tokyo to Paris, Rome, and more, tingling our pal-

lets till tears flow. If you like to play in the kitchen, and whether or not you have skill,

there is something in Ed Engoron's *Choclatique* for you and for everyone.

—GARY GUITTARD
GUITTARD CHOCOLATE COMPANY
BURLINGAME, CALIFORNIA

INTRODUCTION

THERE IS NO EDIBLE SUBSTANCE MORE FANTASTIC THAN CHOCOLATE. IT IS NATURE'S PERFECT FOOD, WHETHER CONSUMED AS A BAR OR USED AS AN INGREDIENT TO MAKE COOKIES, BROWNIES, CAKES, CUSTARDS, ICE CREAMS, DRINKS, AND MORE. IT IS EQUALLY LUSCIOUS AT ALMOST ANY TEMPERATURE—WARM, HOT, CHILLED, OR FROZEN. THERE IS NOTHING I CAN THINK OF THAT EVEN COMES CLOSE TO CHOCOLATE. CHOCOLATE TRULY IS THE NECTAR OF THE GODS.

I owe many of the adventures in my life to food, especially chocolate, strange as that may sound. By a stroke of unparalleled good fortune (and no small amount of hard work, it must be admitted), I have the best job in the world. For more than thirty-five years I have eaten my way through 130 countries, devoured chocolate in most, and have met and been fed by everyone from the locals on an isolated cacao plantation to the royal families of Malaysia and Thailand. I have dined in humble one-room shacks and splendid dining rooms and been welcomed by world-famous chefs, bakers, and chocolatiers.

I have sipped bittersweet, rough-milled chocolate under a jungle canopy in Brazil. I recall a snowy Christmas Eve in Bruges, Belgium, when I bit into fresh, creamy chocolate truffles that brought tears to my eyes. I've eaten chocolate mole in sleepy little Oaxacan towns and in bustling Mexico City restaurants, and enjoyed freshly baked croissants au chocolat at the Lancaster Hotel off the fabled Champs-Élysées in Paris. And I have been fortunate enough to savor each and every one of his wonderful confections with M. Robert Linxe, long worshipped as the premier Paris chocolatier of La Maison du Chocolat.

Chocolate mousses, chocolate ice creams, chocolate crêpes, chocolate cakes, chocolate cookies, even chocolate pasta . . . if it's chocolate, I've been there, seen it, done it, made it, and eaten it. I've circled the globe in my pursuit to understand chocolate and bring its secrets home for an ever-more discerning and demanding American consumer.

You might say that I have an unnatural passion for or even an addiction to chocolate, which I reason is understandable because there are few foods that arouse such passion in people across the globe. It is a passion that goes beyond the love for the "sweetness" of ordinary candies or desserts. After all, most people don't crave caramel, whipped cream, or bubble gum on its own. Chocolate is, well, different—very different for the true chocoholic. Just thinking about chocolate can evoke an extremely pleasurable, almost sexual, response. After all, one of the most pleasant effects of eating chocolate is that "great feeling" that most people experience after indulging. There are more than three hundred known chemicals naturally occurring in chocolate, and these contribute to its ability to elevate moods and satisfy the deepest craving. Since they cracked the cacao (kah KOW) gene, scientists have been working to isolate the specific chemical compounds that may explain some of the pleasurable effects and health benefits of consuming chocolate.

The more than 150 recipes in *Choclatique* all call for simple, available, and inexpensive ingredients, as well as a few extravagant ones, and are all based on chocolate *ganache*, which is the essential building block for our recipes. We rely on five ganaches, and once you master the simple principles of working with ganache, you can produce stunning, professional-looking chocolate creations

as well as simpler luscious chocolate delights just minutes before dinner.

As you venture through the pages, you will see Chef's Secrets, and icons that delineate G gluten free, D dairy free, and V vegan. This book is all about the pure indulgence and the love of chocolate, but because we are sensitive to chocolate lovers with special health needs, those on special diets will also learn about great-tasting chocolate.

Take every opportunity you can to nibble a piece of chocolate or sip a nice cup of hot cocoa. Wouldn't the world be a better and healthier place if everyone had a little chocolate every day?

How about *now*?

1

ALL ABOUT CHOCOLATE

A Little Chocolate History

THE HISTORY OF HOW CHOCOLATE GREW FROM A LOCAL MESOAMERICAN BEVERAGE INTO A GLOBAL INDULGENCE ENCOMPASSING MANY CULTURES AND CONTINENTS IS A "SWEET" STORY. THE EXOTIC SECRETS OF THE CACAO TREE WERE DISCOVERED ABOUT TWO THOUSAND YEARS AGO IN THE VAST TROPICAL RAINFORESTS OF CENTRAL AND SOUTH AMERICA.

The first cultures known to have made chocolate were the ancient Mayans and Aztecs in Mexico and Central America. These people ceremoniously ground cacao beans—aka *cocoa beans*—from the pod of the cacao tree and maize (Indian corn) with various spices (cinnamon and chile peppers) to make a spicy, frothy, somewhat bitter beverage with stimulant and restorative properties. It was rumored that King Montezuma drank *xocolatl* from solid golden goblets fifty times a day, giving him the power to make love to many of his 250 wives nightly. *Xocolatl* was reserved for warriors, nobility, and priests. The Aztecs esteemed its reputed ability to confer wisdom and vitality. Taken as a fermented drink, chocolate was also used in religious ceremonies. The sacred concoction was associated with Xochiquetzal, the goddess of fertility. Who would have imagined that chocolate was the Viagra of yesteryear?

Cacao horticulture started to spread during the colonial age, as did the spread of cacao beans and of chocolate itself. Christopher Columbus was most likely the first European to come in contact with cacao. On August 15, 1502, on his fourth and final voyage to the Americas, Columbus and his crew encountered a large dugout canoe near the island of Guanaja, off the coast of what is now Honduras. The canoe was one of the largest native boats the Spaniards had seen. It was "as long as a galley" and was filled with local goods for trade—including cacao beans. Columbus's crew seized the vessel and its goods, kidnapped its skipper as their guide, and the rest is chocolate history.

What Columbus and the other members of his crew didn't know was that cocoa beans were actually the local currency of the time. Aztec taxation was levied in cacao beans. One hundred cacao beans could buy a slave, and twelve bought the services of a courtesan. As recently as the late nineteenth century, some parts of the New World continued to use cacao beans as currency; they held a value higher than gold. Fortunately for the Spaniards, the Catholic Church categorized chocolate as a drink and not a food, which allowed them to enjoy the brown almonds from the Americas even during periods of fasting.

Eventually, the chocolate drink's popularity spread throughout Europe, and within a hundred years, the love of chocolate spread throughout the rest of world. After all these years, chocolate still remains one of the world's favorite flavors.

DOES CHOCOLATE HAVE A TEMPER?

Turning the treasure of the cacao bean harvest into great chocolate starts with a great tree and requires time, effort, knowledge, and much artistry. We have contracts with cacao plantations around the world. Once we have the beans in hand, converting the cacao into chocolate is a complex and time-consuming process. An individual piece of chocolate can take anywhere from two to six days to complete.

The key to excellent chocolate flavor is the roasting process, very similar to that used for coffee beans. Large, rotating ovens roast the beans at temperatures below 250°F to release the rich aromas slowly and to enhance the delicious flavors. Many of our chocolate blends contain up to seventeen different types of beans, all slowly roasted for maximum flavor. Roasting can take up to two and a half hours, depending on the variety of cacao and the amount of internal moisture.

As the beans toss about in the oven, they lose much of their moisture. Eventually, they turn a deep brown color. The roasting process makes the cacao shells brittle so that when the beans cool, the winnowing machine can begin its job. The blades crack the thin shells to get at the interior of the beans. Fans blow away, or "winnow," the empty husks, and the remaining broken bean bits, called *nibs*, pass through a series of sieves, which strain and sort the nibs according to size.

The nibs themselves are made up of about 53 percent cocoa butter and 47 percent pure cocoa solids. Separating these two substances takes a lot of work and high pressure. The nibs are milled—crushed by heavy steel rollers and discs. This process generates enough friction and heat to liquefy the nibs into a thick paste called *chocolate liquor*. The chocolate liquor is placed in a huge, hydraulic press that squeezes out the cocoa butter. The ivory-colored fat drains away through metallic sieves and is held so that it can be added to dark or milk chocolate formulations or used as the base for white chocolate. (At Choclatique, it is called Snowy White Chocolate—and is as rich, creamy, and sublime as the best white chocolate should be.) Once the cocoa butter is extracted and pressed, the remaining solid cocoa is ground into cocoa powder—the product used in our chocolate beverages and baking chocolate.

As do all chocolate makers, our Chocolate Studios blend chocolate liquor with sugar, vanilla, and reserved

DID YOU KNOW?

It takes about twenty-five to thirty-five cacao beans to make one ounce of chocolate.

cocoa butter (and milk solids, in the case of milk or white chocolate) to form our basic chocolates. The cocoa butter keeps the chocolate solid at room temperature, which explains why chocolate doesn't spoil—and why it melts in the warmth of your mouth with a lush and indescribable sensation.

The raw mixture of ingredients is churned until it becomes a coarse, brown powder called "crumb." The chocolate crumb goes through a series of steel rollers stacked one on top of another. These fuse the tiny milk, cocoa, and sugar particles within the crumb. (We blend this mixture very carefully and precisely to prevent the chocolate from becoming coarse and grainy on the one hand, or pasty and gummy on the other.)

The refined chocolate paste is poured into a vat, where a large, heavy roller kneads, blends, and grinds the mixture. This is the conching process. Agitating this paste smooths out the sugar grains, giving the chocolate a silky texture. It also aerates the paste to allow acids and moisture to evaporate to create our mellow, well rounded, authentically American flavor. This process can take up to four days to complete!

Finally, the refined chocolate is cooled and warmed repeatedly in a process called "tempering." This gives chocolate its glossy sheen and ensures that it will melt properly when we are ready to make our confections.

THE CARE AND WELFARE OF CHOCOLATE

Chocolate should be stored in its original wrapping in a cool, dry, airy place, at a recommended temperature of 62°F to 70°F.

Since chocolate is notorious for absorbing odors, it should not be stored in any container or near any items that might impart an aroma. Avoid storing chocolate in the refrigerator or in a warm room. Try to avoid sudden changes of temperature. If stored properly, most solid chocolate has a shelf life of more than one year—darker varieties will keep a little longer.

Sometimes chocolate will develop white or gray surface clouds or casts called "bloom." This is the result of

The flavor complexities of dark chocolate are like red wine . . . on steroids. Exploring each of these flavor thrills can be an enlightening, educational experience—and lots of fun. Tasting chocolate involves all of the senses: sight, smell, touch, hearing, and, of course, taste.

I find the best time to taste chocolate is between meals, when you are neither hungry nor satiated. At Choclatique, we do our most serious tasting at ten o'clock in the morning. Don't try to taste too many chocolate samples at

DID YOU KNOW?

No state in the continental U.S. grows cacao. Hawaii is the only state that grows it and only a small amount of high-quality cacao beans are cultivated there to produce chocolate.

improper storage and is harmless. If your chocolate blooms, you can get rid of it by melting the chocolate. While it won't regain its sheen unless you temper it, you can use the chocolate in baking. The bloom does not render the chocolate unusable or inedible.

HOW TO TASTE CHOCOLATE

Good dark chocolate should always be shared, so grab your favorite chocolate-loving friend, light a candle or two, open a bottle of red wine, and experience something new with our dark chocolate-tasting kit. Go to www.Choclatique.com/products/tasting-kit and type in the username "Great Tasting Chocolate" for more information.

the same time. The palate is very sensitive to rich flavors and fat; depending on the tolerance of the individual, it may quickly lose its tasting edge.

Try to limit your tasting to no more than six to eight dark chocolate samples, four to six milk chocolate samples, and four to six white chocolate samples at a time.

Chocolate samples should not touch one another and should be spaced about a half inch apart to avoid any flavor transference. When setting up the tasting, don't touch the samples with your bare fingers; use a pair of tongs or, if you want to be a little fussy, wear a pair of clean, white cotton gloves (we call them "chocolate gloves"). Let the following serve as your guide, so that you can extract the full flavor potential from dark chocolate.

WHERE CACAO GROWS

Cacao trees grow naturally with little seasonality in lowland, tropical rainforest areas along the banks of rivers. They need a fairly consistent climate with temperatures ranging from 70°F to 90°F year-round, and never any lower than 60°F. They require between forty and one hundred inches of annual rainfall, well distributed throughout the year, with no fewer than four inches of rainfall in any single month. Finally, cacao trees grow best below one thousand feet above sea level, and never higher than three thousand feet.

All of this means that they grow only in the tropics—with the best chocolate coming from trees that grow almost exclusively within ten degrees latitude of the equator, between the Tropics of Cancer and Capricorn, and only in places that are not too mountainous and do not have monsoons or droughts.

Unlike coffee and coca, cacao does not damage the rainforest—it doesn't require open land and, in fact, needs the shade of the rainforest to grow. Some larger, commercial plantation owners may clear some of the forest to facilitate harvesting the pods.

- Find a quiet place away from extraneous background noises and aromas. Being able to concentrate on what you are tasting will facilitate flavor detection.

- Cleanse your palate. To fully taste the subtleties of dark chocolate's complex flavor, your mouth, cheeks, and tongue should not contain leftover flavors. Brush your teeth about thirty minutes before starting your tasting and, if necessary, eat a slice of apple or an unsalted cracker between tastes.

- You should start with a minimum of a quarter ounce of chocolate for each flavor tasted. A chocolate piece that is too small will not allow you to detect all of the subtle nuances as the chocolate slowly melts in your mouth. Flavor notes gradually evolve and unfold on the tongue rather than open up in one large flavor explosion.

- The chocolate should be kept at room temperature.

- Look at the quality of the chocolate. Dark chocolate should be deeply shiny and blemish-free. There should be no evidence of bloom.

- Break the chocolate, listening for a resounding snap. That's the sign of fine dark chocolate.

- Smell the chocolate at the break point. As with most foods, aroma is an important indicator of flavor. Deeply breathe in the scent. Inhaling will prime the tongue for the incoming chocolate.

- Place the chocolate on the middle of your tongue and let it melt. This allows the chocolate flavor to distribute evenly in the mouth and excite all the taste receptors. As the chocolate begins to melt, concentrate on the flavors coating your tongue and enveloping your mouth

- Notice the developing of flavors and how the flavors evolve. Is the chocolate too sweet or too bitter? Is it heavy or light in flavor? Do any changes in flavor occur? Is there a strong reminder lingering in your mouth, or does it quickly vanish? Note any metallic or unpleasant flavors in the finish. This is a sign of old, stale, or poorly made chocolate.

• Take note of how the chocolate leaves the palate feeling. Is the texture smooth or grainy? Is the texture constant? This is called mouthfeel.

• Do it again: Repeat the process with a different dark chocolate. Be sure to cleanse your palate thoroughly with room-temperature water before moving on to the next chocolate.

HEALTH AND CHOCOLATE?

You've Got to Be Kidding!

Recent medical research has linked the antioxidants found in cacao—the fruit from which chocolate is made—to decreases in blood pressure and reductions of "bad" cholesterol levels.

Chocolate is a known stimulant and is also thought to be an aphrodisiac. The darker the chocolate, the richer it is in flavanols, which many physicians and nutritionists say are beneficial to your health.

The small amount of caffeine found in chocolate (1.4 ounces of chocolate = 1 cup of decaffeinated coffee) combined with theobromine, a weak stimulant also present in chocolate, provides the "lift" that chocolate eaters experience. Although no conclusive medical proof exists yet, phenylethylamine, also present in chocolate, is reputed to be a mood elevator and an antidepressant.

Scientists are still developing their opinions on the health benefits of dark chocolate. It is probably not a good idea to replace your daily intake of fruits and vegetables with a six-layer frosted chocolate cake, whether dark or milk chocolate—but the research has certainly reduced the stigma of a moderate daily chocolate habit.

WOMEN ARE HOT FOR GOURMET CHOCOLATE

According to Italian scientists (you've got to love the Italians when it comes to *amore* and chocolate), women who eat chocolate have better sex lives than those who don't. A group of urologists at the San Raffaele Hospital in Milan questioned 163 women about their chocolate consumption and found that women who had a daily intake of chocolate showed higher levels of desire than women who didn't indulge. The study also revealed that chocolate is less like a food and more like a drug. Italian doctors believe eating chocolate may actually improve a woman's sexual functions and attitude.

So, don't wait for Valentine's Day to buy a box of chocolate, or you might miss out on a lot of romance, love, and sex.

2

THE CHOCOLATIQUE METHOD

THE RECIPES IN THIS BOOK ARE BASED ON FIVE DIFFERENT GANACHES THAT BECOME ESSENTIAL BUILDING BLOCKS. THE GANACHES ARE EASY TO MAKE AND KEEP FOR MONTHS IN THE REFRIGERATOR. IF YOU CAN BOIL WATER, YOU CAN MAKE A PROFESSIONAL-TASTING GANACHE. BEST OF ALL, WITH ONE OR TWO OF THESE AT YOUR FINGERTIPS, YOU CAN CREATE A CHOCOLATE DESSERT IN A FLASH.

I first discovered this method of working with chocolate while preparing a chocolate banquet on the Mexican Riviera one hot, humid summer afternoon. I was cooking for three of the top female celebrity chefs in the country, so a lot was at stake. As anyone who has worked with chocolate knows, heat and humidity wreak havoc with it. Even moderate temperatures can cause chocolate to melt, discolor, and fail to set up. So, faced with the relentless Mexican sun beating in the kitchen window, I was forced to be resourceful and reach deep into my training and experience to come up with a solution—the concept of basing recipes on more stable ganaches.

This was my "aha!" moment. I discovered that no matter where I was working—whether it was in the humid tropical climate of the island of Bali or the milder environs of San Diego—the end results when I relied on ganache were the same . . . always fantastic!

The five ganaches I use here are Dark Chocolate Ganache; Velvety Smooth Milk Chocolate Ganache; Snowy White Chocolate Ganache; Old-Fashioned Hot Fudge Ganache; and Spiced Aztoc Chocolate Ganache.

"Ganache" is not a scary concept, although the word may not be immediately familiar to the American reader. It's a blend of chocolate, creams, and syrups that results in a velvety, ultrasmooth paste. In the case of my Dairy-Free Dark Chocolate Ganache, the dark chocolate is blended with light corn syrup, cocoa powder, and chocolate extract, and whipped until smooth. With no sacrifice of taste or texture, this dark ganache is the perfect building block for those who are lactose intolerant or those on a vegan diet.

Ganache is the soft filling everyone has bitten into when they have eaten a chocolate truffle or another confection enrobed with shiny chocolate. The filling transforms these confections into bites from heaven. When heated, ganache liquefies to a sauce; when chilled and beaten, it becomes frosting, and it assumes every texture in between. Ganache lends itself to a near-infinite number of flavors, from citrus, raspberry, mint, hazelnut, and champagne, to coffee, praline, and tropical fruits—including açaí, pomegranate, and even blueberry, all loaded with antioxidants.

Tips for Beginners

All our recipes have been thoroughly tested many times. I have added three inches to my waistline to prove it! I always recommend that the first time you make a recipe you follow the directions exactly as written, so you have a good idea of all the touch points to look for. Once you have done so, feel free to adjust the recipes to your own tastes. The exception to this is the ratios of baking ingredients, which you should follow closely. You can change the flavor of the ganache or add a little bit more chocolate if you want a richer flavor, but if you have a problem, remember: when everything else fails, go back and follow the recipe.

Use only the best, freshest, highest quality ingredients as specified in the recipe—"good stuff in, good stuff out!" In our Chocolate Studios, I insist on using the best quality chocolate. Luckily, I own a chocolate company and have a wide choice of chocolate options, but there are plenty of very good to great chocolates available worldwide from which to choose. France, Germany, Belgium,

Switzerland, Spain, and, of course, the United States all have different flavor and textural characteristics that have become the standard of each country.

For the recipes in this book, I used our blends of Choclatique Chocolate Couverture: Private Reserve Dark Chocolate (64 percent cacao), Prestige Milk Chocolate (32 percent cacao), and Snowy White Chocolate (33 percent cacao). I have blended all of our Choclatique chocolates to appeal to American tastes and to complement the centers of our Authentically American truffles.

I prefer chocolate higher in mass and lower in fat so that I can use the desired amounts of butter and cream in my recipes without the fear of collapse or failure in the baked products. I find that chocolate with a 64 percent cacao content will blend better with butter, cream, and other ingredients containing fat than those with a lower or higher cacao content. Experiment and follow your own tastes, and have fun discovering the hidden flavors in chocolate.

Milk and white chocolate are not inferior! Let me say it another way: milk and white chocolate are great! They are both wonderful ingredients to work with as you create desserts and other sweets for various occasions. Variety is the spice of life. The recipes in this book use all five ganaches made with a variety of our chocolate. In most cases you can substitute one for another. This means that for every recipe in this book, there are four easy alternatives. Simply use a different ganache and you will get a different outcome. What a bargain—five for the price of one!

For best results, I suggest using only chocolate *couverture*, as it produces the finest flavors and smoothest textures. I don't usually use or recommend inexpensive baking chocolate sold in supermarkets.

All About Cocoa Powder

For the most decadent chocolate desserts and confections, you should use the finest quality, premium cocoa powders. For the recipes in this book, I also used our Choclatique unsweetened cocoa powders—Natura (all-natural), Red Rouge (lightly Dutched), and Black Onyx

Dutch-processed, or alkalized, cocoa powder requires another step. Natural cocoa powder is treated with an alkali. The alkali is solely to control the flavor and color of the cocoa, which now is smoother and darker than natural cocoa.

In some instances, it does not matter which you use—non-alkalized or alkalized—but more often I specify one or the other. Nearly all imported brands of cocoa are Dutch-processed (alkalized); domestically, Hershey's and Nestlé make brasher tasting, natural (non-alkalized) cocoa powders. It is best to use the type specified in the recipe.

DID YOU KNOW? Chocolate is the most common craving in North America, affecting 40 percent of women and 15 percent of men.

(ultra-Dutched), the latter used largely for color rather than flavor. It is great for those deep, rich devil's food and blackout cakes and really dark, dark, rich chocolate ice cream. Please do not substitute drinking chocolate mixes for unsweetened baking cocoa, as it will adversely affect the flavor of your finished chocolate recipe.

Before I go any farther, let me explain the differences between Dutch-processed cocoa and natural cocoa. All cocoa powder is made by using hydraulic pressure to remove just about all the cocoa butter from the chocolate liquor (the thick, dark mass produced from the cocoa beans). At this point, the cocoa is considered "natural" or non-alkalized.

When cocoa powder is the only chocolate used in a cake, it imparts a full, rich chocolate flavor and dark color. Cocoa powders can also be used in concert with other chocolate ingredients, such as unsweetened chocolate or chocolate ganache, to improve the texture and flavor of the finished product. This result is a cake with a more complex and intense chocolate flavor. Many recipes call for sifting the cocoa powder with the flour. Other recipes suggest combining the cocoa powder with a small amount of boiling water or hot coffee to develop the full flavor of the cocoa powder. You may prefer one method over the other, but until you are comfortable with both, follow the recipe's instructions.

You may notice that recipes that rely on cocoa powder also call for more butter than other recipes, and a leavening agent, such as baking powder or baking soda. This is to offset the cocoa powder's drying and structural effects.

Due to these differences, never substitute one kind of cocoa for another without making these adjustments:

IF THE RECIPE CALLS FOR	SUBSTITUTE
3 tablespoons Dutch-processed cocoa powder	3 tablespoons natural cocoa powder plus a pinch (about $\frac{1}{8}$ teaspoon) of baking soda
3 tablespoons natural cocoa powder	3 tablespoons Dutch-processed cocoa powder plus a pinch ($\frac{1}{8}$ teaspoon) of cream of tartar or lemon juice

Stuff to Make Chocolate

In "Where Can I Find That Keen Stuff?" on page 252, there are great sources for premium chocolate, chocolate couverture, and other essential ingredients and tools for the curious and serious dessert makers, budding chocolatiers, and bakers. I think you will find that if you have questions, you can call or e-mail any of these suppliers. I have never had anyone turn me down for information.

If all else fails, send me an e-mail at chocolatedoctor@choclatique.com, and I will respond promptly.

How to Melt Chocolate

It's time to forget everything you ever learned about melting chocolate and chocolate ganache!

I used to recommend the old-fashioned, "traditional" way of melting chocolate. You know: Break or chop the bar chocolate into small pieces and put them in a bowl set over a saucepan of barely simmering water, stirring gently with a wooden spoon, until the chocolate is completely melted. Be sure that the water does not touch the bottom of the bowl, and be very careful that not even a drop of water or a puff of steam mixes with the melting chocolate. If this happens, the chocolate will seize up, a condition that renders it unusable. By the same token, if you accidentally burn the chocolate, you will have to discard it.

STOP!

Wrong, wrong, wrong! It's time to start over using the Swiss Method, an approach that will not destroy the delicate beta-5 crystalline structure so very important for perfect chocolate desserts. And best of all, it is so much easier and faster to do . . . no hot pans . . . no hot water. All you need is an instant-read thermometer and a microwave oven.

Melting chocolate in a microwave is the quickest and most efficient method. Although you may be tempted to melt it at 100 percent power, lower power (50 percent is a good level) guarantees even melting and avoids scorching. The length of time it takes to melt the chocolate depends on the strength of the microwave's wattage, and the size and thickness of the container you use to hold the chopped chocolate. Another factor is the percentage of cocoa butter in the chocolate.

It's more important to watch the chocolate than to watch the clock with this method, because the chocolate will never melt into a liquid pool in the microwave, as it does when melted in the top of a double boiler. Instead, it will soften and look wet and shiny, so you can stir it into that satisfying puddle. With the power level set for 50 percent, begin cautiously. Open the door every ten or fifteen seconds to stir the chocolate with a wooden spoon or spatula, until the chocolate reaches 116°F to 118°F.

Once the chocolate is melted and smooth, let it cool for ten to fifteen minutes, to about 88°F, before adding the rest of the liquid ingredients. For best results, when you add these ingredients to melted chocolate, make sure they, too, are at 88°F, so that all will blend smoothly and easily.

Ingredient Clues

- **Butter**—I find it best to use softened, room-temperature, unsalted, European-style butter. It has a lower water content than American butter. This gives the best results when the butter is beaten with sugar or eggs. Do not put the butter in the microwave or on a warm surface unless the recipe says so, as it will materially change the texture of your chocolate products.

- **Chocolate**—For my recipes I use only the same quality of chocolate that I would eat. It makes licking the beaters and the bowl so much more rewarding.

- **Cocoa powder**—Use only unsweetened cocoa, and sift it with the flour and other dry ingredients. Pure cocoa powder is a fiber and doesn't melt or dissolve; it is just absorbed by the liquids. Some recipes call for mixing the cocoa powder with a little hot water to make sure the texture of the final recipe isn't grainy. Turn to page 17 for more on cocoa and definitions of alkalized (Dutch-processed) and non-alkalized (natural) cocoa powders.

- **Dairy**—Use only the freshest, just-bought milk and cream. If you wouldn't drink it, don't use it in your recipes.

- **Eggs**—Use the freshest, just-bought, large eggs, unless otherwise directed in the recipe. Egg whites should be brought to room temperature before whipping. Remember, you can't successfully whip egg whites with any yolk present in the bowl. Always begin with impeccably clean and dry bowls and beaters.

- **Flour**—Use only all-purpose flour that has been sifted, unless otherwise directed.

- **Salt**—Use ordinary table salt in your recipes, unless otherwise directed.

Tool Time

I am no longer allowed to go shopping for culinary tools in any of the very cool kitchen stores, such as Williams-Sonoma or Sur la Table, without adult supervision. I have been known to exceed an unlimited budget when outfitting a new restaurant's pastry kitchen. In our Chocolate Studios and test kitchens, we have every gadget and appliance known to man for the preparation, cooking, and baking of anything edible. We have even dug an imu pit (Hawaiian underground oven) in the atrium of our building to bake a white chocolate coconut cake while roasting a wild boar. My feeling is you can't get the job done without the right tools.

We have listed specific pieces of equipment in the Special Toolbox at the top of each recipe. In addition to those, there are some very basic items that every home kitchen should have available to make wonderful desserts and confections.

Why is this so important? The right tools help you achieve the success you want. There are tools for measuring and weighing precisely the right amount of ingredients; pots and pans for cooking and baking; bowls for mixing and whisking. There are boards, pans, trays, liners, sifters, and . . . I'm getting too excited and way ahead of myself. Let me start from the beginning.

Measuring and Weighing

- **Measuring spoons.** These are used for measuring tablespoons, teaspoons, and, if you get a complete set, even a pinch of a dry ingredient or a dash of a liquid. For sticky stuff, like honey, corn syrup, and peanut butter, I suggest a set of nonstick measuring spoons. A few companies even make long-handled spoons that are great for getting into the box of baking soda or reaching the bottom of a canister, which can be very handy at times.

- **Dry measuring cups.** These come in graduations from $1/8$ cup to 2 cups. These are used to measure larger quantities of bulk ingredients, such as sugar and flour. The top of each cup when level or packed is the correct amount. Once again, my preference is metal rather than plastic cups for a few reasons: they are more accurate, are easier to clean, and never pick up off aromas.

- **Liquid measuring cups.** These are usually made of clear glass, or translucent, heavy-weight plastic. The cups should have clean, legible graduations in both ounces and cups. One-, 2-, and 4-cup measures are indispensable; 8- and 12-cup measures are handy. My preference is for old-fashioned Pyrex cups that can safely be used in a microwave and are wide enough to act as a small mixing bowl.

- **A kitchen scale.** A scale is very handy to have in a kitchen. Some recipes are written for pounds and ounces rather than cups. I prefer an electric scale, simply because the display is so much easier to read, and I believe it tends to be more accurate. When you purchase a scale, buy one that reads in both ounces and grams, ranging from 0.1 to 80 ounces and from 1 to 2,000 grams.

- **Thermometers.** Cooking thermometers come in several forms—dial, instant-read, and standing bulb-type candy thermometers. I use them all for different purposes. They are valuable for determining the temperature of cooked sugars and finished baked goods. I also have an oven thermometer in each of our ovens as a double check for the oven thermostat. I highly recommend that home cooks do the same, as kitchen ovens do not always stay accurately calibrated.

Preparation

- **Parchment paper.** It is great for lining baking sheets and cake pans and makes cleanup a breeze. We have a standard practice of lining all baking sheets with parchment to cut down on scrubbing time. (Make sure your parchment is for cooking and baking purposes only.)

- **Waxed paper.** Like parchment paper, waxed paper is also handy for lining pans that will be filled with batter. (Do *not* use it for lining baking sheets, as it can be a fire hazard.) You can also spread waxed paper on a countertop and sift and portion ingredients on top of it. This makes it easy to transfer the ingredients to a nearby mixing bowl: just bend and lift the paper.

- **Nonstick silicone baking sheets.** These are great for lining pans when you bake fragile cookies and tender biscuits. They are made from food-grade silicone reinforced glass weave. They are fairly expensive but well

worth the money. Remember, these are used for baking, not cutting. Never use any sharp object that will puncture or cut the liners, and always store them flat.

- **Cake circles (cake rounds).** These tools are what we use to assemble layer cakes. Without them, you couldn't move the layers from the decorating turntable to the serving plate. They can be made out of cardboard or laminated corrugated plastic.

Pots, Pans, and Bakeware

- **Saucepans.** Buy the best cookware you can afford; I prefer All-Clad. A heavy-gauge, well-constructed pot will last a lifetime, while inexpensive ones tend to dent and warp and will never conduct heat as efficiently and effectively.

- **Baking dishes.** I like using Pyrex glassware, and I turn to Nordic Ware Bundt pans. Baking dishes come in a variety of sizes.

- **Heavy-duty baking pans** or restaurant sheet pans made by Lincoln. These carefully made pans have good heft, which prevents uneven cooking and burning. They come in full-size, which is too large for nearly all home ovens; half-sheet; and quarter-sheet pans—the last two sizes are perfect for the home cook.

- **Springform pans.** If you like cheesecake as much as I do, I suggest you have a 4-, 9-, and 10-inch springform pan in your arsenal. For layer cakes, stock 8- and 9-inch round pans that are two inches deep. These will suffice for any cake in this book and most others.

- **Muffin tins.** I have a variety of pans to make mini to jumbo muffins and cupcakes. I even own a muffin top pan, which is perfect for making whoopie pies. Standard muffin (cupcake) pans have six or twelve cups, each able to hold six or seven tablespoons of batter.

- **Heavy-duty metal pie pans** are better because they produce a more evenly browned piecrust. I also have a variety of torte or tart pans with removable bottoms and fluted sides for fancier desserts.

As a special note: I don't recommend dark anodized-aluminum bakeware. It attracts heat and tends to burn the outside edges before the middle is fully baked. You won't get as much browning from coated, nonstick (such as Teflon-coated) bakeware as you will from traditional bright aluminum products.

Mixing

- **Mixing bowls.** I keep a variety of nesting mixing bowls, both glass and stainless-steel, handy in several places in my kitchen. It's always a good idea to use a bigger bowl than you think you will need.

- **Stand mixer.** A quality standing mixer is one of the best investments you can make, and one that will last for decades. Many retailers sell KitchenAid and other stand mixers, so shop carefully to find the best deal.

- **Handheld electric mixer.** Sometimes a handheld electric mixer is more appropriate, depending on the task.

A handheld is essential when you need to beat a batter or emulsion on a heated surface. I also like immersion blenders, which look like straight wands, for blending mixtures in deep pans and bowls.

- **Food processors.** I can't imagine a kitchen without one. It makes the perfect piecrust when you follow directions and don't overprocess the dough.

Small Jobs

- **Hand utensils.** To make kitchen tasks easier, you must have the right hand tools for the job: a collection of wooden spoons and flat paddles, rubber spatulas, offset stainless-steel spatulas, traditional straight-edge spatulas, and all sizes of whisks.

- **Rolling pin.** A good rolling pin is necessary for turning out the perfect crust.

- **Knives.** Good quality knives are essential. I have used J. A. Henckels knives since cooking school. It's important to keep your knives sharp and to wash and dry them by hand. Use the sharpening steel every time you use them, and get them professionally sharpened when they get dull.

- **Cutting wheel.** I use a large diameter cutting wheel (the kind used in pizza restaurants for cutting pies into slices) for cutting piecrusts. I also like using it to trim dough and to cut sheet cakes, among other tasks.

- **Pastry scrapers.** I use rubber, plastic, and soft metal scrapers for getting every last drop of frosting out of bowls, and hard metal scrapers for cleaning work surfaces and pushing scraps of pie pastry together.

- **Pastry brushes.** These are essential for applying glazes, washes, butters, and oils. I have every size imaginable. Only purchase brushes that are certified food-safe—and segregate brushes used for sweet purposes from those used for savory ones.

- **Pastry bags.** I have given up traditional coated, linen pastry bags and now rely solely on disposable, plastic pastry bags. In a pinch you can use a sturdy plastic food storage bag as well. Fill it with frosting or filling and snip off one of the bottom corners to squeeze it through.

3

THE FIVE BASIC GANACHES

THE STORIES OF THE ORIGINS OF GANACHE (GAH-NOSH) VARY. SOME BELIEVE IT CAME FROM SWITZERLAND IN THE MID-1850S AND WAS USED AS A BASE FOR CHOCOLATE TRUFFLES. OTHERS CLAIM IT WAS INVENTED IN PARIS AT THE PATISSERIE SIRAUDIN. THE IMPORTANT THING IS THAT A CHOCOLATIER DISCOVERED THAT WHEN HOT CREAM IS POURED OVER CHOPPED CHOCOLATE (TRADITIONALLY SEMISWEET OR BITTERSWEET), AND THE MIXTURE IS STIRRED UNTIL VELVETY SMOOTH, AN INGREDIENT IS CREATED THAT CAN BE USED IN A TEMPTING AND MOUTHWATERING VARIETY OF DESSERTS, PASTRIES, AND CONFECTIONS. AS YOU WILL SEE, GANACHE CAN BE MADE WITH DARK, MILK, OR WHITE CHOCOLATE; AND DIFFERENT FLAVORINGS CAN BE ADDED, SUCH AS LIQUEURS, SPICES, AND EXTRACTS. BUTTER, OIL, OR CORN SYRUP CAN ALSO BE ADDED FOR DARK SHINY GLAZES.

Ganache is nothing short of miraculous—a thing of beauty. When warm and liquid, it can be poured over a cake or torte for a smooth, seamless, shiny glaze. If cooled to room temperature, ganache becomes a spreadable filling or topping for cakes, cookies, and bars. Once chilled, ganache can be whipped into swirlable frostings or formed into truffles. In my experience, ganache is the ubiquitous chocolate ingredient that never fails.

A slightly more complicated version is called *ganache soufflé*, which is a basic ganache to which flavorings have been added before it is whipped at room temperature until doubled in volume. Ganache soufflé is generally used to fill pastry layers and to frost, finish, and decorate cakes.

The taste and quality of ganache depend entirely on the quality of chocolate and the freshness of the milk or cream used. Not all chocolates are created equal. Chocolate with higher cocoa butter content produces a ganache that is firmer than one made with a chocolate that has a low cocoa butter content. A chocolate with a velvety smooth texture will produce a ganache that is equally velvety. The most important point to consider when choosing a chocolate for making ganache is whether you like the taste and texture of the chocolate when you eat it out of hand. If you wouldn't eat it, don't use it.

Velvety Smooth
Milk Chocolate Ganache

Milton Hershey popularized milk chocolate in America. He felt so strongly about his conviction to blend great chocolate with fresh milk that he built his factory adjacent to the cow pastures in Western Pennsylvania. This basic milk chocolate ganache is designed to be rich and creamy to satisfy North American preferences. Just a tablespoon or two is a wonderful addition to store-bought chocolate cake mixes, and to brownies.

Makes about 2 pounds of ganache

Prep Time: 10 minutes
Cooking Time: 15 minutes
Cooling Time: 2 hours
Chilling Time: 3 to 4 hours
Level: *

In a large, heavy saucepan, bring the cream to a boil over medium-high heat. Remove the pan from the heat.

Immediately add the chocolate to the pan and whisk until smooth. Set aside for about 2 hours to cool completely, whisking every 15 minutes or so to keep the ganache emulsified.

When cool, transfer the ganache to a rigid plastic or glass container, cover, date, and refrigerate overnight before using. Ganache will keep refrigerated for up to three months.

ChefSecret: Cream doubles in size when it is brought to a boil; be sure to use a large enough saucepan. For 1½ cups of cream, you will need a 3-quart saucepan or larger.

Variations:

Azteca-style milk chocolate ganache: Add 1 tablespoon ground cinnamon and ½ teaspoon finely ground cayenne pepper to the cream and bring to a boil. Continue with the remaining directions.

Chocolate Peanut Butter Ganache: Warm ½ cup creamy peanut butter in a microwave until slightly pourable, about 20 seconds. Combine the peanut butter with 1 tablespoon peanut oil and 1 cup Velvety Smooth Milk Chocolate Ganache and mix with an electric mixer until thoroughly blended.

G gluten free

special toolbox:

large, heavy saucepan (3 quarts or larger)

plastic sealable storage container

1½ cups heavy cream

1½ pounds milk chocolate (at least 32 percent), chopped

ED'S BOX-TOP WISDOM
Complexity

We crave complexity that adds dimension and vistas to the fresh confections we artistically prepare—the depth and vitality to our ganaches; creativity and robustness of our designs, warmth and fullness of our flavors; and soul and heritage to our guests partaking.

Dark Chocolate Ganache

This wonderful, dark ganache enriches any recipe with true dark chocolate European flavor. It is the chocolate ganache "workhorse" of this cookbook. I love the intensity of the rich, deep chocolate flavor. It is perfect in the Dark Chocolate Ganache Cheesecake (page 86), Devil's Food Cake (page 55), and Dark Chocolate Ganache Ice Cream (page 192). It's dairy and gluten free, and while it is not as sweet as other ganaches, it possesses all the benefits and "flavor thrills" that appeal to many intense chocolate lovers.

Makes about 2 pounds of ganache

Prep Time: 10 minutes
Cooking Time: 15 minutes
Cooling Time: 1 hour
Chilling Time: 3 to 4 hours
Level: *

In a large, heavy saucepan, bring the water, corn syrup, cocoa powder, and salt to a boil over medium-high heat. Whisk until blended. Remove the pan from the heat.

Immediately add the chocolate and chocolate extract to the pan and whisk until smooth. Set aside for about 1 hour to cool completely, whisking every 15 minutes or so to keep the ganache emulsified.

When cool, transfer the ganache to a rigid plastic or glass container, cover, date, and refrigerate for up to three months.

ChefSecret: Chocolate extract is sold in most supermarkets and confectionery shops. I like to use Star Kay White's Chocolate Extract, which will keep in the refrigerator for up to three months.

G gluten free

V vegan

D dairy free

special toolbox:

large, heavy saucepan
(3 quarts or larger)

plastic sealable storage container

1¼ cups water

⅔ cup light corn syrup

2 tablespoons unsweetened
Dutch-processed cocoa powder

¼ teaspoon salt

1¼ pounds bittersweet chocolate
(at least 64 percent), coarsely
chopped

1¼ teaspoons chocolate extract
(see ChefSecret)

Snowy White
Chocolate Ganache

Visiting second-year pastry students from trade/technical cooking schools preferred this white chocolate ganache to the dark and milk chocolate ganache in truffles. This is an incredible addition of light chocolate flavor and richness when no color is desired. White chocolate ganache is perfect for the Blushing White Chocolate Brownies on page 128, and other white chocolate confections.

Makes about 2 pounds of ganache

Prep Time: 10 minutes
Cooking Time: 15 minutes
Cooling Time: 2 hours
Chilling Time: 3 to 4 hours
Level: *

In a large, heavy saucepan, bring the cream, corn syrup, and salt to a boil over medium-high heat. Whisk until blended. Remove the pan from the heat.

Immediately add the white chocolate and vanilla to the pan and whisk until smooth. Set aside for about 2 hours to cool completely, whisking every 15 minutes or so to keep the ganache emulsified.

When cool, transfer the ganache to a rigid plastic or glass container, cover, date, and refrigerate overnight before using. Ganache will keep refrigerated for up to three months.

ChefSecret: Only use pure vanilla extract, which is true in rich vanilla flavor and does not leave a tinny, artificial aftertaste.

Variations:

For the flavor of a Scandinavian Christmas treat, add 1 teaspoon ground cardamom and ½ teaspoon ground cinnamon to the ganache when it has been whisked until smooth and before it is cooled. Stir well and then let the ganache cool. It will taste like it came from Copenhagen's Tivoli Gardens or Stockholm's Cookbook Café.

G gluten free

special toolbox:

large, heavy saucepan (3 quarts or larger)

plastic sealable storage container

2 cups heavy cream

¼ cup light corn syrup

¼ teaspoon salt

1 pound white chocolate (at least 33 percent), chopped

2 teaspoons pure vanilla extract

DID YOU KNOW? The melting point of cocoa butter is just below the human body temperature—which is why chocolate literally "melts in your mouth."

Old-Fashioned
Hot Fudge Ganache

Let's go for ice cream! Wil Wright's Ice Cream Parlor in Beverly Hills was the high school weekend date place in the '60s. They used to serve wonderful, small macaroons with every fountain order, and to my taste, they made the best homemade hot fudge sauce. That sauce is my benchmark for this ganache recipe. When rich, dark chocolate is simply not enough, this Old-Fashioned Hot Fudge Ganache is best used as a topping for ice cream, an enrichment for chocolate malts and shakes, and as a base ingredient for the wonderful Malted Fudge Frosting on page 231.

Makes about 2 pounds of ganache

Prep Time: 10 minutes
Cooking Time: 15 minutes
Cooling Time: 2 hours
Chilling Time: 3 to 4 hours
Level: *

In a large, heavy saucepan, bring the cream, corn syrup, and salt to a boil over medium-high heat. Whisk until blended. Remove the pan from the heat.

Immediately add the chocolate and vanilla to the pan and whisk until smooth. Set aside for about 2 hours to cool completely, whisking every 15 minutes or so to keep the ganache emulsified.

When cool, transfer the ganache to a rigid plastic or glass container, cover, date, and refrigerate overnight before using. Ganache will keep refrigerated for up to three months.

G gluten free

special toolbox:

large, heavy saucepan (3 quarts or larger)

plastic sealable storage container

2 cups heavy cream

¼ cup light corn syrup

¼ teaspoon salt

1 pound semisweet dark chocolate (at least 64 percent), chopped

2 teaspoons pure vanilla extract

MAKING CHOCOLATE SAUCES FROM GANACHE

Everyone knows what Milton Hershey's Famous Chocolate Syrup tastes like and the good it can do for a dish of plain vanilla ice cream. It's the flavor you grew up with if you were born in the United States after 1928. But for grown-up tastes, nothing beats the richer, deeper flavors of premium chocolate syrups and sauces, which are as easy to make as melting one of my classic ganaches.

• Homemade Dark, Milk, White, Azteca (Mexican), and Hot Fudge Chocolate sauces can be easily made by just melting the ganache, without adding any more liquid.

• Gently warm the ganache to about 105°F over hot water or in a microwave for only a few seconds. Stir the sauce to ensure it's smooth.

• Pour the warm chocolate ganache sauces into squeeze bottles or pans set in a warm water bath (bain-marie) and use them for a topping, to garnish or decorate, or to add great flavor to any dessert or sweet.

CHOCOLATE ON THE AMAZON

My trip down the Amazon began back in Mrs. B's tenth grade United States history class and our study of President Theodore Roosevelt (T. R.). Mrs. B had a gift for bringing history to life, and after two weeks of Roosevelt, I was captivated by his life, creativity, interests, and travels, especially his trip down the Amazon River.

Like Roosevelt, I became addicted to adventure travel. I spent three weeks in Xian, China, on an anthropological dig; two weeks cruising down the Nile in search of temples, pyramids, and the lasting legacy of the pharaohs; and three months camping in Tanzania's Serengeti Plain. It wasn't a stretch to convince myself and a few buddies that a trip to South America to explore the mysteries of the Amazon River Basin was just what the doctor ordered. I planned the trip so that it followed as closely as possible the route taken by Roosevelt.

Roosevelt's fellow adventurers included the famous Brazilian explorer Cândido Rondon, and the self-proclaimed naturalist and thirty-year veteran of the Amazon, George Cherrie. By contrast, my crew included ten of my high school and college friends and five hired guides and canoe handlers. Our adventure downriver soon shifted from an interesting tour of the famous tributary of the Amazon to a serious quest for survival. We quickly learned why the Rio da Dúvida—The River of Doubt—was so aptly named as the stream turned suddenly into a surging, pulsating passage of rapids and boiling white water.

During our trip, I discovered some of the most self-sufficient people in the world and came to understand the culture of the world of cacao. One hot, humid evening, our gang of exhausted "river rats" stumbled onto a member of the Yanomami tribe, in the middle of a tree-canopied clearing that was peppered with cacao plants. (The Yanomami are one of the largest remaining indigenous peoples of the Amazon River Basin.) The heavy forest air was perfumed with the light scent of chocolate. A Yanomami shaman soon joined us. Were it not for the Grateful Dead T-shirt he wore, the year could have been 1483. The shaman cut into a mature cacao pod and tempted us to taste the fresh, raw, bittersweet sacred fruit of the forest. He then invited us to join him and his companions for a meal. Our guides were reluctant. There were rumors that many of the tribes along the river still practiced cannibalism, so we weren't really sure if they were planning to feed us or eat us (no kidding).

We quickly learned that the Yanomami were not at all threatening. The tropical rainforests have long been home to indigenous peoples who have shaped cultures based on their environments since, some believe, the Siberian migration thousands of years ago. Great civilizations like the Mayas, Incas, and Aztecs developed complex societies and made significant contributions to science. Living from nature, without the technology to dominate their environment, native peoples such as the Yanomami learned to observe their rainforest surroundings, understand the intricacies, and grow cacao, used for both ceremony and currency.

A regional boat navigates the Amazon River.

As many as fifty indigenous tribal groups live so far in the depths of Brazil's rainforest that even today they have little, if any, contact with the outside world. Totally self-sufficient, these amazing Amazonian tribes have called the rainforest home for centuries. Besides hunting, gathering wild fruits and nuts, and fishing, the indigenous people plant small gardens, using sustainable farming methods. While cacao grows naturally along riverbanks in the Amazon River Basin, tribespeople also cultivate it under the rainforest canopy, protected by banana trees or cassava (tapioca) shrubs and other large-leaf plants and looming, treelike grasses. This makes perfect sense, since cacao thrives only when shaded.

We traveled five hundred miles down the river and spent a little more than five weeks in the rainforest. We saw harmless, eighteen-foot snakes, and six-inch baby surucucu snakes that could kill you in seconds with a single bite. There were hundreds of mysterious plants, and the friendliest and most colorful birds in the world swooped down on our heads, teasing us down the river. At times, the rapids were so violent that I was sure we would all drown; at other times the waters were so calm that we were tempted to let our fingers dangle near the glassy surface, despite the ever-present danger of the piranha.

The Roosevelt party suffered injuries and deaths during their expedition of the Amazon. Roosevelt's own illnesses later ravaged his body and ultimately took his life. We were far more fortunate. We lost some gear and some weight, but that was nothing compared to what we gained—treasured memories, a heaping helping of humility, and a wonderful, healthy tan.

Spiced Azteca
Dark Chocolate Ganache

I chose to name this recipe Spiced Azteca Chocolate Ganache because the combination of flavors (cinnamon and chili) is a treasure commonly paired with chocolate in Aztec culture. For additional depth of flavor, squeeze some freshly cut orange zest over the melted mixture to release the oils from the skin and complement the fruitiness of the dark chocolate. This is definitely a recipe for which you'll want to spring for the best chocolate you can afford, as you can easily transform this ganache into truly gourmet truffles.

Makes about 2 pounds of ganache

Prep Time: 10 minutes
Cooking Time: 15 minutes
Cooling Time: 2 hours
Chilling Time: 3 to 4 hours
Level: *

In a large, heavy saucepan, bring the cream, cinnamon sticks, and chili powder to a boil over medium-high heat. Whisk until blended. Remove the pan from the heat. Remove the cinnamon sticks and discard.

Immediately add the chocolate and vanilla to the pan and whisk until smooth. Set aside for about 2 hours to cool completely, whisking every 15 minutes or so to keep the ganache emulsified.

When cool, transfer the ganache to a rigid plastic or glass container, cover, date, and refrigerate overnight before using. Ganache will keep refrigerated for up to three months.

G gluten free

special toolbox:
large, heavy saucepan (3 quarts or larger)
plastic sealable storage container

1½ cups heavy cream

2 cinnamon sticks, about 3 inches long

½ teaspoon ground chipotle chili powder

1 pound bittersweet or semisweet chocolate (at least 64 percent), chopped

½ pound white chocolate (at least 33 percent), chopped

2 teaspoons pure vanilla extract

DID YOU KNOW? Alfred Hitchcock used chocolate syrup instead of fake blood in the famous shower scene in the movie *Psycho*. It photographed better in black and white when going down the drain.

4

CHOCOLATES

OUT OF THE BOX!

WHEN IT COMES TO MAKING GREAT CHOCOLATE, WE HAVE BECOME KNOWN FOR THINKING OUTSIDE THE BOX. MY GOOD FRIEND ALLAN WHITE, AN ACCOMPLISHED CHOCOLATIER HIMSELF AND REPRESENTATIVE FOR GUITTARD CHOCOLATE COMPANY, IS ALWAYS AMAZED AT WHAT WE ARE DEVELOPING IN OUR CHOCOLATE STUDIOS. HE FREQUENTLY LEAVES ME WITH, "YOU MUST BE OUT OF YOUR MIND!"

That I get to "play with" talented people each day is one of the biggest bonuses of working with chocolate. In what other job can you fantasize about chocolate all day long and work side-by-side with such talented chocolatiers and artisans making chocolaty dreams come true? So when we were hired to produce a chocolate fantasy birthday party menu for a customer, our little brainstorming group came up with some of the following recipes. If you want to get attention at one of your parties, here are several sure bets.

HOW TO MAKE CHOCOLATE CURLS

Chocolate curls are wonderful little decorations that make the ordinary look and taste extraordinary by adding additional chocolate accent and flair. They can be made from dark, milk, or white chocolate and can be large, luscious twists or small, sprinkle-like curls. Or something in between. While you can purchase them in many kitchenware stores, they are easy to make.

To make large curls, use a room-temperature bar of chocolate—dark, milk, or white. Using a vegetable peeler, make long strokes over the chocolate to scrape slivers of chocolate from the bar. The slivers will curl as you remove them. Let the curls drop onto a plate as you form them. To make small curls, freeze the bar of chocolate. Make short strokes with the vegetable peeler, and collect the curls in a bowl.

Chocolate Puffs

Many people think that working with puff pastry is a real chore. I don't! The good people at Pepperidge Farm have made it easy with their excellent-quality frozen dough, which you can find in almost any supermarket in America. I always have a package in my home freezer. With just five or six ingredients and a garnish of your choice, you can turn out a professional-looking and -tasting dessert in just about a half hour. I love it when the melted chocolate ganache mixes with the sugar-topped, baked puff.

Makes 8 puffs

Prep Time: 20 minutes
Baking Time: 35 minutes
Level: **

special toolbox:

pastry brush

parchment paper–lined baking sheet

medium saucepan

4 sheets puff pastry (from a 17.3-ounce package), thawed

2 large eggs

1 teaspoon heavy cream

8 (1-inch) Dark Chocolate Ganache (page 28) balls, frozen or at least very well chilled

2 tablespoons crystalline sugar (sugar with large crystals)

½ cup Milk Chocolate Ganache (page 26)

White Chocolate Ganache Whipped Cream (page 238)

Fresh strawberry slices, for garnish

Mint sprigs, for garnish

Preheat the oven to 350°F. Unfold the puff pastry sheets and cut into two 8-inch squares.

Beat the eggs and cream together in a small bowl to create an egg wash. Brush the pastry squares with the egg wash. Place a Dark Chocolate Ganache ball in the center of each pastry square. Repeat with the remaining ganache balls.

Pull the corners of the square over the chocolate, brushing the edges with more egg wash, if necessary. Press the edges of the square together, enclosing the chocolate completely. Brush the outside of the chocolate puff with additional egg wash. Repeat with the remaining puffs.

Place the puffs on a baking pan lined with parchment paper. Sprinkle with the sugar. Bake for about 35 minutes, or until golden brown.

In a saucepan, melt the Milk Chocolate Ganache over medium-low heat, whisking until smooth. Spoon the ganache evenly onto eight dessert plates and place 1 chocolate puff on each plate. Top with White Chocolate Ganache Whipped Cream and additional Milk Chocolate Ganache, if desired. Garnish with strawberry slices and mint. Repeat with the remaining puffs.

ChefSecret: To make ganache balls, using a melon baller or a tablespoon, scoop chocolate ganache and roll into a ball. Place in the freezer for at least 10 minutes.

Chocolate-Peanut Butter Wontons

Dim sum chefs are among the highest paid and most capable artisans of Chinese cuisine and are understandably proud that their little "love cakes" have a history dating back nearly two centuries.

It may be an ancient tradition but nevertheless is one that is open to change and new ideas as younger chefs introduce western ingredients to the cuisine. Whoever would have thought of Chocolate-Peanut Butter Wontons during the Ming Dynasty?

Makes 8 servings

Prep Time: 15 minutes
Cooking Time: 30 minutes
Assembly Time: 1 minute
Level: *

Blend the peanut butter and Azteca Chocolate Ganache together in a food processor.

Spread the wonton wrappers on a work surface. Brush the edges of the wrappers lightly with the beaten egg and spoon about 1 heaping teaspoon of the chocolate-peanut butter mixture onto the center of each wrapper.

Fold each wonton wrapper diagonally in half over the filling to form a triangle, pressing the edges of the wrapper to seal. Bring the ends around to form that distinctive wonton shape. As they are formed, place the wontons on a baking sheet lined with parchment paper.

Add enough oil to a deep, large, heavy skillet to reach a depth of 2 inches. Heat the oil over medium heat until it registers 350°F on a thermometer.

Working in batches, carefully submerge the wontons into the hot oil and cook until golden brown, about 45 seconds on each side.

Using a slotted spoon, transfer the wontons to a plate lined with paper towels to drain. Then, transfer the cooked wontons to a baking sheet and keep warm in a low (about 200°F) oven while frying the remaining wontons.

Spray the pomegranate seeds very lightly with nonstick spray and dredge to coat lightly with the granulated sugar.

To serve, place two fried wontons on each plate. Dust the wontons with confectioners' sugar and garnish with the sugar-coated pomegranate seeds.

ChefSecret: For a sweeter flavor, use Milk or White Chocolate Ganache (pages 26 and 29).

special toolbox:

food processor

pastry brush

parchment paper–lined baking sheets

large, heavy skillet

slotted spoon

deep-fry thermometer

½ cup creamy peanut butter

½ cup Azteca Chocolate Ganache (page 33)

16 wonton wrappers

1 large egg, beaten

Vegetable oil, for frying

¼ cup pomegranate seeds

Flavorless vegetable oil spray

Granulated sugar, for dredging

Confectioners' sugar, for dusting

Chocolate Dumplings

The Central European cuisines of Germany, Hungary, Austria, Poland, the Czech Republic, and Slovakia boast a large variety of dumplings, both sweet and savory. Whether known as *kola* in Northern Germany, or *spaetzle*, knöpfle, or knödel in Southern Germany and Austria, these are flour dumplings, the most common. They may be thin or thick and usually are either made with eggs and semolina flour and then boiled in water, or, as are these chocolate dumplings, made with all-purpose flour and cooked in a boiling blueberry mixture. In this recipe I have taken the liberty of adding chocolate ganache to create a new sweet dumpling dessert.

Makes 6 to 8 servings

Prep Time: 15 minutes
Cooking Time: 20 to 30 minutes
Assembly Time: 5 minutes
Level: **

In a medium bowl, stir together the flour, 1 tablespoon of the sugar, the baking powder, and salt. Cut the butter and chocolate ganache into the dry ingredients using a pastry cutter or two knives. Add the milk to form dough. Set aside.

In a large saucepan, combine the berries, the remaining 1½ cups sugar, and the water and bring to a boil. Drop the dumpling dough into the hot boiling berries by the tablespoonful. Cover, reduce the heat to low, and cook slowly for 20 minutes. The dumplings are done when they bob to the surface of the poaching liquid. If they are not done, simmer for 8 to 10 minutes longer or until they float to the surface of the pot. Remove with a slotted spoon and let drain in a colander.

Divide evenly among 6 to 8 serving plates and serve warm with chocolate ice cream or whipped cream.

special toolbox:

pastry cutter, fork or food processor

large, heavy saucepan with lid
(3 quarts or larger)

1 cup all-purpose flour

1 tablespoon plus 1½ cups
    granulated sugar, divided

1 teaspoon baking powder

Pinch of salt

¼ pound (1 stick) unsalted butter,
    softened

¼ cup Dark Chocolate Ganache
    (page 28)

¼ cup whole milk

1 quart fresh or frozen blueberries,
    raspberries, or boysenberries (not
    strawberries)

2 cups water

Chocolate ice cream, for serving

Freshly whipped cream, for serving

THE KING AND I

Thailand is one of the most unique societies in the modern world: a Theravada Buddhist monarchy with a parliamentary system and a clarinet-playing king believed to be the living incarnation of the Hindu god Vishnu and a direct descendent of Rama I (the king Yul Brynner played in the movie *The King and I*). The king presides via lèse majesté laws over a hedonistic and technology-obsessed Asian Tiger economy, centered in one of the most sophisticated urban cultures on earth. No one has ever been able to understand how it all holds together, but, trust me, it does.

I met Onn and seven other beautiful, off-duty flight attendants on a flight from Hong Kong to Bangkok. I invited them to join me for dinner the next night at the Oriental Hotel's exotic Sala Rim Naam restaurant on the legendary Chao Phraya River. They arrived wearing traditional Thai dresses. We feasted for hours on both the food and the entertainment.

Onn met me the next day to give me a guided tour of the Grand Palace (Phra Borom Maha Ratcha Wang), covering many areas normally off limits to tourists. The two-hundred-year old structures are beautiful in a peculiar sort of way. From a distance, they look like a palace cast in gold and precious gems, but up close they are a collection of traditional wooden buildings adorned with gold leaf and broken bits of mirrors and glass.

Her mother was one of the aides to the king and had arranged an invitation to visit the Dusit Palace (the Little Palace), where the king actually lives. Because of her position I was allowed to tour the personal residence and meet the king—my first time meeting royalty. The tour of the royal home was interesting, but not quite as fascinating as His Majesty, King Bhumibol Adulyadej himself.

The third and youngest child of Prince Mahidol of Songkla was born in December 1927, at Mount Auburn Hospital, in Cambridge, Massachusetts. The sudden death of his older brother, King Ananda Mahidol, in Bangkok on June 9, 1946, changed the course of his life. The law of succession bestowed on him the challenging function of the Thai Crown. As he had not yet finished his education, he agreed to complete his studies in Switzerland before returning to Thailand. He earned degrees in political science and law before he was crowned the king of Thailand.

I told the king that a friend of mine, Chef David Thompson, had once cooked for him and found him to be a very appreciative diner. He smiled wisely, and his eyes danced a bit as he described one of Chef David's best dishes. He asked me if, while staying in Bangkok, I would prepare one of my famous chocolate desserts for him. I couldn't refuse a royal command. Three days later I was making my Show-Stopping Chocolate Pasta (page 40) for an intimate royal party of fifty dinner guests.

Show-Stopping
Chocolate Pasta

In the late 1990s, I was frequently invited to do on-air, live cooking segments on AMLA. I always wanted to do something remarkable . . . a recipe that would tempt the tastebuds of the hosts, Cristina Ferrare and Steve Edwards. On one occasion Cristina was being a bit difficult. While she loved all the ingredients I had chosen for the recipe, she didn't think they should be mixed together. She made such a fuss, but in the end decided to let the audience decide my fate with a tasting. They loved it! After this, I was invited back often to produce outrageous chocolate desserts, including this one.

Makes 4 to 6 servings

Prep Time: 10 minutes
Cooking Time: 15 minutes
Level: **

Fill a large pot three-fourths full with water and bring to a boil over high heat. Add the sugar and oil. Return to a rolling boil, then add the fettuccini and cook for 10 minutes or until the pasta is al dente. Drain the pasta in a colander.

Return the pot to the stovetop and melt the butter over medium heat until it turns light brown and nutty. Return the pasta to the pot and cook gently, tossing to coat with the butter.

Reduce the heat and add the fruit, tossing lightly with the pasta just to heat. Do not overcook the fruit.

Remove from the heat and add the Dark Chocolate Ganache. Lightly toss with the pasta and fruit until coated with ganache.

To serve, divide the pasta and fruit evenly among four to six plates. Top with a scoop of ice cream and a dollop of White Chocolate Ganache Whipped Cream and garnish with the almonds.

special toolbox:

8-quart pot

ice cream scoop

1 cup granulated sugar

1 tablespoon canola or other unflavored vegetable oil

8 ounces fettuccini

4 tablespoons unsalted butter

1 cup fresh raspberries, blueberries, boysenberries, sliced strawberries, or canned cherries, drained

¾ cup Dark Chocolate Ganache (page 28), at room temperature

4 to 6 scoops strawberry ice cream

½ cup White Chocolate Ganache Whipped Cream (page 238)

¼ cup toasted, slivered almonds, for garnish

Chocolate Salami

The French have perfected the art of making miniature fruits and vegetables out of marzipan. Some confectionery shops in Paris look like small produce stalls stocked with perfect tiny, colorful fruits and vegetables. At Choclatique, we are always looking for new, artistic, and interesting things to do with chocolate that look a lot like something else, so I was pleasantly surprised when one of our team members came up with this recipe for Chocolate Salami. Chocolate salami is commonly found in Spain, Portugal, and Italy.

Makes about 20 slices

Prep Time: 15 minutes
Chilling Time: 8 hours
Level: **

In a large, heatproof bowl, melt the ganache in a microwave oven (being careful not to scorch) or set over hot water.

Add the almonds, cookies, and raisins and blend well. Take care not to break up the cookies too much.

Chill in the refrigerator for about 2 hours or until the chocolate will no longer stick to your fingers. Roll the chocolate into a salami shape and tightly wrap in plastic wrap, twisting the ends to make it look like a real salami. Chill for at least 8 hours.

When ready to serve, coat in confectioners' sugar and cut into slices.

ChefSecret: Please, don't hold the mustard. If you're looking for the complete effect, soften and tint White Chocolate Ganache with yellow and red vegetable coloring until it looks like real mustard and wait for the unusual comments.

2 cups Dark Chocolate Ganache (page 28)

½ cup crushed toasted almonds or hazelnuts

12 soft fruit-filled, oatmeal, or ginger cookies, cut into quarters

¼ cup golden raisins

1 tablespoon confectioners' sugar, for rolling

Chocolate Ganache
Toas-Tites

For as long as I can remember, our family had a Toas-Tite sandwich grill—the kind that heats up on the range top or over a campfire. I used to make "tites" with American cheese or peanut butter and jelly on Wonder Bread. The edges came out wonderfully crisp and crunchy. My brother, Roy, inherited the family heirloom, so imagine my pleasure when I found a vintage one on eBay for only ten dollars. It was delivered while I was traveling in Asia, and the only ingredients suitable for grilling when I arrived home were a package of frozen waffles and Old-Fashioned Hot Fudge Ganache on page 30. What a great way to beat the jet lag blues!

Makes 1 serving (or 2 if served with ice cream)

Prep Time: 2 minutes
Cooking Time: 2 minutes
Level: *

Lightly butter one side of each waffle. Place one of the waffles, butter side down, on the Toas-Tite sandwich grill. Spread the Chocolate Peanut Butter Ganache on the unbuttered side of the waffle. Top with the remaining waffle, butter side up.

Close the grill and cut off any exposed edges with a sharp knife.

Toast on low heat on the stovetop until the edges start to char and the delicious aroma of chocolate spreads through the kitchen. Serve immediately.

ChefSecret: You can use any flavor of Chocolate Ganache or, if you are really desperate, you can fill the waffles with Nutella, a chocolate bar, or chocolate chips and peanut butter. If you don't have waffles, use brioche, challah (egg bread), an English muffin, or just plain Wonder Bread.

special toolbox:

Toas-Tite sandwich grill (or a griddle or frying pan, but it's not the same)

2 teaspoons unsalted butter

2 small, round, frozen waffles, thawed

5 tablespoons Chocolate Peanut Butter Ganache (page 26)

Orgasmic
Chocolate Soup

special toolbox:

double boiler

fondue dish and flame set up

fondue forks

condiment dishes

2 pounds mixed fresh fruit, such as
grapes, figs, strawberries, bananas,
apples, apricots, plums, or peaches

⅓ cup chopped toasted almonds

⅓ cup chopped toasted hazelnuts

½ cup desiccated coconut

4 cups Milk Chocolate Ganache
(page 26), at room temperature

1 cup heavy cream

I first heard Jack Cakebread talk about pairing wines with chocolate at a food conference. I believed that they should never be consumed together. I changed my tune when we began to develop our Napa Valley Wine Chocolates. I discovered that not only did wine and chocolate have complementary health benefits, but they tasted great blended together.

I was preparing a dessert for a wine dinner and accidentally dropped some grapes into a large bowl of dark chocolate ganache. I wasn't at all surprised when some of my cooks came over and began popping them into their mouths. The oohs and aahs that followed were happily revealing.

Makes 6 to 8 servings

Prep Time: 15 minutes
Cooking Time: 15 minutes
Level: *

Rinse and dry the fruit. Cut the larger pieces into bite-size chunks. If using apples, pears, or bananas, immerse the chunks in lemon-water for a few seconds to prevent the flesh from browning. Rinse and dry carefully. Arrange the fruit in an attractive bowl or serving dish. Place the almonds, hazelnuts, and coconut in small individual serving bowls.

Melt the Milk Chocolate Ganache in a double boiler over barely simmering water. As the ganache melts, stir in the cream. Pour the chocolate mixture into a fondue bowl and keep warm over the flame. Place the bowls filled with the nuts on the table. Have your guests dip pieces of fruit into the chocolate and then into the nuts.

S'Mores Pizza

The first recorded version of a s'more was found in the publication *Tramping and Trailing with the Girl Scouts* in 1927. Although it is unknown when the name was shortened, recipes for Some Mores appeared in various Girl Scout publications until 1971. Using the same ingredients, we have come up with our own version of s'mores in the form of a pizza. Starting with a store-bought pizza crust, you can have this campfire-style treat even if you're not a Girl Scout.

Makes 1 pizza

Prep Time: 10 minutes
Baking Time: 10 minutes
Level: *

Preheat the oven to 350°F.

Spread the Hot Fudge Ganache over the pizza crust, leaving a ¼-inch border around the edge.

Drizzle the White Chocolate Ganache and peanut butter over the Hot Fudge Ganache and then scatter the marshmallows evenly over the pizza.

Bake until golden brown, rotating as needed, for about 10 minutes. Remove from the oven and top with the graham cracker pieces. Slice and serve immediately.

special toolbox:

pizza pan or baking sheet

pizza cutter

pizza paddle

¼ cup Hot Fudge Ganache, melted (page 30)

1 ready-made, pre-baked pizza crust

¼ cup White Chocolate Ganache, melted (page 29)

¼ cup creamy peanut butter, warmed and pourable

1 cup miniature marshmallows

¼ cup coarsely broken graham crackers (2½ to 3 crackers)

Chocolate Marshmallows

Homemade chocolate marshmallows introduce an additional dimension to Chocolate Soup (page 44). They are great for dipping along with some pound or angel food cake. Chocolate marshmallows also make a great topping for hot chocolate drinks, and they're wonderful to eat on their own, too!

Makes about 48 marshmallows

Prep Time: 20 minutes
Cooking Time: 10 to 15 minutes
Setting Time: 4 to 6 hours
Level: **

Place the gelatin and water in the bowl of an electric mixer, stir, and let stand until softened, about 3 minutes.

Place the sugar, corn syrup, water, and salt in a saucepan over medium heat. Bring to a boil. Reduce the heat and simmer until a candy thermometer inserted into the syrup registers 235°F (soft-ball stage). Remove from the heat and let cool for a few minutes.

In the meantime, add the cocoa to the gelatin mixture and beat until frothy with the whisk attachment. With mixer on low speed, slowly and carefully pour in the hot sugar mixture. Add the vanilla extract and continue to beat until glossy and smooth, about 10 minutes.

Using a spatula, transfer the mixture to a buttered heatproof pan. Top with buttered parchment paper and let stand for 4 to 6 hours until the marshmallow firms up.

Cut into 1-inch squares and roll in confectioners' sugar.

ChefSecret: When the mixture reaches the soft-ball stage, the sugar syrup, when dropped into cold water, it will form a soft, flexible ball. If you remove the ball from the water, it will flatten after a few moments in your hand.

G gluten free

D dairy free

special toolbox:
electric stand mixer, bowl, and whisk
medium saucepan
candy thermometer
11 x 8 x 2-inch heatproof dish
parchment paper

3 tablespoons gelatin
1/2 cup warm water
2 1/4 cups granulated sugar
1/3 cup light corn syrup
1/4 cup water
1/4 teaspoon salt
1/2 cup unsweetened Dutch-
  processed cocoa powder
1 tablespoon pure vanilla extract
1/2 cup confectioners' sugar,
  for dusting

Chapter

5

LET THEM EAT CHOCOLATE CAKE
AND CUPCAKES

THERE ARE SO MANY VARIETIES OF CHOCOLATE CAKE THAT I HARDLY KNEW WHERE
TO BEGIN OR WHAT TO INCLUDE IN THIS CHAPTER. I STARTED WITH WHAT I CON-
SIDER TO BE THE ORIGINAL CHOCOLATE LAYER CAKE—THE SACHER TORTE (PAGE
58), WHICH I LEARNED TO MAKE IN VIENNA—AND A CONTEMPORARY VERSION OF THE HOT
LAVA CAKE (PAGE 62), WHICH I BASED ON ONE I CREATED FOR MY CHAIN OF RESTAURANTS,
THE CUSTOMS HOUSE. AND THEN I FILLED IN WITH CAKES THAT FALL IN BETWEEN THE
TWO! THIS INCLUDES MY FAVORITE COCA-COLA CHOCOLATE CAKE (PAGE 60).

THERE IS ALSO A SECTION ON THE "SPRINKLES PHENOMENON," WHICH IS WHAT I
CALL THE RECENT POPULARITY OF YUMMY CUPCAKES. CUPCAKES SEEM TO BE THE HULA
HOOPS OF THIS MILLENNIUM, WITHOUT ALL THE REQUIRED MOVEMENT. I NEVER COULD
MAKE A HULA HOOP STAY UP ON MY HIPS; THE SOLUTION: EAT MORE CUPCAKES! OF
COURSE, THERE ARE CUPCAKES AND THEN THERE ARE CHOCOLATE CUPCAKES. WHEN CON-
TEMPORARY BAKERIES SUCH AS SPRINKLES CAME ALONG WITH THEIR GOURMET-FLAVORED
BAKED GOODIES, IT WAS A GAME CHANGER, AND THE LATEST CHAPTER WAS WRITTEN ON THE
BRIEF BUT DELICIOUS HISTORY OF THE CUPCAKE.

special toolbox:

2 (9-inch) round cake pans

flour sifter

electric stand mixer, bowl, and whisk

cake tester

wire cooling rack

$^{3}/_{4}$ cup unsweetened Dutch-
processed cocoa powder, sifted

2 cups all-purpose flour

2 cups granulated sugar

$1^{1}/_{2}$ teaspoons baking powder

$1^{1}/_{2}$ teaspoons baking soda

$^{1}/_{4}$ teaspoon salt

2 large eggs

1 cup whole milk

$^{1}/_{2}$ cup vegetable oil

2 teaspoons pure vanilla extract

$^{1}/_{4}$ cup Dark Chocolate Ganache
(page 28), at room temperature

1 cup boiling water

Chocolate Cream Cheese Frosting
(pages 232–235)

Dark Chocolate Ganache Layer Cake

This fabulous cake is very simple to make. Eat it on its own, fill and frost it, or use it for layers in Hot Fudge Nut Trifle recipes. A dark chocolate cake frosted with a lighter White Chocolate Cream Cheese Frosting (page 234) is the perfect ending for a springtime dinner.

By filling the cake with whipped ganache and enrobing it with a ganache of the same flavor, you can also turn these chocolate layers into a decadent, satiny treat. It is made easy with one of our ganache building blocks, resulting in a thick, rich, chocolaty concoction with a heavenly taste. The next time you make this chocolate cake, try dressing it up with ganache.

Makes 1 (9-inch) layer cake, serving 8 to 10

Prep Time: 25 minutes
Baking Time: 30 to 35 minutes
Cooling Time: 1 hour
Level: *

Preheat the oven to 350°F. Coat two 9-inch round cake pans with butter and dust with cocoa powder. Set aside.

In a large mixing bowl, combine the cocoa powder, flour, sugar, baking powder, baking soda, and salt until blended. Add the eggs, milk, oil, and vanilla and beat well on medium speed until thoroughly combined, about 2 minutes. Add the Dark Chocolate Ganache. Add the boiling water and stir until completely blended. The batter will be thin.

Pour the batter into the prepared pans and bake for 30 to 35 minutes or until the cake pulls away from side of the pan, the top springs back when lightly touched, and a cake tester inserted in the center comes out clean.

Cool for about 5 minutes in the pans set on a wire cooling rack. Invert onto the wire rack and let cool completely.

Spread one of the Chocolate Cream Cheese Frostings over the layers and the top and side of the cake.

Variations:

Milk Chocolate Ganache Layer Cake with Milk Chocolate Frosting: Substitute ¼ cup Milk Chocolate Ganache (page 26) and Milk Chocolate Cream Cheese Frosting (page 233).

White Chocolate Ganache Layer Cake with Dark Chocolate Frosting: Substitute ¼ cup White Chocolate Ganache (page 29) and Dark Chocolate Cream Cheese Frosting (page 232).

Azteca Dark Chocolate Ganache Layer Cake with Milk Chocolate Frosting: Substitute ¼ cup Azteca Dark Chocolate Ganache (page 33) and Azteca Milk Chocolate Cream Cheese Frosting (page 235) and add 1 teaspoon cinnamon.

Reduce the baking time to 20 to 25 minutes or until the cake pulls away from side of the pan, the top springs back when lightly touched, and a cake tester inserted in the center comes out clean.

Classic Chocolate Génoise

A génoise is a basic building block for much French patisserie and is used for making several different types of cakes. The batter is usually baked to form thin sheets. It is perfect for making chocolate jelly rolls or for cutting and stacking in layers to line a mold to be filled with a frozen dessert. A variety of fillings can be used, such as fruit sauces, chocolate, fruit, chocolate pastry cream, and chocolate whipped cream. Génoise batter can be piped into molds to make madeleines (page 111).

Makes 2 sheet cakes

Prep Time: 15 minutes
Baking Time: 10 minutes
Cooling Time: 10 minutes
Level: **

special toolbox:

2 parchment paper–lined génoise pans or 1 (16 x 11-inch) sheet pan

electric stand mixer, bowl, and paddle

thermometer

sifter

Wire cooling rack

15 large eggs

2 cups granulated sugar

2 tablespoons Dark Chocolate Ganache (page 28), melted

4$\frac{1}{2}$ teaspoons pure vanilla extract

1$\frac{1}{2}$ teaspoons grated lemon zest

3$\frac{1}{4}$ cups pastry flour, sifted

$\frac{1}{4}$ cup ultra unsweetened Dutch-processed cocoa powder or another high-quality cocoa powder

4$\frac{1}{2}$ ounces clarified butter

Preheat the oven to 325°F. Butter and flour two parchment paper–lined génoise pans or one 16 x 11-inch baking sheet; tap out the excess flour.

In a heatproof bowl, combine the eggs and sugar using an electric mixer fitted with the paddle attachment. Continue mixing and add the melted Dark Chocolate Ganache until fully incorporated. Place the bowl over simmering water in the bottom of a double boiler until the mixture reaches 100°F to 110°F. It will feel warm when you insert your finger in the batter.

Return the bowl to the electric mixer and beat on high until whipped and cool. Add the vanilla and lemon zest and mix for 1 minute longer. Fold in the sifted flour, cocoa powder, and clarified butter. Do not overmix. Pour the batter into the prepared pans and smooth the surface with a rubber spatula.

Bake for 10 minutes, or until the cakes are slightly spongy to the touch.

Cool the cakes in the pans set on wire cooling racks. When completely cool, invert the pans and turn the cakes out. The cakes may be wrapped in plastic wrap and stored for up to three days in the refrigerator or three months in the freezer.

Variations:

Classic White Chocolate Génoise: Substitute 3 tablespooons of White Chocolate Ganache (page 29) for the Dark Chocolate Ganache. Omit the cocoa powder and increase the amount of pastry flour by $\frac{1}{3}$ cup. Proceed with the recipe.

Sour Cream Chocolate Cake

The elements in both sour cream and chocolate are perfect for making an ideal cake that is always moist, never oily, and always divinely rich and delicious. If you are looking for the single chocolate cake to become your own, then this is the one to master.

Makes 1 (9-inch) layer cake, serving 8 to 10

Prep Time: 20 minutes
Baking Time: 25 to 30 minutes
Cooling Time: 30 minutes
Level: **

For the cake: Adjust the oven rack so that it is in the center of the oven. Preheat the oven to 350°F. Coat two 9-inch round cake pans with butter and dust with flour. Tap out any excess flour.

Into a medium bowl, sift together the flour, cocoa powder, baking powder, baking soda, and salt. In a small bowl, whisk together the sour cream, water, and vanilla.

In the bowl of an electric mixer fitted with the paddle attachment, beat together the butter, Milk Chocolate Ganache, and brown sugar until light and fluffy. Beat in the eggs, one at a time, beating well after each addition. Add the flour mixture and the sour cream mixture alternately in three batches, beginning and ending with the flour mixture and mixing until just combined. Do not overbeat the batter.

Divide the batter between the prepared pans and smooth the tops. Bake for 25 to 30 minutes, or until a tester inserted into the center comes out clean.

Cool the cake layers in the pans on wire cooling racks for about 10 minutes before turning out onto the racks to cool completely. The cake layers may be made one week ahead, wrapped in plastic wrap, and frozen.

For the frosting: In a bowl of an electric mixer fitted with the paddle attachment, beat together the butter, Dark Chocolate Ganache, and cream cheese until light and fluffy. Add the confectioners' sugar and vanilla and beat until well combined.

To assemble: Arrange 1 cake layer on a large plate and spread with about ¾ cup of the frosting. Top the frosting with remaining cake layer. Spread the side and top of the cake with the remaining frosting.

ChefSecret: We had difficulty finding good, fresh sour cream in Berlin when we opened a new restaurant, so we made our own. It tastes great and the process is so simple that you'll never want to use store-bought sour cream again. In a large glass jar, mix 2 cups half-and-half with 2 tablespoons buttermilk. Put the lid on the jar and shake well. Let the jar stand in a warm place for 24 to 48 hours at room temperature. It will thicken once refrigerated.

special toolbox:

electric stand mixer, bowl, and paddle
2 (9-inch) round cake pans
cake tester
wire cooling rack

cake:

1½ cups all-purpose flour

¼ cup natural cocoa powder

1½ teaspoons baking powder

¾ teaspoon baking soda

½ teaspoon salt

1 cup sour cream

⅓ cup water

2 teaspoons pure vanilla extract

¼ pound (1 stick) unsalted butter, at room temperature

½ cup Milk Chocolate Ganache (page 26)

1⅓ cups firmly packed light brown sugar

3 large eggs

frosting:

4 tablespoons unsalted butter, at room temperature

⅓ cup Dark Chocolate Ganache (page 28), at room temperature

1 cup whipped cream cheese

2½ cups confectioners' sugar

1 teaspoon pure vanilla extract

Old-Fashioned Six-Layer Devil's Food Cake

As urban legend has it, devil's food cake originated at the famed Waldorf Astoria Hotel in New York City in the 1950s, although no one can find any evidence or records of this in the hotel's archives. Another rumor is that at some time in the 1940s, a customer asked for a copy of the recipe and was given a bill in the amount of $100. According to the story, the angry customer, to get revenge, then circulated the recipe, along with her story.

This recipe was a favorite with the customers of our Customs House Restaurants in Northern California, where we sold as many as ten a day.

Makes 1 (9-inch) layer cake, serving 6 to 10

Prep Time: 15 minutes
Baking Time: 25 minutes
Cooling Time: 1 hour
Resting Time: 30 minutes
Level: ***

For the cake: Adjust the oven rack so that it is in the center of the oven. Preheat the oven to 350°F. Butter three 9-inch cake pans and line the bottoms with circles of parchment paper.

Sift together the cake flour, cocoa powder, baking soda, baking powder, and salt in a bowl.

In the bowl of an electric mixer fitted with the paddle attachment, beat together the sugar and Dark Chocolate Ganache until smooth and creamy, about 5 minutes. Add the eggs, one at a time, beating after each addition until fully incorporated. Stop the mixer as necessary to scrape down the sides of the bowl.

In a small bowl, mix together the coffee, milk and vinegar. Add the flour mixture and the coffee mixture to the Ganache alternately in three batches, beginning and ending with the flour mixture and mixing until just combined.

Divide the batter among the cake pans and bake for 25 minutes, or until a cake tester inserted into the center comes out clean. Cool the cakes in the pans set on wire racks for about 10 minutes. Turn out onto the racks to cool completely before frosting.

Ingredients and directions continued on page 56.

special toolbox:

3 (9-inch) cake pans

parchment paper

sifter

electric stand mixer, bowl, and whisk

cake tester

wire cooling rack

medium bowl and saucepan
or a double boiler

serrated knife

offset metal spatula

cake:

3 cups cake flour (not self-rising)

½ cup unsweetened
   Dutch-processed cocoa powder

2 teaspoons baking soda

1 teaspoon baking powder

1 teaspoon salt

2½ cups granulated sugar

1 cup Dark Chocolate Ganache
   (page 28), at room temperature

4 large eggs, at room temperature

1 cup strong hot coffee

1 cup whole or low-fat milk,
   at room temperature

1 teaspoon white vinegar

frosting:

4 cups Hot Fudge Ganache
  (page 30), at room temperature

1 cup heavy cream

$1/2$ pound (2 sticks) unsalted butter,
  cut into small pieces

$1/2$ cup sour cream, at room
  temperature

For the frosting: In a heatproof bowl set over a pan of barely simmering water, melt the Hot Fudge Ganache and the cream together, stirring occasionally until melted. Remove the bowl from the pan of water. Whisk the butter into the warm ganache mixture until completely melted and the ganache is smooth. Set aside for about 1 hour or until cooled and spreadable.

When ready to frost the cake, transfer the frosting to the bowl of an electric stand mixer. Add the sour cream. Using the whisk attachment, whip well to incorporate enough air to double the volume of the frosting.

To assemble: Halve each cake layer horizontally using a long serrated knife. On a cake stand, arrange 1 cake layer cut side up. Spread about 1 cup of the frosting over the top. Top with the next layer, cut side down. Repeat four more times so that you have six layers. Decoratively spread the top and side with the remaining frosting.

ChefSecret: Devil's food cake is best eaten the day it is made, although it will be fine the next day. Do not refrigerate. Place a piece of plastic wrap on the cut portions of the cake and store at room temperature under a cake dome or cover the whole cake completely with plastic wrap. Just be sure to keep the cake out of the direct sun or heat.

The Wall Came Tumbling Down

On November 9, 1989, the Iron Curtain was pried open when the Berlin Wall toppled, ending the separation between East and West Germany. It was the end of nearly three decades of forced partition and marked a new beginning for a united Germany. My business partner and friend Joan and I were working in West Berlin at the time. We watched people enter the city from all directions without restrictions.

The atmosphere was electric as thousands of excited East and West Germans gathered for huge parties of cheering citizens—citizens now of one country. People applauded and grinned spontaneously, dazzled by thousands of popping flashbulbs. The traffic was spectacular. Streams of people walked hand in hand between car-jammed lanes, talking, chanting, and singing together. Musicians played trumpets, clarinets, and accordions, while men and women danced in the streets. Despite the brilliantly cold night, car windows were open, and everyone waved and yelled fond greetings to one another.

Joan and I and the hotel management set up street-side banquet tables and handed out hot coffee and hastily baked chocolate cupcakes—the first ever seen in Berlin—right in front of the Mövenpick Hotel. The cupcakes were made in muffin tins because they baked quickly and were easy to give away.

Finally, we couldn't contain ourselves. We headed to the former East Berlin. We saw police standing near the famed wall, which was quickly mobbed by large, excited, singing crowds who started to tear it down, literally piece by piece. In what had been forbidden territory just hours earlier, cars were abandoned. At the wall, smiling, friendly West German police stood in rows, armed with tall shields, trying to prevent chaos. On top of the wall, East German soldiers lined up at parade rest. We could hear the sounds of heavy equipment—a giant drill, a jackhammer, a backhoe—punching holes in the wall. Every time a drill poked through, everyone cheered. People shot off firecrackers, emergency flares, and rescue rockets. We spotted a few East German border guards huddled together, looking through a narrow hole; we reached through and shook their hands.

Thousands of people were walking everywhere, going in and out of stores, looking around, drinking, laughing, and crying. Empty champagne and beer bottles littered the streets. Everything was open—restaurants, bars, discos. Nearly two million East Germans entered Berlin between the evening of one day and the early morning of the next! Berlin's population swelled from three million to five million that day, with everyone joyfully and deliriously filling the streets. Germany was reunited in the streets of Berlin, and Joan and I were there—celebrating with chocolate!

The Original Sacher Torte

In 1832, Prince Klemens Wenzel von Metternich asked his personal chef to create a special dessert for a couple of his royal friends. The head chef had fallen that afternoon and was out sick, so the assignment was given to the sixteen-year-old pastry apprentice, Franz Sacher. The prince was a bit put off when he learned that Sacher was only in his second year of training at the royal's kitchen, and is reported to have declared, "Let there be no shame on me or this house tonight!" In other words, Herr Sacher, "Don't mess it up!" The young man outdid himself, and here is the result—the original Sacher torte.

Makes 8 to 10 servings for princes or princesses

Prep Time: 27 minutes
Baking Time: 45 minutes
Cooling: 10 minutes
Chilling Time: 1 hour
Waiting Time: 30 minutes
Level: ***

special toolbox:

9-inch springform pan

food processor fitted
with a metal blade

double boiler

flour sifter

electric stand mixer, bowl, paddle,
and whisk

cake tester

wire cooling rack

serrated knife

cake:

6 tablespoons unsalted butter,
  at room temperature, divided

12 ounces Dark Chocolate Ganache
  (page 28)

1 cup granulated sugar

1 dozen large eggs, separated

1⅓ cups all-purpose flour, sifted

For the cake: Preheat the oven to 325°F. Coat a 9-inch springform pan with 2 tablespoons of the butter and dust with flour. Tap out any excess flour.

In a double boiler over barely simmering water, melt the Dark Chocolate Ganache, stirring occasionally. Set aside to cool.

In the bowl of an electric mixer fitted with the paddle attachment, beat the remaining 4 tablespoons of butter and sugar until creamy. Add the egg yolks, one at a time, beating until just blended after each addition.

Using a large rubber spatula, fold the cooled ganache and the flour into the batter.

Using the whisk attachment, in a separate mixing bowl beat the egg whites on high speed until stiff peaks form. Gently fold the egg whites, about one-third at a time, into the cake batter, being careful not to deflate them.

Pour the batter into the prepared pan. Hold a large spoon over the pan, upside down, so that the batter pours over the back of the spoon so as to ensure that the batter remains light and airy.

Bake for 45 minutes or until a cake tester inserted in the center of cake comes out clean. Cool in the pan on a wire rack.

For the filling: Pureé the apricot preserves in a food processor for about 1 minute. Add the brandy and pulse until blended.

Using a long serrated knife, slice the cake horizontally into 4 equal layers. Spread one fourth of the apricot filling on the bottom layer. Top with a second layer of cake and spread one fourth of the apricot filling over this layer. Repeat until all four layers are stacked on top of each other.

Place the cake on a wire rack set over a jelly roll pan and refrigerate for at least 30 minutes.

For the glaze: Melt the Dark Chocolate Ganache and butter in a heatproof bowl set over simmering water. In a separate saucepan, bring the cream to a simmer over medium heat. Stir the cream into the melted chocolate mixture. Cool until the glaze reaches a consistency that coats the back of a wooden spoon.

Pour the glaze over the cake so that it drips down the side. Use a spatula to spread the glaze over the side of the cake. Chill for another 30 minutes before serving to allow the glaze to set.

Remove the cake from the refrigerator 30 minutes before serving so that the glaze regains its shine. Serve each cake slice with a dollop of Dark Chocolate Ganache Whipped Cream.

filling:

1 cup apricot preserves

2 tablespoons apricot brandy

glaze:

12 ounces Dark Chocolate Ganache (page 28)

3 tablespoons unsalted butter, at room temperature

1/2 cup heavy cream

Dark Chocolate Ganache Whipped Cream (page 238)

Coca-Cola® Chocolate Cake

For more than 120 years, The Coca-Cola Company has provided a wide variety of refreshing beverages, but soft drinks aren't just for drinking. We don't know exactly where or when, but many newspaper articles confirm that this genre of baking with carbonated beverages started in the South. Little wonder: Coca-Cola (Atlanta) and Dr. Pepper/7UP (Dallas) started in the South. Most of these recipes generally refer to the Coca-Cola Chocolate Cake as "traditional" or "grandma's Sunday special cake."

We were looking for a special, signature chocolate dessert for Disneyland's Plaza Inn. Coca-Cola was one of the park's paid sponsors. So it was easy to go back to Main Street and rediscover this favorite recipe.

Makes 1 (17 x 11-inch) cake, serving 20 to 24

Prep Time: 15 minutes
Baking Time: 45 minutes
Cooling Time: 10 minutes
Level: *

For the cake: Preheat the oven to 350°F. Butter and flour a 17 x 11-inch pan.

Sift together the flour, sugar, cocoa powder, baking soda, and salt. Set aside.

In a saucepan, heat the butter, Coca-Cola, and Dark Chocolate Ganache over medium heat until the butter and ganache melt. Transfer to the bowl of an electric mixer fitted with the paddle attachment.

With the mixer on medium speed, add the eggs, one at a time, mixing well after each addition. Add the buttermilk and vanilla and mix well. Add the dry ingredients and beat until smooth. The batter should be very thin.

Pour the batter into the prepared pan and bake for 45 minutes or until a cake tester comes out clean.

Let the cake cool slightly in the pan set on wire cooling racks.

For the icing: Using the same saucepan, heat the ganache and Coca-Cola over medium heat until the ganache melts. Do not boil. Transfer the mixture to the bowl of an electric mixer fitted with the paddle attachment. Add the confectioners' sugar, malt balls, cocoa powder, and vanilla and beat well.

Pour the warm icing over the warm cake, still in the pan. Allow the cake and icing to cool and set before cutting.

ChefSecret: This recipe works equally well and is as delicious using Pepsi-Cola or Dr. Pepper, but under no circumstance should you use any diet beverages. They just don't work as well.

special toolbox:

17 x 11-inch baking pan

sifter

offset metal spatula

electric stand mixer, bowl, and paddle

cake tester

wire cooling rack

cake:

4 cups all-purpose flour

4 cups granulated sugar

1 cup unsweetened Dutch-processed cocoa powder

2 teaspoons baking soda

1 teaspoon salt

1 pound (4 sticks) unsalted butter, at room temperature

2 cups Coca-Cola

1/4 cup Dark Chocolate Ganache (page 28)

4 large eggs

1 cup buttermilk

4 teaspoons pure vanilla extract

icing:

1/2 cup Milk Chocolate Ganache (page 26)

1/2 cup Coca-Cola

2 pounds confectioners' sugar

1 cup crushed malt balls

1/2 cup unsweetened Dutch-processed cocoa powder

2 teaspoons pure vanilla extract

Triple Chocolate Glazed
Mini-Bundt Cakes

In 1950, David Dalquist, founder of Nordic Ware, trademarked the *Bundt* name when he manufactured the first pan. The pan sold somewhat slowly until 1966, when the Pillsbury Bake-Off judges awarded a Bundt cake recipe second place in the contest. Since then, more than 50 million Bundt pans have been sold.

These pans come in a number of detailed, decorative shapes and sizes, ranging from a mini muffin to a layer cake. Bundt cakes can be glazed or not, filled or unfilled, split and frosted, or just served with a dusting of confectioners' sugar. They are suitable for the fanciest brunch buffet or, gussied up, for dessert with ice cream and chocolate sauce.

Makes 6 mini-Bundt cakes

Prep Time: 20 minutes
Baking Time: 20 to 25 minutes
Cooling Time: 30 minutes
Level: **

Preheat the oven to 350°F. Coat a 6-cavity mini Bundt pan with vegetable oil spray.

In the bowl of an electric mixer fitted with the paddle attachment, beat the butter and the Milk Chocolate Ganache until creamy. Gradually beat in the sugar until light and fluffy, about 2 minutes. Add the eggs, one at a time, beating well after each. Beat in the vanilla.

In a separate bowl, mix together the flour, cocoa powder, baking powder, and salt. Gradually beat the flour mixture into the butter mixture on medium speed for about 3 minutes or until thick and creamy.

Using a rubber spatula, fold in the chocolate chips and evenly divide the batter among the prepared Bundt pan. Bake for 20 to 25 minutes or until a cake tester inserted in centers comes out clean.

Let the cakes cool in the pan on a wire cooling rack for about 10 minutes. Gently loosen the edges with a dull kitchen knife and transfer the cakes to the rack to cool completely.

Before serving, drizzle the cakes with Chocolate Ganache. Decorate with chocolate curls, if desired.

special toolbox:

6-cup swirl cake pan (or mini 6-cup Bundt pan)

electric stand mixer, bowl, and paddle

wire cooling racks

cake tester

Flavorless vegetable oil spray

12 tablespoons (1$^1/_2$ sticks) unsalted butter, at room temperature

$^1/_2$ cup Milk Chocolate Ganache (page 26)

1$^1/_4$ cups granulated sugar

3 large eggs

2 teaspoons pure vanilla extract

1$^1/_2$ cups all-purpose flour

$^1/_4$ cup natural cocoa powder

2 teaspoons baking powder

$^1/_2$ teaspoon salt

$^1/_4$ cup milk chocolate chips

$^1/_4$ cup bittersweet or semisweet chocolate chips

1 cup Dark Chocolate Ganache (page 28), melted, for drizzling

Dark or white chocolate curls (page 35), for decoration (optional)

Never-Fail
Molten Lava Cakes

I was told that Molten Lava Cakes were created by master chef Joël Robuchon when he owned Jamin, his first restaurant in France, for a special Valrhona Chocolate Company dinner. Chef Joël is a master of complex textures and flavors and was really at his best with this recipe.

Prepared in the traditional manner, these are basically underbaked chocolate cakes; the batter in the center is soft and liquid. They can be somewhat temperamental if the oven temperature is a little off or if they are baked a little too long. Our recipe is perfect every time and never disappoints. It calls for placing a tablespoon-sized ball of Dark Chocolate Ganache in the center of each little cake to ensure a lavalike effect when you cut into the cake.

Makes 6 cakes

Prep Time: 30 minutes
Baking Time: 16 minutes
Level: **

Preheat the oven to 425°F. Butter six custard cups.

In a heatproof bowl, melt the chocolate and butter in a microwave or in a double boiler over simmering water, stirring until smooth. Add the confectioners' sugar and flour to the chocolate mixture and stir until well mixed and the batter is no longer hot. Stir in the whole eggs and egg yolks until smooth. Stir in the wine, if using, and the vanilla.

Pour an inch of the batter into each prepared custard cup. Place 1 tablespoon of Dark Chocolate Ganache in each cup, centering it on top of the batter. Divide the remainder of the batter evenly among the custard cups. Bake for about 16 minutes. The edges should be firm, but the center will be wonderfully fluid.

Run a knife around the edges to loosen and carefully invert the cakes onto dessert plates. Top with a dollop of White Chocolate Ganache Whipped Cream.

Variations:

You can use any flavored ganache or even caramel sauce for the center of the cakes. For additional impact, deeply color the White Chocolate Ganache with red food coloring and blend 3 tablespoons roasted cocoa nibs and ¼ teaspoon cayenne pepper to create your own red-hot rocky lava centers.

special toolbox:

6 (6-ounce) custard cups or ramekins

8 ounces bittersweet chocolate

¼ pound (1 stick) butter

1½ cups confectioners' sugar

½ cup all-purpose flour

3 large eggs

3 large egg yolks

2 tablespoons cabernet sauvignon (optional)

1 teaspoon pure vanilla extract

6 tablespoons Dark Chocolate Ganache (page 28)

1 cup White Chocolate Ganache Whipped Cream (page 238)

special toolbox:

9-inch square baking pan

cake tester

wire cooling rack

1 pound (4 sticks) unsalted butter

1½ cups heavy cream

15 ounces bittersweet or
  semisweet chocolate

2 tablespoons Dark Chocolate
  Ganache (page 28)

¾ cup granulated sugar

8 large eggs

Confectioners' sugar or cocoa
  powder, for decoration

ED'S BOX-TOP WISDOM

Negativity

We have no use for Vanity,
Infidelity, Sloppiness, Dirt, or
Greed. After all, negative
things like these can spoil a
great chocolate dessert.

Chocolate Ganache Cake

In 1982, my friend David Christy and I adventured on the plains of the Serengeti for three months. Toward the end of the trip, we were in "need" of something made with chocolate but were left with just a little baking flour and a case of evaporated milk. We found some freshly laid duck eggs by the river, and I was able to make this Chocolate Ganache Cake in a cast-iron skillet over an open fire. Fortunately, you won't have to work that hard to make this gluten-free cake.

Makes 8 to 10 servings

Prep Time: 15 minutes
Baking Time: 40 minutes
Chilling Time: best overnight
Level: ***

Preheat the oven to 350°F. Butter the baking pan.

In a heatproof bowl, melt the butter, cream, chocolate, and Dark Chocolate Ganache in a microwave or in a bowl set over simmering water. Stir with a wooden spoon until smooth. Add the granulated sugar to the warm mixture and stir until completely dissolved to prevent crystallization.

In a large bowl, beat the eggs with a fork. Add to the chocolate mixture, stirring until smooth. Pour into the baking pan and bake for 40 minutes, or until a cake tester inserted in the center comes out with just a few crumbs. Remove from the oven and let cool on a wire cooling rack.

When the cake is completely cool, invert it and wrap in plastic wrap. Refrigerate overnight.

To serve, remove the cake from the refrigerator and let it reach cool room temperature on the kitchen counter. The cake is meant to be served slightly chilled. Decorate with confectioners' sugar or cocoa powder before serving.

Spicy Chocolate Swirl Cakes

Any time that I can bring some of the original ingredients used by the native Mayan culture (circa sixth century) together to complement chocolate, I do. My friend's uncle owned a pre-Columbian art gallery in Amsterdam. When Morty invited me to the opening of an exhibit where the pieces dated back to the Olmec civilization—which flourished around 1200–400 BC—he asked me to "invent" a dessert that would bring balance to the exhibit. The Mayan art exhibit focused on rain, agriculture, and fertility. My Spicy Chocolate Swirl Cakes featured cinnamon, cloves, black pepper, sea salt, and, of course, cacao.

Makes 12 cakes

Prep Time: 20 minutes
Baking Time: 25 to 35 minutes
Cooling Time: 25 to 30 minutes
Level: **

Position the rack to the lower third of the oven. Preheat the oven to 325°F. Butter and flour the cavities of a swirl cake pan, tapping out any excess flour.

Sift the cake flour, cocoa powder, baking powder, cinnamon, cloves, pepper, and salt onto a sheet of waxed paper; set aside.

In the bowl of an electric mixer with a paddle attachment, beat the butter on medium speed until creamy, 45 to 60 seconds. Add the sugar and beat until light and fluffy, 4 to 5 minutes, occasionally scraping down the sides of the bowl.

Add the eggs, one at a time, beating well after each addition. Add the vanilla and beat just until mixed.

Add the dry ingredients and the milk alternately in three batches, beginning and ending with the dry ingredients and mixing on low speed until just combined. Scrape down the sides of the bowl as needed. Divide the batter among the prepared cake pan.

Bake for 25 to 35 minutes or until the cakes pull away from sides of the pans and spring back when gently touched. Transfer the pan to a wire cooling rack and let the cakes cool in the pan for about 10 minutes. Remove the cakes from the pan and let cool for 15 to 20 minutes longer, swirl side up. Drizzle tops with White Chocolate Sauce.

special toolbox:
12-cup swirl cake pan (or mini 12-cup Bundt pan)
sifter
electric stand mixer, bowl, and paddle
wire cooling rack

2 cups cake flour
(not self-rising), sifted

⅔ cup unsweetened
Dutch-processed cocoa powder

2 teaspoons baking powder

1 teaspoon ground cinnamon

¼ teaspoon ground cloves

¼ teaspoon ground black pepper

¼ teaspoon salt

½ pound (2 sticks) unsalted butter,
at room temperature

1¾ cups granulated sugar

2 large eggs

1 teaspoon pure vanilla extract

¾ cup whole milk

Tres Leches Chocolate Cake

Cinco de Mayo ("fifth of May") is the commemoration of the Mexican army's unexpected victory over the French at the Battle of Puebla on May 5, 1862. Celebrating the battle is important for at least two reasons. It gives us a chance to celebrate the victory by drinking lots of margaritas, and it's a good excuse to make our Tres Leches Chocolate Cake. This recipe may require that you clear out space in the freezer, which is a good idea to do before you begin.

Makes 1 (9-inch) 4-layer cake

Prep Time: 1 hour
Chilling Time: 50 minutes
Level: ****

Place the milk and white chocolate cake layers upside down on two baking sheets lined with parchment paper. Using a fork, poke holes evenly over the cake layers.

Pour 6 tablespoons of the evaporated milk over each cake layer and let it soak into the cake, approximately 1 to 2 minutes.

Pour 6 tablespoons of the condensed milk over each layer and spread evenly with a spatula. Transfer the baking sheets to the freezer for about 20 minutes to firm up the cake layers.

Put a small dab of ganache in the center of a cake-decorating turntable and place a cake circle on top of it. This will keep the cardboard centered and the cake layers stable while assembling. Apply another dab of ganache on top of the cake circle to secure the doily.

Center one milk chocolate cake layer on the doily, crown side down. Cut a strip of parchment paper and tuck it just under the bottom of the cake to keep the doily clean. The parchment should be able to be easily removed once the cake is assembled.

Evenly spread 1½ cups of Azteca Dark Chocolate Pastry Cream over the cake layer. Place a white chocolate cake layer over the Azteca Dark Chocolate Pastry Cream. Evenly spread the White Chocolate Pastry Cream over the cake layer.

Place a milk chocolate cake layer over the White Chocolate Pastry Cream and evenly spread the remaining 1½ cups Azteca Dark Chocolate Pastry Cream over the cake layer. Finally, top with a white chocolate cake layer over the Azteca Dark Chocolate Pastry Cream. Run a spatula around the sides to clean up the edges.

Carefully place the assembled cake in the freezer for 30 minutes.

Remove from the freezer and immediately frost the entire cake with the whipped Milk Chocolate Ganache.

special toolbox:

2 baking sheets

parchment paper

cake-decorating turntable
or lazy Susan

cake circle

10-inch cut paper doily

offset metal spatula

1 (9-inch) Milk Chocolate Ganache
  Layer Cake (page 51), at room
  temperature

1 (9-inch) White Chocolate Ganache
  Layer Cake (page 51), at room
  temperature

1½ cups (12 ounces)
  evaporated milk

1½ cups (12 ounces) sweetened
  condensed milk

3 cups Azteca Dark Chocolate
  Ganache Pastry Cream (page 237)

1½ cups White Chocolate Ganache
  Pastry Cream (page 237)

6 cups Milk Chocolate Ganache
  (page 26), whipped

Chocolate Gingerbread

Ginger is found on almost every continent and is used to flavor the foods of many cultures. Here in America, we seem to confine our use to baking familiar Christmas goodies, like gingerbread cake, gingerbread men, cookies, and even the popular edible ginger architecture, the gingerbread house.

The familiar deep color and moistness of gingerbread comes in large part from molasses—that dark, thick syrup made from sugarcane juice. When I was in Germany, working on desserts for a client in Berlin, my executive chef, Wayne Chidester, discovered that we could enhance the flavor of the beloved gingerbread by adding Old-Fashioned Hot Fudge Ganache.

Makes 6 to 8 servings

Prep Time: 15 minutes
Baking Time: 30 minutes
Level: *

Preheat the oven to 325°F. Butter an 8-inch square pan.

In a large bowl, mix the flour, ginger, baking powder, salt, pepper, and cloves. Stir in the brown sugar; set aside.

In a small saucepan, combine the butter, Hot Fudge Ganache, and water. Heat over medium, stirring frequently to blend.

Pour the wet ingredients into the dry ingredients and stir until smooth. Add the molasses and egg, stirring until just blended. Spoon the batter into the prepared pan. Bake until a cake tester inserted into the center comes out clean, about 30 minutes.

Cool in the pan on a wire cooling rack for 15 minutes and then turn the cake out onto the rack to cool completely.

Variations:

Add a Secret Center: Pour 1 inch of batter in each of eight custard cups. Put 1 tablespoon White Chocolate Ganache (page 29) in each cup. Divide the remaining batter evenly among the custard cups and bake for 20 minutes. The edges should be firm but the center will be wonderfully fluid. Run a knife around the edges to loosen and carefully invert onto dessert plates. Top with a dollop of White Chocolate Ganache Whipped Cream (page 238).

special toolbox:

8-inch square baking pan

cake tester

wire cooling rack

1¾ cups all-purpose flour

1½ teaspoons ground ginger

1 teaspoon baking powder

¼ teaspoon salt

⅛ teaspoon freshly ground black pepper

⅛ teaspoon ground cloves

½ cup firmly packed dark brown sugar

4 tablespoons unsalted butter

¼ cup Hot Fudge Ganache (page 30)

½ cup water

½ cup molasses

1 large egg, lightly beaten

Boston-Steamed Chocolate Cake

Okay, I admit it: I love the steamed pumpernickel bread you buy in a can from B&M, the baked beans people. A few years back I saw a recipe for making Boston-style steamed pumpernickel in the King Arthur Baker's catalog. I thought that if I could steam something as finicky as bread, it should be easy to steam a pudding-style chocolate cake. It took only a couple of attempts before we had a simple, no-fuss, steamed chocolate cake recipe. The best part is you don't even need a mixer.

Makes 4 to 6 servings

Prep Time: 15 minutes
Steaming Time: 1 hour
Level: *

In a large saucepan, bring the water to a boil over medium-high heat. Add the cocoa powder and sugar and stir until they are well absorbed.

Remove from the heat. Add the flour, sweetened condensed milk, Milk Chocolate Ganache, vegetable oil, eggs, vanilla, baking soda, and baking powder. Stir until smooth.

Pour the batter into a steamer container. Place a piece of aluminum foil loosely over the top to prevent condensations, which will ruin the cake's beautiful look.

Place the container on a steaming trivet in an 8 quart pot. Be sure the steamer container does not sit in the water. Bring the water to a low boil to produce steam. Cover and steam for 1 hour, making sure that the water does not boil away. If it does, add more water. The cake is done when a cake tester inserted in the center comes out clean.

Gently remove the cake from the container, slice, and serve hot.

ChefSecret: If you don't have a Pyrex cylinder, use a clean, tall, 16-ounce tin can. You can serve Steamed Chocolate Cake over a pool of melted White Chocolate Ganache (page 29), Hot Fudge Ganache (page 30), or Burnt Caramel Sauce (page 242).

special toolbox:

Pyrex steaming cylinder
8-quart pot with lid
steaming trivet
cake tester

1 cup water

1 cup unsweetened
  Dutch-processed cocoa powder

1 cup granulated sugar

2 cups all-purpose flour

1 cup sweetened condensed milk

¼ cup Milk Chocolate Ganache
  (page 26), melted

¼ cup vegetable oil

6 large eggs, lightly beaten

1 tablespoon pure vanilla extract

1 teaspoon baking soda

1 teaspoon baking powder

Scan for Ed's ChefSecret

Deep, Dark Chocolate
Ganache Cupcakes

This batter produces perfect rich, dark, moist chocolate cupcakes. If you're looking for a never-fail, basic cupcake recipe, you are in luck! The cupcakes are great frosted with any whipped chocolate ganache or buttercream frosting. You can drop a ball of frozen ganache into the unbaked batter spooned into the baking cups for molten chocolate cupcakes and eat them warm right out of the oven. You can also marble the cakes by substituting white or milk chocolate ganache for half of the recipe and swirling it through the dark chocolate batter.

Makes 16 cupcakes

Prep Time: 15 minutes
Baking Time: 20 to 25 minutes
Cooling Time: 20 minutes
Level: *

Preheat the oven to 350°F. Arrange 16 foil or paper muffin cups on a baking sheet or in muffins pans.

Whisk together the flour, cocoa powder, baking powder, baking soda, and salt in a large bowl.

Using an electric stand mixer on high speed, beat the sugar, butter, and Dark Chocolate Ganache in a large bowl. Scrape down the sides of the bowl with a rubber spatula as needed. Add the eggs, one at a time, mixing until just combined, and then beat in the vanilla.

With the mixer on low speed, add the dry ingredients and the milk alternately in three batches, beginning and ending with the flour mixture and mixing until just combined. Scrape down the sides of the bowl occasionally with a rubber spatula and mix just until the batter is incorporated.

Spoon the batter into the muffin cups, filling each about two-thirds full. Bake for 20 to 25 minutes or until a cake tester inserted into the center of a cupcake comes out clean.

special toolbox:

16 paper or foil baking cups
(2$\frac{1}{2}$-inch diameter)

muffin tins (optional)

2 large bowls

electric stand mixer, bowl, and paddle

cake tester

wire cooling rack

offset metal spatula

2 cups all-purpose flour

$\frac{1}{2}$ cup unsweetened
   Dutch-processed cocoa powder

2 teaspoons baking powder

1 teaspoon baking soda

$\frac{1}{4}$ teaspoon salt

1$\frac{1}{4}$ cups granulated sugar

$\frac{1}{4}$ pound (1 stick) unsalted butter,
   at room temperature

3 tablespoons Dark Chocolate
   Ganache (page 28),
   at room temperature

2 large eggs

1 teaspoon pure vanilla extract

$\frac{3}{4}$ cup whole milk

2 cups Dark Chocolate Cream
   Cheese Frosting, softened and
   whipped (page 232)

$\frac{1}{2}$ cup small chocolate curls
   (page 35) or decoratifs, for garnish

Transfer the cupcakes to a wire cooling rack or set the muffin pans directly on the rack and let cool for about 10 minutes. Remove the cupcakes from the muffin pans and cool completely.

When cool, frost with the Dark Chocolate Cream Cheese Frosting using an offset metal spatula. Garnish with chocolate curls or decoratifs.

ChefSecret: I like to use a 2-ounce (#16) ice cream scoop to measure the batter evenly when I spoon it into the cups.

Variations:

Substitute the Dark Chocolate Ganache with Milk Chocolate Ganache for a lighter chocolate flavor.

CUPCAKES

Of course the cupcake was invented in the United States. Where else could something so ingenious have been created? It was considered revolutionary at first because of the amount of time it saved in the nineteenth-century kitchen. There was a shift from weighing ingredients for baking to measuring them. This explains why cupcakes were sometimes called "number cakes." The measurements were easy to remember: one cup of butter, two cups of sugar, three cups of flour, four eggs, one cup of milk, and one spoonful of soda. Now, in the twenty-first century, cupcakes are enjoying a renaissance, and I couldn't be happier! The offerings out there include a staggering variety of fillings, frostings, flavors, and shapes.

Mile-High Meringue Chocolate Cupcakes

This is my version of a high-hat cupcake, baked Alaska, and a chocolate Italian meringue cake all rolled into one. The ingredients come together to make one of the most beautiful and memorable desserts you will find in this book—which is saying a lot! You may want to practice once or twice before attempting this for an important occasion, but no matter how the cupcakes come out, no one will turn one down, even if it's from a "practice round."

Makes 12 jumbo cupcakes

Prep Time: 15 minutes
Baking Time: 20 to 25 minutes
Cooling Time: 20 minutes
Level: ***

For the cupcakes. Position a rack in the middle of the oven and preheat to 350°F. Set 12 foil or paper cupcake liners on a baking sheet or line a large 12-cup muffin pan with the liners.

Melt the baking chocolate and Hot Fudge Ganache in a bowl in a microwave oven or in a bowl set over hot water, stirring until smooth and melted. Set aside.

Sift the flour, cocoa powder, baking powder, baking soda, and salt into a medium bowl. Set aside.

Using an electric stand mixer on medium speed, beat the sugar and butter in a large bowl until light and creamy, about 3 minutes. Scrape down the sides of the bowl with a rubber spatula once or twice.

Reduce the speed to low and mix in the melted chocolate.

With the mixer on medium speed, add the eggs, one at a time, beating after each addition until well blended into the batter. Add the vanilla and continue to beat until the mixture is creamy, about 2 minutes.

Mix in the sour cream until no white streaks remain. Stop the mixer and scrape down the sides of the bowl with a rubber spatula.

Reduce the mixer speed to low. Add half the flour mixture, mixing until just incorporated. Add the water and then the remaining flour, being careful not to overmix the batter.

Ingredients and directions continued on page 74.

special toolbox:

12 large paper or foil baking cups (3½-inch diameter)

muffin tins (optional)

sifter

electric stand mixer, bowl, and paddle

cake tester

wire cooling rack

handheld electric mixer

double boiler

instant-read thermometer

pastry bag fitted with a plain tip

cupcakes:

3 ounces unsweetened baking chocolate, chopped

2 tablespoons Hot Fudge Ganache (page 30)

1 cup all-purpose flour

2 tablespoons unsweetened ultra Dutch-processed cocoa powder or another high-quality cocoa powder

½ teaspoon baking powder

½ teaspoon baking soda

¼ teaspoon salt

1¼ cups granulated sugar

¼ pound (1 stick) unsalted butter, at room temperature

2 large eggs

1 teaspoon pure vanilla extract

½ cup sour cream

½ cup water

meringue topping:

1¾ cups granulated sugar

¼ cup cold water

3 large egg whites

¼ teaspoon cream of tartar

1 teaspoon pure vanilla extract

½ teaspoon almond extract

coating:

2 cups Dark Chocolate Ganache
(page 28)

3 tablespoons vegetable oil

Using a #12 scoop or a ⅓-cup measure, fill each baking cup with batter to just below the top of the paper liner.

Bake until the tops feel firm and bounce back and a cake tester inserted into the center comes out clean, about 20 minutes. Cool the cupcakes on a wire rack for 10 minutes. Remove the cupcakes from the pan and let them cool completely on the wire rack.

For the meringue topping: While the cupcakes are cooling, combine the sugar, water, egg whites, and cream of tartar in a metal mixing bowl with at least a 2-quart capacity. Beat with a handheld electric mixer on high speed until opaque, white, and foamy, about 3 minutes.

Transfer the egg whites to the top of a double boiler set over barely simmering water. You may also set the metal mixing bowl over a saucepan filled partially with barely simmering water. The mixing bowl should sit firmly over the pan of hot water.

Using the same handheld electric mixer, beat the whites on high speed until the meringue forms stiff peaks, about 12 minutes. The topping will be done by then, and its temperature will register 165°F on an instant read thermometer. If not, keep beating until the temperature is right. (Take care to keep the cord of the electric mixer away from the stovetop burner.)

Remove the bowl from the water, add the vanilla and almond extracts, and continue to beat for 2 minutes to further thicken the topping. The topping will become firmer as it cools.

Carefully spoon the topping into a large pastry bag fitted with a large plain pastry tip. Pipe a spiral of topping into a 2-inch-high cone-shaped mound on top of each cupcake using about ½ cup of topping per cupcake. Leave a ⅛-inch edge around each cupcake. Transfer the cupcakes to a plate and refrigerate. Do not cover the cupcakes.

For the coating: Heat the Dark Chocolate Ganache with the oil in a microwave oven or in a bowl set over hot water, stirring until the ganache is smooth and melted. Set aside.

Transfer the chocolate coating to a small, deep bowl, which will make it easy to dip the cupcakes. Cool slightly, about 15 minutes.

Remove the cupcakes from the refrigerator. Holding each cupcake by its bottom, dip the top of the meringue topping into the chocolate coating, letting any excess drip off. Spoon more coating over the rest of the topping to coat and over the unfilled edge of the cupcake; none of the white topping should show. Let the cupcakes sit at room temperature for about 15 minutes for the coating to firm slightly.

Peel off the paper liners and discard. This will give you a smooth chocolate-coated edge if any coating has run over the paper liner. Refrigerate for 30 minutes to set the coating. When the coating is set, cover and refrigerate for at least 2 hours.

Before serving, remove the cupcakes from the refrigerator and let sit at room temperature for 15 minutes. Serve slightly chilled. The cupcakes will keep in the refrigerator for up to two days if covered with plastic wrap.

ChefSecret: If you don't have a pastry bag, substitute a sturdy plastic bag, such as a freezer bag. Snip one of the bottom corners off the bag, fill it partially with the meringue topping, and gently squeeze into the cupcakes.

MY BEST CUPCAKE MEMORY

My most memorable birthday was my tenth because I had a Hopalong Cassidy birthday party. For anyone who doesn't know who Hopalong was, he was a beloved television cowboy in the era of Roy Rogers and Gene Autry. My mother made a cupcake tree for the event, and while I don't quite know what cupcakes had to do with cowboys, I still smile when I think about that magical party.

Chocolate-Pumped Cupcakes

Some people go to Gold's Gym and pump iron. I make cupcakes that are pumped with chocolate ganache—the ultimate party-stopping dessert. It's as easy to do as baking a traditional cupcake, with a little gussying up for company. This recipe gets a smidge more difficult when it comes to cutting a small cone out of the middle and filling it with Chocolate Ganache whipped cream, but because just a little effort turns this basic cupcake into something very special, I hope you won't find it too daunting.

Makes 12 jumbo cupcakes

Prep Time: 15 minutes
Baking Time: 20 minutes
Cooling Time: 20 minutes
Level: **

Position a rack in the middle of the oven and preheat to 350°F. Line a large 12-cavity muffin pan with paper or foil liners.

Melt the baking chocolate and the Hot Fudge Ganache in a bowl in a microwave oven or in a bowl set over hot water. Stir the mixture until the chocolate has melted and it has a smooth consistency. Set aside.

Sift the flour, cocoa powder, baking powder, baking soda, and salt into a medium bowl. Set aside.

Using an electric stand mixer on medium speed, beat the granulated sugar and butter, and scrape down the sides of the bowl with a rubber spatula once or twice. Reduce the speed to low and beat in the melted chocolate just until blended.

With the mixer on medium speed, add the eggs, one at a time, beating after each addition until well blended. Add the vanilla and continue to beat until the mixture is

special toolbox:

12 large paper or foil baking cups (3½-inch diameter)

12-cup muffin tin

sifter

electric stand mixer, bowl, and paddle

cake tester

wire cooling rack

pastry bag fitted with a star tip

3 ounces unsweetened baking chocolate, chopped

2 tablespoons Hot Fudge Ganache (page 30)

1 cup all-purpose flour

2 tablespoon unsweetened ultra Dutch-processed cocoa powder or another high-quality cocoa powder

½ teaspoon baking powder

½ teaspoon baking soda

¼ teaspoon salt

Ingredients continued on page 77.

creamy, about 2 minutes. Mix in the sour cream until no white streaks remain. Scrape down the sides of the bowl with a rubber spatula once or twice.

Reduce the mixer speed to low. Add half the flour mixture, and beat just until just incorporated. Add the water and then the remaining flour mixture, being careful not to overmix the batter.

Using a #12 scoop or a ⅓-cup measure, fill each baking cup with batter to just below the top of the paper liner.

Bake until the tops feel firm and bounce back and a cake tester inserted into the center comes out clean, about 20 minutes. Cool the cupcakes in the pan on a wire cooling rack for 10 minutes. Remove the cupcakes from the pan and cool completely on the wire rack.

Using a sharp paring knife, cut a large, cone-shaped piece from the middle of each cupcake. Set the cone aside. The cones should be about 1 inch in diameter at the crown.

Fill a pastry bag fitted with a star tip with Hot Fudge Ganache Whipped Cream. Fill the hole in each cupcake with the whipped cream. Replace the cone, inserting the pointed end into the cream and allowing the top to protrude above the cupcake. Sift confectioners' sugar over the top.

ChefSecret: If you don't have a pastry bag, substitute a sturdy plastic bag, such as a freezer bag. Snip one of the bottom corners off the bag, partially fill it with whipped cream, and gently squeeze into the cupcakes.

1¼ cups granulated sugar

¼ pound (1 stick) unsalted butter, at room temperature

2 large eggs

1 teaspoon pure vanilla extract

½ cup sour cream

½ cup water

2 cups Hot Fudge Ganache Whipped Cream (page 238)

¼ cup confectioners' sugar

Scan for Ed's ChefSecret

Light and White Chocolate Ganache Chocolate Chip Cupcakes

Each year I host a class for the aspiring chefs of Los Angeles Trade Tech, where we conduct a chocolate tasting. We start with the various dark chocolates and then move up to taste the milks and, finally, the white chocolates. Judging from the moans of pleasure that accompany each bite, each chocolate seems to be progressively more orgasmic. To my surprise, when the students are asked their favorite, white is always the winner. This recipe is versatile and highlights our smooth and satisfying Snowy White Chocolate. I like to add macadamia nuts, pineapple bits, and coconut to give it a Hawaiian flair.

Makes 16 cupcakes

Prep Time: 15 minutes
Baking Time: 15 to 20 minutes
Cooling Time: 20 minutes
Level: *

Preheat the oven to 350°F. Arrange 16 foil or paper muffin cups on a baking sheet or in muffins pans.

In a large bowl, whisk together the flour, baking powder, baking soda, and salt. Set aside.

Using an electric stand mixer on high speed, beat the sugar, butter, and White Chocolate Ganache in a large bowl. Scrape down the sides of the bowl with a rubber spatula once or twice. Add the eggs, one at a time, mixing until just combined. Beat in the vanilla.

With the mixer on low speed, gradually beat in the dry ingredients, alternating with the milk. Scrape down the bowl occasionally with a rubber spatula and mix until the batter is just blended. Fold in the white chocolate chips.

Spoon the batter into the muffin cups, filling each about two-thirds full. Bake for 15 to 20 minutes or until a cake tester comes out clean.

Transfer the cupcakes to a wire rack or set the muffin pans directly on the rack and let cool for about 10 minutes. Remove the cupcakes from the muffin pans and cool completely.

When cool, frost with the White Chocolate Cream Cheese Frosting using an offset metal spatula.

ChefSecret: For even baking, rotate the baking sheet holding the cupcakes or the muffin pans in the oven about halfway through the baking process.

special toolbox:

16 paper or foil baking cups
(2 1/2-inch diameter)

muffin tins (optional)

electric stand mixer, bowl, and paddle

cake tester

wire cooling rack

offset metal spatula

2 1/2 cups all-purpose flour

2 teaspoons baking powder

1 teaspoon baking soda

1/4 teaspoon salt

1 1/4 cups granulated sugar

4 tablespoons unsalted butter,
at room temperature

1/4 cup White Chocolate Ganache
(page 29), at room temperature

2 large eggs

2 teaspoons pure vanilla extract

3/4 cup whole milk

1/2 cup white chocolate chips

2 cups White Chocolate Cream
Cheese Frosting, softened and
whipped (page 234)

The Chocolate Bombe Cupcakes

This is one of those desserts you can't mess up—even if you already have. Just bake the cupcakes, turn them upside down, slather them with Old Fashioned Hot Fudge Sauce, and then drizzle them with a little White Chocolate Ganache Sauce. Voilà!

These didn't start out so fancy, but evolved when I discovered that the tops had broken off nearly every cupcake I was preparing for a catered banquet. We had baked one thousand cupcakes, and while at first I panicked, I ended up making the best of what could have been a bad situation, and the result is yummy!

Makes 12 jumbo cupcakes

Prep Time: 15 minutes
Baking Time: 20 to 25 minutes
Cooling Time: 20 minutes
Level: **

Position a rack in the middle of the oven and preheat to 350°F. Set 12 foil or paper cupcake liners on a baking sheet or line a large 12-cup muffin pan with the liners.

Melt the baking chocolate and Hot Fudge Ganache in a bowl in a microwave oven or in a bowl set over hot water, stirring until smooth and melted. Set aside.

Sift the flour, cocoa powder, baking powder, baking soda, and salt into a medium bowl. Set aside.

Using an electric stand mixer on medium speed, beat the sugar and butter in a large bowl until smooth and creamy, about 3 minutes. Scrape down the sides of the bowl with a rubber spatula once or twice. Reduce the speed to low and mix in the melted chocolate.

With the mixer on medium speed, add the eggs, one at a time, beating after each addition until well blended into the batter. Add the vanilla and continue to beat until the mixture is creamy, about 2 minutes. Mix in the sour cream until no white streaks remain. Stop the mixer and scrape down the sides with a rubber spatula.

Reduce the speed to low. Add half the flour mixture, mixing until just incorporated. Add the water and then the remaining flour, being careful not to overmix the batter.

Using a #12 scoop or a 1/3-cup measure, fill each baking cup with batter to just below the top of the paper liner.

Directions continued on page 81.

special toolbox:

12 large paper or foil baking cups (3 1/2-inch diameter)

muffin tins (optional)

saucepan

sifter

electric stand mixer, bowl, and paddle

wire cooling rack

2 microwave-safe bowls

mixing spoon

pastry bag with a narrow tip

3 ounces unsweetened baking chocolate, chopped

2 tablespoons Hot Fudge Ganache (page 30)

1 cup all-purpose flour

2 tablespoons unsweetened ultra Dutch-processed cocoa powder or another high-quality cocoa powder

1/2 teaspoon baking powder

1/2 teaspoon baking soda

1/4 teaspoon salt

1 1/4 cups granulated sugar

1/4 pound (1 stick) unsalted butter, at room temperature

2 large eggs

1 teaspoon pure vanilla extract

1/2 cup sour cream

1/2 cup water

12 (1-inch) White Chocolate Ganache (page 29) balls, frozen

3 cups Hot Fudge Ganache (page 30), at room temperature

1/2 cup White Chocolate Ganache (page 29), at room temperature

Carefully place a frozen White Chocolate Ganache ball into the center of each cupcake and bake until the tops feel firm and bounce back, about 20 minutes. The center will be creamy because of the ganache ball.

Transfer the cupcakes from the baking sheet to a wire rack or set the muffin pans directly on the rack and cool completely.

While the cupcakes are cooling, in a microwave-safe bowl melt the Hot Fudge Ganache in a microwave oven until pourable. In a separate bowl melt the White Chocolate Ganache until pourable.

When ready to serve, remove the paper liners from the cupcakes and turn the cupcakes upside down on a wire rack. Spoon 3 or 4 tablespoons of the melted Hot Fudge Ganache over each cupcake. Let the ganache set for about 15 minutes and then glaze again. Let this second coating set before proceeding.

Spoon the melted White Chocolate Ganache into a pastry bag fitted with a narrow tip. Drizzle lines over the Hot Fudge Ganache. Serve immediately.

ChefSecret: To make ganache balls, using a melon baller or a tablespoon, scoop chocolate ganache and roll into a ball. Place in the freezer for at least 10 minutes.

You can prepare the cupcakes up to three days ahead. When ready to serve, microwave each cupcake for about 10 seconds to soften the White Chocolate Ganache center; then follow the glazing instructions.

If you don't have a pastry bag, substitute a sturdy plastic bag, such as a freezer bag. Snip one of the bottom corners off the bag, fill it partially with the ganache, and gently squeeze over the cupcakes.

Chapter

6

SMOOTH AND CREAMY
CHOCOLATE CHEESECAKES

THE ANCIENT ROMANS SERVED CHEESECAKES DURING RELIGIOUS CEREMONIES. IT MAKES PER-
FECT SENSE: WHO HASN'T HAD A RELIGIOUS EXPERIENCE EATING A GREAT PIECE OF CHEESE-
CAKE? WHETHER YOU ARE A FAN OF JUNIOR'S IN BROOKLYN OR YOU HEAD TO THE CHEESECAKE
FACTORY AT EVERY OPPORTUNITY, CHEESECAKE AFICIONADOS HAVE A HARD TIME RESISTING THE DESSERT.

Cheesecakes are both sweet and savory and made from a variety of cheeses. Most cheesecakes in the United States use cream cheese as a base; in Italy, it's ricotta; in Germany and Poland, quark.

When you blend chocolate with cream cheese and heavy cream, something magical happens—and when the chocolate is one of my chocolate ganaches, the results are beyond sublime. Cheesecakes are easy to dress up. You can add chocolate chips, pieces of leftover cake, or ripples of fruit-flavored ganache to the batter.

They are always a crowd pleaser, which is why I devote an entire chapter to this all-American favorite. I am sure you won't be surprised to learn that cheesecake has outdistanced apple pie as America's number-one dessert. I know I wasn't!

Not every cheesecake in this chapter is a classic, by any stretch of the imagination. Instead, they are tempting hybrids of the original, old-fashioned, New York–style cheesecake originally found in Jewish delis and bakeries, primarily in the Northeast. Most are easily baked in a springform pan, and all contain chocolate ganache.

New York–Style cheesecakes require patience. They are not difficult to make—really!—but it's hard to wait to eat them while they cool. And cool they must, because cheesecakes are best eaten after being allowed to chill overnight and then brought back to room temperature.

Ultimate White Chocolate Cheesecake

"This is so pretty and delicious that I want you to make this for my wedding," said my good friend Beth about six weeks before getting married in Chicago. This cake is perfect for a bridal luncheon or wedding shower, but I had never thought of it as a wedding cake. Figuring out how to support the sheer weight of the layers would be as challenging as any Food Network competition. But how can you say no to a blushing bride? I couldn't! The lemon-blueberry topping enhances the flavor of both the cream cheese and the White Chocolate Ganache . . . and the bride and groom lived happily ever after.

Makes 8 to 10 servings

Prep Time: 30 minutes
Baking Time: 1 hour 30 minutes
Cooling Time: 30 minutes
Chilling Time: 6 hours or overnight
Assembly Time: 10 minutes
Level: **

special toolbox:

10-inch springform pan

10-inch parchment paper circle

electric stand mixer, bowl, and paddle

roasting pan

wire cooling rack

cake plate

crust:

2 cups finely ground, store-bought chocolate wafers (about 35 wafers)

¼ pound (1 stick) unsalted butter, melted

½ teaspoon ground cinnamon

For the crust: Line the bottom of a 10-inch springform pan with a 10-inch parchment paper circle. Lightly coat the bottom and side of the pan with nonstick cooking spray. Wrap the bottom of the springform pan with a layer of plastic wrap and then a layer of foil to prevent leaking during baking.

In a medium bowl, combine the wafers, butter, and cinnamon and stir with a fork until evenly moistened. Pour the crumbs into the springform pan and, using the bottom of a measuring cup or the smooth bottom of a glass and your fingertips, press the crumbs into the bottom and up the side of the pan about 1 inch. Refrigerate while making the filling.

For the cheesecake: Preheat the oven to 325°F. In the bowl of an electric mixer fitted with the paddle attachment, beat the cream cheese on low speed for 1 minute until smooth and free of any lumps. Add the eggs, one at a time, beating slowly after each addition until combined. Gradually add the sugar and beat until creamy, for 1 to 2 minutes. Add the sour cream, White Chocolate Ganache, lemon zest, and vanilla and beat until incorporated, scraping down the sides of the bowl and the paddle with a rubber spatula occasionally. The batter should be well mixed, but not overbeaten.

Pour the batter into the crust in the springform pan. Smooth the top with a rubber spatula. Place the springform pan in a large roasting pan and set the pan on the middle rack of the oven. Pour enough boiling water into the roasting pan to reach halfway up the side of the springform pan. The foil and plastic wrap will keep the water from seeping into the cheesecake.

Bake for 1 hour 30 minutes or until the top of the cheesecake jiggles slightly in the center. The cheesecake will become firm after chilling. Remove the cheesecake from the water and let cool in the pan on a wire cooling rack for 30 minutes. Loosely cover the cheesecake with plastic wrap and transfer to the refrigerator for at least 6 hours or overnight before serving.

For the topping: In a small saucepan, heat the blueberries, sugar, lemon zest, and lemon juice to a simmer over medium heat and cook for 5 minutes or until the fruit begins to break down slightly. Stir gently with a wooden spoon. Let the sauce cool slightly for about 20 minutes before spreading on the top of the cheesecake.

Loosen the cheesecake from the side of the pan by running a thin paring knife around the inner edge of the pan. Release the clip from the rim of the pan and carefully remove it from the cheesecake. Transfer the cheesecake to a cake plate, leaving the bottom of the springform pan underneath the cake. Using an offset metal spatula, spread a layer of the warm topping over the top of the cheesecake.

To serve, dip a thin paring knife (do not use a serrated knife) in hot water and dry, then slice the cheesecake.

cheesecake:

2 (8-ounce) packages cream cheese, at room temperature

3 large eggs

2/3 cup granulated sugar

1 cup sour cream

1 cup White Chocolate Ganache (page 29), at room temperature

Zest of 1 lemon

1/2 teaspoon pure vanilla extract (or the seeds from 1/2 vanilla bean)

topping:

1 pint blueberries

2 tablespoons granulated sugar

Zest and juice of 1 lemon

Dark Chocolate Ganache Cheesecake

I love to make this über-decadent chocolate cheesecake as the finale for Sunday brunch . . . it literally melts in your mouth. It is so ultra creamy and sinfully rich, it becomes the pièce de résistance at the end of any meal. One piece and your guests will love you forever!

The most common complaint I hear about cheesecakes is that they're too difficult to make. Don't believe it. For best results, read the recipe completely and have all of the ingredients measured out in front of you before even turning on the oven. Then be prepared for everyone you know to ask you for your secret recipe!

Makes 8 to 10 servings

Prep Time: 30 minutes
Baking Time: 1 hour 30 minutes
Cooling Time: 1 hour
Chilling Time: 6 hours or overnight
Level: **

special toolbox:

food processor fitted
with a metal blade

10-inch springform pan

10-inch parchment paper circle

electric stand mixer, bowl, and paddle

roasting pan

wire cooling rack

cookie crust:

1 cup whole almonds, toasted

2 cups finely ground, store-bought
chocolate wafers (about 35 wafers)

4 tablespoons unsalted butter, melted

1/2 teaspoon almond extract

For the cookie crust: Preheat the oven to 350°F. Line the bottom of a 10-inch springform pan with a 10-inch parchment paper circle. Spray the bottom of the pan with flavorless vegetable spray.

In the bowl of a food processor fitted with the metal blade, pulse the almonds, cookie crumbs, butter, and almond extract until well mixed and nicely moist. Pour the crumbs into the pan and, using the bottom of a measuring cup or the smooth bottom of a glass and your fingertips, press the crumbs into the bottom of the pan. Bake for 10 minutes. Remove from the oven and let cool on a wire cooling rack.

When cool, wrap the bottom of the springform pan with a layer of plastic wrap and a layer of aluminum foil to prevent leaking during baking.

Reduce the oven temperature to 325°F.

For the cheesecake: In the bowl of an electric mixer fitted with the paddle attachment, beat half of the cream cheese, one-third of the sugar, and 2 tablespoons of the cornstarch on low speed until creamy, about 3 minutes. Beat in the remaining cream cheese and the Dark Chocolate Ganache.

Increase the mixer speed to high and beat in the remaining sugar, the remaining cornstarch, and the coffee, cocoa powder, and vanilla. Add the eggs, one at a time, beating well after each addition. Scrape down the sides of the bowl with a rubber spatula. Add the cream and sour cream and mix only until completely blended, being careful not to overmix the batter.

Pour the batter into the crust in the springform pan. Smooth the top with a spatula. Place the springform pan in a large roasting pan and set the pan on the middle rack of the oven. Pour enough boiling water into the roasting pan to reach about halfway up the side of the springform pan. The foil and plastic wrap will keep the water from seeping into the cheesecake.

Bake for about 1 hour 30 minutes. The cheesecake should still jiggle slightly in the center. It will become firm after chilling. Remove the cheesecake from the water and let cool in the pan on a wire cooling rack for 10 minutes.

For the topping: Increase the oven temperature to 400°F

In a medium mixing bowl, whisk together the sour cream and sugar. Pour over the cheesecake and return to the oven for 10 minutes. Cool the cheesecake on a wire rack for 1 hour. Cover with plastic wrap and refrigerate for at least 6 hours or overnight until completely chilled.

When ready to serve, loosen the cheesecake from the side of the pan by running a thin paring knife around the inner edge of the pan. Release the clip from the rim of the pan and carefully remove it from the cheesecake. Transfer the cheesecake to a cake plate, leaving the bottom of the springform pan underneath the cake.

To serve, dip a thin paring knife (do not use a serrated knife) in hot water and dry, then slice the cheesecake. Dip and dry between each cut. Place a light pool of Red Raspberry Sauce on each serving plate and drizzle each piece with additional Red Raspberry Sauce.

cheesecake:

4 (8-ounce) packages cream cheese, at room temperature, divided

1⅔ cups granulated sugar, divided

¼ cup cornstarch, divided

¾ cup Dark Chocolate Ganache (page 28)

2 tablespoons cold, strong coffee

1 tablespoon unsweetened cocoa powder

2 teaspoons pure vanilla extract

3 large eggs

½ cup heavy cream

¼ cup sour cream

topping:

2 cups sour cream

½ cup granulated sugar

¼ cup Red Raspberry Sauce (page 243)

Marble Chocolate Cheesecake

Do I want white chocolate or do I want dark chocolate? Here is a marbleized cheesecake that offers a taste of three chocolates—bittersweet, milk, and white—to make the decision easier. Back in the day, I made this cheesecake with three different batters, but now I make one batter, divide it in thirds, and simply add melted ganache to flavor it. The result is an extra-tall, rich, moist cheesecake with beautiful swirls of white and chocolate ganache eddying through the cheesecake batter.

Makes 8 to 10 servings

Prep Time: 30 minutes
Baking Time: 1 hour 30 minutes
Cooling Time: 1 hour
Chilling Time: 6 hours or overnight
Level: ***

For the graham cracker crust: Preheat the oven to 375°F. Line the bottom of a 10-inch springform pan with a 10-inch parchment paper circle. Butter the bottom and side of the pan. In a large bowl, mix together the graham cracker crumbs, butter, sugar, almond extract, and cinnamon, if using, with a wooden spoon until well blended. Pour the crumbs into the springform pan and, using the bottom of a measuring cup or the smooth bottom of a glass and your fingertips, press the crumbs into the bottom and up the side of the pan about 1 inch.

Reduce the oven temperature to 325°F and bake the crust for 7 minutes. Cool on a wire cooling rack for at least 20 minutes before filling. When cool, wrap the bottom of the springform pan with plastic wrap and aluminum foil to prevent leaking during baking.

For the cheesecake: In the bowl of an electric mixer fitted with the paddle attachment, beat half of the cream cheese, one-third of the sugar, and all of the cornstarch on low speed until creamy, about 3 minutes. Beat in the remaining cream cheese.

special toolbox:

10-inch springform pan

10-inch parchment paper circle

electric stand mixer, bowl, and paddle

4 small mixing bowls

roasting pan

wire cooling rack

graham cracker crust:

2 cups finely ground graham cracker crumbs (about 16 whole crackers)

¼ pound (1 stick) unsalted butter, melted

½ cup granulated sugar

1 teaspoon almond extract

½ teaspoon ground cinnamon (optional)

Increase the mixer speed to high and beat in the remaining sugar and the vanilla. Add the eggs, one at a time, beating well after each addition. Scrape down the sides of the bowl with a rubber spatula. Add the cream and mix until smoothly blended, being careful not to overmix.

Equally divide the batter among three separate bowls. Pour the melted Dark Chocolate Ganache into one bowl, the White Chocolate Ganache into a second bowl, and the Milk Chocolate Ganache into a third bowl. Gently fold the ganache into the batter with a rubber spatula.

Pour the dark chocolate batter into the crust in the springform pan. Next, pour in the white chocolate batter. Finally, pour in the milk chocolate batter. Using a table knife, gently swirl to create a marbled design.

Place the springform pan in a large roasting pan and set the pan on the middle rack of the oven. Pour enough boiling water into the roasting pan to reach about halfway up the side of the springform pan. The foil and plastic wrap will keep the water from seeping into the cheesecake.

Bake for about 1 hour 30 minutes, or until the edges looked baked and the center is set but it should not jiggle in the middle. Remove the cheesecake from the water and cool in the pan on a wire cooling rack for 2 hours. Cover with plastic wrap and refrigerate for at least 6 hours or overnight until completely chilled.

When ready to serve, loosen the cheesecake from the side of the pan by running a thin paring knife around the inner edge of the pan. Release the clip from the rim of the pan and carefully remove it from the cheesecake. Transfer the cheesecake to a cake plate, leaving the bottom of the spingform pan underneath the cake.

To serve, dip a thin paring knife (do not use a serrated knife) in hot water and dry, then slice the cheesecake. Dip and dry between every cut. Drizzle each piece with Dark Chocolate Sauce.

cheesecake:

4 (8-ounce) packages cream cheese, at room temperature

1²⁄₃ cups granulated sugar

¼ cup cornstarch

1 tablespoon pure vanilla extract

3 large eggs

¾ cup heavy cream

¼ cup Dark Chocolate Ganache (page 28), melted

¼ cup White Chocolate Ganache (page 29), melted

¼ cup Milk Chocolate Ganache (page 26), melted

¼ cup Dark Chocolate Sauce (see box on page 30), warmed

New York Sponge Cake

When I first started making cheesecakes with sponge cake crusts, I was concerned that the sponge might get soggy or gummy. Even though many New York restaurants favor the sponge base over cookie or cracker crusts, I remained skeptical until I had mastered it.

At first, I believed the sponge would be complicated to make, but after four or five tries, I discovered sponges were really quite easy and, of course, totally delicious. I add a little white ganache to this recipe just to make sure there is more than enough chocolate.

Makes 1 (10-inch) cheesecake or 8 (4-inch) mini cheesecakes

Prep Time: 20 minutes
Baking Time: 10 to 11 minutes
Cooling Time: 10 minutes
Level: *

special toolbox:

10-inch springform pan or 8 (4-inch) springform pans

10-inch parchment paper circle or 8 (4-inch) parchment paper circles

sifter

electric stand mixer, bowl, and whisk

whisk

wire cooling rack

1/2 cup all-purpose flour

1 teaspoon baking powder

Pinch of salt

3 large eggs, separated

1/3 cup plus 2 tablespoons granulated sugar, divided

2 teaspoons pure vanilla extract

1 teaspoon grated lemon zest

2 tablespoons unsalted butter, melted

1 tablespoon White Chocolate Ganache (page 29), melted

1/4 teaspoon cream of tartar

Preheat the oven to 350°F. Line the bottom of a 10-inch springform pan with a 10-inch parchment paper circle and spray with flavorless vegetable oil spray. If using 8 small springform pans, line and spray each of them with parchment rounds cut to fit. Wrap the bottom of the springform pan with plastic wrap and aluminum foil to prevent leaking during baking.

Whisk together the flour, baking powder, and salt in a medium bowl and set aside.

In the bowl of an electric mixer fitted with the paddle attachment, beat the egg yolks on high speed for about 3 minutes.

Reduce the speed to medium and gradually add 1/3 cup of the sugar. Continue beating until thick, light yellow ribbons form when the beaters are lifted, about 5 minutes more. Beat in the vanilla and lemon zest. Remove the bowl from the mixer.

Sift the flour mixture over the batter and stir just until there are no white flecks. Slowly stir the butter and the White Chocolate Ganache into the batter with a spatula.

In a separate mixing bowl using the whisk attachment, beat the egg whites and cream of tartar together on high speed until frothy. Gradually add the remaining 2 tablespoons sugar and continue beating until stiff peaks form. Stir about one-third of the egg whites into the batter and then gently fold in the remaining egg whites.

Spoon the batter into the prepared springform pan or pans and smooth the top with the rubber spatula. Bake just until the center of the cake springs back when lightly touched, 10 to 11 minutes; Cool in the pan set on a wire cooling rack.

When cool, pour the cheesecake batter of your choice into the sponge and bake according to the recipe.

"MR. ENGORON, THIS IS THE WHITE HOUSE CALLING."

In 1983 I got a call at four o'clock in the morning. I had just closed one of my restaurants two hours earlier and wasn't in the mood to be bothered. The voice on the other end said it was the White House. I hung up, thinking it was a joke. Finally, on the third try I realized that the voice at the other end was that of Ed Meese, counselor to President Reagan. I had met Mr. Meese a few months earlier in San Francisco. "President Reagan heard that you frequently travel to the Philippines on business, and he'd like you to deliver a package and communiqué to President Marcos this week. Are you available?" I was and I did.

I flew to Washington on a special Air Force jet later that day. I temporarily traded my personal passport for a diplomatic one and was entrusted with two gifts to be given to President Marcos—a commemorative Theodore Roosevelt Winchester 30-30 rifle and a pictorial book on the Spanish-American War, with hand-painted pictures. I was also handed a sealed envelope marked "Secret," with the presidential seal prominently displayed on the exterior.

Upon arrival in Manila, I was whisked off to the embassy, where I met Ambassador Dick Murphy. We discussed the required protocol for the trip, and subjects that were considered taboo. At the presidential palace, we were met by the First Lady's pastry chef, and a bodyguard who looked like Oddjob from the movie *Goldfinger*. Madame Marcos was a frequent guest at one of my San Francisco restaurants and loved our cheesecakes. She wanted one of my best ones to be served at the following night's dinner party. Working together, the chef and I created the White Chocolate Raspberry Cheesecake that you will find on page 96.

The evening was to include a small formal dinner and entertainment at the Malacañang Palace the following night and I was an in-residence guest of the president. My companion for the evening was a female news anchor from the Philippine television studio Associated Broadcasting Company. When dinner was first served, I was seated directly to the right of the president. Just before the first dessert course and coffee were served, the president and the First Lady switched seats, placing me between the two beautiful Filipino women.

The cheesecake was a big hit. As good as it was though, it could hardly compare with the magic of that special tropical evening in Manila.

Azteca Mini Chocolate Ganache Cheesecakes

On the West Coast, we "party hearty" on May 5, with frosty pitchers of margaritas to celebrate the Mexican holiday of Cinco de Mayo. I was in need of a dessert for Cinco de Mayo one year when I was cooking on the cruise ship *Island Princess*, headed for the Mexican Riviera. I could have made a fresh key lime or tequila cheesecake and everyone would have been happy, but as we weren't wasting away in Margaritaville, I instead opted for these Azteca Mini Chocolate Ganache Cheesecakes. Mexico is, after all, the birthplace of cinnamon and chocolate, and this cake is rich with both, as well as a touch of honey.

Makes 8 servings

Prep Time: 30 minutes
Baking Time: 1 hour
Cooling Time: 1 hour
Chilling Time: 3 to 4 hours or overnight
Level: *

special toolbox:

8 (4-inch) mini-springform pans

8 (4-inch) parchment paper circles

electric stand mixer, bowl, and paddle

roasting pan

wire cooling rack

Batter for New York Sponge Cake
   (page 90), uncooked

4 (8-ounce) packages cream cheese,
   at room temperature

1²/₃ cups granulated sugar, divided

¼ cup cornstarch

1 teaspoon ground cinnamon

½ cup Azteca Chocolate Ganache
   (page 33)

1 tablespoon honey

1 tablespoon pure vanilla extract

3 large eggs

¾ cup heavy cream

¼ cup sour cream

Mango-Pineapple Chutney
   (page 249)

Preheat the oven to 350°F. Line the bottom of each of the springform pans with 4-inch parchment paper circles and spray the bottom with flavorless vegetable oil spray. Wrap the bottoms of the springform pans with a layer of plastic wrap and then a layer of foil to prevent leaking during baking.

Evenly divide the New York Sponge Cake batter among the springform pans and bake until the center of the cakes spring back when lightly touched, 10 to 11 minutes. Let the cakes cool in the pans on a wire cooling rack while you make the cheesecake filling.

Reduce the oven temperature to 325°F.

In the bowl of an electric mixer fitted with the paddle attachment, beat the cream cheese, one-third of the sugar, the cornstarch, and cinnamon on low speed until creamy, about 3 minutes. Beat in the remaining cream cheese and the Azteca Chocolate Ganache.

Increase the mixer speed to high and beat in the remaining sugar, honey, and vanilla extract. Add the eggs, one at a time, beating well after each addition. Scrape down the sides of the bowl with a rubber spatula. Beat in the cream and sour cream. Mix the filling only until completely blended, being careful not to overmix.

Divide the batter evenly among the prepared pans, pouring gently on top of the sponge cake. Smooth the top of each with a rubber spatula.

Place the springform pans in a roasting pan large enough to hold them without touching. Set the roasting pan on the middle rack of the oven. Pour enough boiling water into the roasting pan to reach about halfway up the sides of the springform pans. The foil and plastic wrap will keep the water from seeping into the cheesecakes.

Bake for 45 to 60 minutes or until set. Remove the cheesecakes from the water and let cool in the pans on a wire cooling racks for about 1 hour. Cover with plastic wrap and refrigerate for 3 to 4 hours or overnight until completely chilled.

When ready to serve, loosen the cheesecakes from the sides of the pans by running a thin paring knife around the inner edge of the pan. Release the clip from the rim of the pan and carefully remove it from the cheesecakes. Transfer the cheesecakes to eight serving plates, leaving the bottom of the springform pans underneath the cakes. Spoon some of the Mango-Pineapple Chutney over each cheesecake and serve.

Caramel Cheesecake Brûlée

This is one impressive dessert that is made with minimum effort—your guests will be in awe of your extraordinary culinary skills. Make the cheesecake a day ahead of time, as you would any other cheesecake recipe, and just before serving, top it with a layer of granulated sugar, which is then heated, for a crunchy brûlée crust.

To achieve the desired thin layer of caramelized sugar, you will have to apply direct heat to the sugar with a kitchen torch, which you can find at any kitchenware shop. Typically, crème brûlée is served in individual ramekins, and that is how I recommend that you serve this picture-perfect dessert.

Makes 8 servings

Prep Time: 30 minutes
Baking Time: 15 to 20 minutes
Cooling Time: 30 minutes
Chilling Time: 3 to 4 hours or overnight
Level: **

For the crust: Preheat the oven to 325°F. Coat the bottoms and sides of eight (8-ounce) crème brûlée ramekins with butter.

In a mixing bowl, combine the graham cracker crumbs, pecans, sugar, and melted butter and stir until blended. Divide the mixture evenly among the prepared ramekins and, using your fingers, pat the crumbs into the bottom of each ramekin. You will need about 3 tablespoons of crumbs for each ramekin. Bake for 5 minutes to set the crust. Cool on wire cooling racks. When completely cool, drizzle 1 tablespoon of the Burnt Caramel Sauce over each crust.

For the cheesecake: In the bowl of an electric mixer fitted with the paddle attachment, beat the cream cheese, sour cream, and White Chocolate Ganache on medium speed until smooth.

Add the eggs, one at a time, beating well after each addition. Scrape down the sides of the bowl with a rubber spatula. Add the cream and ½ cup of the sugar until the batter is blended and smooth. Divide the batter evenly among the ramekins (about ⅓ cup of batter for each). Bake until the filling is set, 15 to 20 minutes.

Transfer the ramekins to wire racks and let cool to room temperature. When cool, refrigerate for at least 3 hours.

To serve, sprinkle 2 teaspoons of the remaining sugar over the top of each cheesecake. Using a kitchen torch, melt the sugar until it browns and caramelizes. Serve right away.

ChefSecret: If you do not have a kitchen torch, broil about 3 inches from the heat source for 2 minutes until the sugar caramelizes. Watch closely!

special toolbox:

8 (8-ounce) crème brûlée ramekins

electric stand mixer, bowl, and paddle

wire cooling rack

butane kitchen torch

crust:

¾ cup graham cracker crumbs (6 or 7 whole crackers)

⅓ cup ground toasted pecans

3 tablespoons granulated sugar

2 tablespoons unsalted butter, melted and cooled

½ cup Burnt Caramel Sauce (page 242)

cheesecake:

2 (8-ounce) packages cream cheese, at room temperature

2 tablespoons sour cream

¼ cup White Chocolate Ganache (page 29), at room temperature

2 large eggs

¼ cup heavy cream

1 cup granulated sugar, divided

Scan for Ed's ChefSecret

White Chocolate Raspberry Cheesecake

I received an e-mail from one of my customers, Suzie Johnson, requesting a recipe for White Chocolate Raspberry Cheesecake. I couldn't find a single one that fit the bill. Great! A challenge! The next morning I met with our chef, Wayne Chidester, at the Chocolate Studio to brainstorm this very tempting-sounding dessert. We love cheesecakes at the studio, which is a good thing, as Wayne and I tried six variations before coming up with an absolute winner. When we passed the recipe on to Suzie, she was thrilled and told us it was the hit of the party!

Makes 8 to 10 servings

Prep Time: 30 minutes
Baking Time: 1 hour 40 minutes
Cooling Time: 1 hour 20 minutes
Chilling Time: 6 hours or overnight
Level: **

special toolbox:

food processor

12-inch springform pan

12-inch parchment paper circle

electric stand mixer, bowl, and paddle

saucepan

roasting pan

wire cooling rack

crust:

1 cup whole almonds, toasted

2 cups graham cracker crumbs (about 16 whole crackers)

6 tablespoons unsalted butter, melted

cheesecake:

1½ cups Snowy White Chocolate Ganache (page 29), at room temperature

4 (8-ounce) packages cream cheese, at room temperature

½ cup granulated sugar

4 large eggs

2 large egg yolks

2 tablespoons cornstarch

1 teaspoon pure vanilla extract

3 cups fresh raspberries

For the crust: Line a 12-inch springform pan with a 12-inch parchment paper circle. Lightly coat the bottom and side of the pan with nonstick cooking spray. Wrap the bottom of the springform pan with a layer of plastic wrap and then a layer of foil to prevent leaking during baking.

Finely grind the almonds and graham cracker crumbs in a food processor. Add the butter and pulse just until combined. Pour the crumbs into the springform pan and using the bottom of a measuring cup or the smooth bottom of a glass and your fingertips, press the crumbs into the bottom and up the side of the pan about 1 inch. Set aside.

For the cheesecake: Preheat the oven to 325°F.

Melt the White Chocolate Ganache in a heatproof mixing bowl set over a saucepan of barely simmering water and stir until melted and smooth. Remove from the heat.

In the bowl of an electric mixer fitted with the paddle attachment, beat the cream cheese at medium speed until fluffy. Add the sugar and beat until smooth.

With the mixer on low, add the whole eggs and the yolks, one at a time, beating well and scraping down the bowl with a rubber spatula after each addition. Beat in the cornstarch and vanilla until just combined; do not overmix.

With the mixer running, drizzle the melted ganache into the batter in a slow stream, beating until well combined.

Arrange the raspberries in a single layer over the crust and then pour the batter over the berries.

Place the springform pan in a large roasting pan and set the pan on the middle rack of the oven. Pour enough boiling water into the roasting pan to come about halfway up the side of the springform pan. The foil and plastic wrap will keep the water from seeping into the cheesecake.

Bake for about 1 hour 30 minutes, until the cake is set around the edge, but the center slightly jiggles. Remove the cheesecake from the water and let cool in the pan on a wire cooling rack for 10 minutes.

For the topping: Increase the oven temperature to 400°F.

In a medium bowl, whisk together the sour cream, sugar, and Red Raspberry Sauce until well blended. Pour over the cheesecake and return the cake to the oven for 10 minutes.

Remove the cheesecake from the oven and cool in the pan for 1 hour on a wire rack. The cake will continue to set as it cools.

Run a thin paring knife around the inner rim of the pan to loosen it from the side, but do not unmold it. Cover with plastic wrap and refrigerate for at least 6 hours or overnight until completely chilled.

When ready to serve, release the clip from the rim of the springform pan and carefully remove it from the cheesecake. Transfer the cheesecake to a serving plate, leaving the bottom of the springform pan underneath the cake. Garnish with fresh raspberries, a drizzle of Red Raspberry Sauce, and a dollop of White Chocolate Ganache Whipped Cream (and a mint leaf, but only if you must).

topping:

2 cups sour cream

1/2 cup granulated sugar

1/4 cup Red Raspberry Sauce (page 243)

garnish:

Fresh raspberries

Red Raspberry Sauce (page 243)

White Chocolate Ganache Whipped Cream (page 238)

Candy Bar Cheesecake

This is a cheesecake for kids of all ages. It combines rich, creamy cheesecake with popular candy bars—a decadent duo designed to please even the most discriminating cheesecake lover's palate. The way I look at it, if you're going to have a cheesecake treat, why not go all the way with an over-the-top combination of chocolate cheesecake and your favorite candy bars? Need I say more? Go for it!

Makes 8 to 10 servings

Prep Time: 30 minutes
Baking Time: 1 hour 40 minutes
Cooling Time: 2 hours
Chilling Time: 4 hours or overnight
Level: **

For the crust: Preheat the oven to 350°F. Line the bottom of a 10-inch springform pan with a 10-inch parchment paper circle. Generously coat the side of the pan with butter. Wrap the springform pan with a layer of plastic wrap and a layer of aluminum foil to prevent leaking during baking.

Spoon the New York Sponge Cake batter into the prepared pan and bake until the center of the cake springs back when lightly touched, 10 to 11 minutes. Let cool on a wire rack until completely cool.

Reduce the oven temperature to 325°F. Sprinkle the toffee pieces over the cooled cake.

special toolbox:

10-inch springform pan

10-inch parchment paper circle

electric stand mixer, bowl, and paddle

chef's knife

roasting pan

wire cooling rack

crust:

Batter for New York Sponge Cake (page 90), uncooked

½ cup Butter Toffee pieces (page 211) or store-bought toffee bar pieces

For the cheesecake: In the bowl of an electric mixer fitted with the paddle attachment, beat one package of the cream cheese, 1/3 cup of the sugar, and the cornstarch on low speed until creamy, about 4 minutes. Scrape down the sides of the bowl with a rubber spatula. Blend in the remaining cream cheese, one package at a time, scraping down the bowl with a rubber spatula after each addition.

Increase the mixer speed to medium and beat in the remaining 1 1/3 cups sugar, the vanilla, and the Milk Chocolate Ganache until well mixed.

Reduce the speed to low and add the eggs, one at a time, beating well after each addition. Beat in the heavy cream and sour cream just until completely mixed, being careful not to overmix.

Layer the batter and the chopped candy over the crust alternately in two or three layers, beginning and ending with the batter. Place the springform pan in a large roasting pan and set the pan on the middle rack of the oven. Pour enough boiling water into the roasting pan to reach about halfway up the side of the springform pan. The foil and plastic wrap will keep the water from seeping into the cheesecake.

Bake for 1 hour 30 minutes or until the edges look baked and the center is set. Remove the cheesecake from the water, transfer to a wire cooling rack, and let cool for 2 hours. Cover loosely with plastic wrap and refrigerate for at least 4 hours or until completely cool.

When ready to serve, release the clip from the rim of the springform pan and carefully remove it from the cheesecake. Transfer the cheesecake to a serving plate, leaving the bottom of the springform pan underneath the cake.

For the topping: Before serving, spread the Milk Chocolate Ganache Whipped Cream over the top of the cooled cheesecake. Press the Butter Toffee pieces into the side of the cake and serve.

cheesecake:

4 (8-ounce) packages cream cheese, at room temperature, divided

1 2/3 cups granulated sugar, divided

1/3 cup cornstarch

1 tablespoon pure vanilla extract

1 cup Milk Chocolate Ganache (page 26), at room temperature

3 large eggs

1/2 cup heavy cream

1/4 cup sour cream

1 cup chopped candy bars, preferably a mixture of 4 different bars or candies, such as Hershey's Kisses, chocolate chips, Reese's Peanut Butter Cups or Pieces, Peppermint Patties, M&Ms, Mounds Bar, Snickers, etc.

topping:

2 cups Milk Chocolate Ganache Whipped Cream (page 238)

3/4 cup broken Butter Toffee pieces (page 211)

Homemade Marshmallow
Cashew Chocolate Cheesecake

I had a bunch of Rocky Road bars left over from Halloween one year and wanted to eat or use them before they got too old. We featured a "cheesecake of the day" at Fanny's Fish Market, my second restaurant located in Foster City, California. I seized the moment and decided to make a cheesecake with chopped-up pieces of the left-over bars. "Wow!" was the exclamation I heard most from our guests that night. This wasn't too surprising because who wouldn't enjoy the mix of cashews, marshmal-lows, and chocolate in a cheesecake?

Makes 8 to 10 servings

Prep Time: 30 minutes
Baking Time: 1 hour 30 minutes
Cooling Time: 2 hours
Chilling Time: 4 hours or overnight
Level: **

For the crust: Preheat the oven to 350°F. Line the bottom of a 10-inch springform pan with a 10-inch parchment paper circle. Generously coat the side and bottom of the pan with butter.

In the bowl of a food processor fitted with the metal blade, blend the cookie crumbs, sugar, and cinnamon. Slowly add the melted butter and pulse until just barely mixed.

Pour the crumbs into the springform pan and, using the bottom of a measuring cup or the smooth bottom of a glass and your fingertips, press the crumbs into the bot-tom of the pan. Bake for 8 minutes, or until the crust is set. Remove from the oven and cool on a wire cooling rack; set aside.

When cool, wrap the springform pan with a layer of plastic wrap and a layer of aluminum foil to prevent leaking during baking.

Ingredients and directions continued on page 102.

special toolbox:

10-inch springform pan

10-inch parchment paper circle

electric stand mixer, bowl, and paddle

food processor

wire cooling rack

roasting pan

pastry bag fitted with a #2 or #3 round tip

chocolate cookie crust:

1 1/2 cups chocolate wafer cookie crumbs or chocolate graham cracker crumbs (25 or 26 chocolate wafers or 12 or 13 whole graham crackers)

1/3 cup granulated sugar

1/2 teaspoon ground cinnamon

1/3 cup unsalted butter, melted

cheesecake:

1 cup Dark Chocolate Ganache (page 28)

3 (8-ounce) packages cream cheese, room temperature, divided

1⅓ cups granulated sugar, divided

¼ cup cornstarch

1 tablespoon pure vanilla extract

2 large eggs

¾ cup heavy cream

¾ cup toasted, roughly chopped cashew pieces

10 to 15 Homemade Marshmallows (page 236) or store-bought marsh-mallows, cut in ½-inch cubes

topping:

1 (7.5-ounce) jar Marshmallow Fluff

1 cup miniature marshmallows

¼ cup toasted, chopped cashews

2 ounces bittersweet or semisweet chocolate, melted

For the cheesecake: In a heatproof bowl, melt the Dark Chocolate Ganache in a microwave or set over a pan of simmering water. When smooth, set aside to cool.

In the bowl of an electric mixer fitted with the paddle attachment, beat one package of the cream cheese, 1/3 cup of the sugar, and the cornstarch on low speed until creamy, about 3 minutes, scraping down the bowl several times with a rubber spatula. Add the remaining cream cheese, one package at a time, scraping down the bowl with a rubber spatula after each addition. Increase the mixer speed to medium and beat in the remaining 1 cup sugar and the vanilla. Add the eggs, one at a time, beating well after each addition. Beat in the melted ganache and the cream just until completely blended. Don't overmix.

Using a wooden spoon, stir in the chopped cashews and the homemade marsh-mallows. Pour the batter into the crust in the springform pan. Place the springform pan in a large roasting pan and set the pan on the middle rack of the oven. Pour enough boiling water into the roasting pan to reach about halfway up the side of the springform pan. The foil and plastic wrap will keep the water from seeping into the cheesecake. Bake for about 1 hour 30 minutes or until the edges look baked and the center appears set.

Remove the cheesecake from the water bath and let cool in the pan on a wire cooling rack for 2 hours. Cover the cheesecake loosely with plastic wrap and refrigerate for at least 6 hours or overnight until completely chilled.

When ready to serve, loosen the cheesecake from the side of the pan by running a thin paring knife around the inner edge of the pan. Release the clip from the rim of the pan and carefully remove it from the cheesecake. Transfer the cheesecake to a cake plate, leaving the bottom of the springform pan underneath the cake.

Spread the Marshmallow Fluff over the top and down the side of the cake, allowing some of the chocolate to show near the bottom of the cake. Scatter the miniature marshmallows over the top of the cheesecake and then sprinkle with the chopped cashews.

Fit a pastry bag with a #2 or #3 round tip and spoon in the melted chocolate. Drizzle decorative lines over the top of the cake at ⅜-inch intervals. Refrigerate until ready to serve.

ChefsNote: You can use store-bought, spongy, puffed marshmallows or make your own and discover the significant difference homemade makes.

Chapter

7

CHOCOLATE COOKIES, BROWNIES, AND BARS—OH MY

I NEVER MET A SOUL WHO DOESN'T LOVE A COOKIE. WHEN WE WERE ON OUR 1980S ADVENTURE IN THE AMAZON, WE PACKED AN ASSORTMENT OF NABISCO COOKIES IN THE RIVERBOAT SUPPLY LOCKER.

ONE LATE AFTERNOON WE MET UP WITH SOME VILLAGERS FROM ONE OF THE LOCAL TRIBES WHO LIVED ALONG THE BANKS OF THE RIVER AND HAD LIMITED EXPOSURE TO NORTH AMERICANS. WE WERE BROUGHT TO MEET THE CHIEF, WHO OFFERED US A HANDFUL OF WIGGLY, SQUIRMY GRUBS AS A GESTURE OF TRIBAL GOODWILL. IN RETURN, I GAVE HIM A PACKAGE OF OREOS. THE CHIEF TASTED THEM, TOOK BACK THE GRUBS, AND PROMPTLY INVITED US TO DINNER. THE CHIEF'S WIVES SET A TABLE WITH A VARIETY OF WONDERFULLY COOKED, FRESH-CAUGHT RIVER FISH (FAR BETTER THAN THOSE GRUBS). WHEN ASKED ABOUT THE GRUBS, HE TOLD US HE WAS JUST MESSING WITH OUR HEADS, AND HENCE TOOK THEM BACK BEFORE THE JOKE WENT TOO FAR. THE AMAZON IS A STRANGE AND WONDROUS PLACE, WHERE A COOKIE AS SIMPLE AS AN OREO TRUMPS GRUBS EVERY TIME— AND GETS YOU INVITED TO A SUMPTUOUS FISH DINNER.

Just-A-Great-Old-Fashioned Chocolate Chip Cookie

Few things are as tasty as a freshly baked chocolate chip cookie, and our recipe is one of the very best there is. It's for big, fat, "Got Milk?" chocolate chip cookies, the kind that my great Aunt Esther baked for me when I got home from school. They are simple to make, and the raw dough can be frozen for up to a month, so you can scoop out the number of cookies you want to bake and save the rest for later.

Makes twelve (5-inch) cookies

Prep Time: 20 minutes
Baking Time: 12 to 15 minutes
Cooling Time: 15 minutes
Level: *

Preheat the oven to 350°F.

Sift together the flour, baking soda, and salt into a medium bowl and set aside.

In the bowl of an electric mixer fitted with the paddle attachment, beat the butter, White Chocolate Ganache, brown sugar, and granulated sugar together on medium speed until light and fluffy. Scrape down the sides of the bowl with a rubber spatula. Beat in the vanilla and eggs. Gradually add the dry ingredients to the creamed mixture and continue to mix until smooth. Turn off the mixer and, using a rubber spatula, fold in the chocolate chips.

Roll about ¼ cup of dough between your hands into a ball. Arrange the balls 3 inches apart on the prepared baking sheets. You should get about 4 cookies on each pan. Flatten the dough slightly. Bake until the cookies are light brown around the edges and golden, about 12 minutes for chewy cookies and about 15 minutes for crispy cookies. If your oven cannot accommodate all three baking sheets, bake the last four cookies after you remove the first eight from the oven.

Allow the cookies to cool on the baking sheets for 5 minutes before transferring to a wire rack to cool completely.

ChefSecret: If you have leftover, day-old cookies, refresh them on a warming tray (we use a Salton warming tray) set on low for about 20 minutes. This will give them that "just-baked" texture and flavor.

special toolbox:

3 baking sheets lined
with parchment paper

electric stand mixer, bowl, and paddle

wire cooling rack

2½ cups all-purpose flour

1 teaspoon baking soda

1 teaspoon salt

¼ pound (1 stick) unsalted butter,
at room temperature

½ cup White Chocolate Ganache
(page 29), at room temperature

¾ cup packed light brown sugar

½ cup granulated sugar

1 teaspoon pure vanilla extract

2 large eggs

1 cup semisweet or bittersweet
chocolate chips

White Chocolate, Pine Nut, and Sesame Cookies

George Zallie is a wonderful independent grocer who owns several ShopRite Stores in the Philadelphia area. When he couldn't find enough people to staff a new store opening in an upscale suburb, I sent several of our cooks to fill the open positions until he could recruit his own. We were joined by an old-world Sicilian baker George was able to hire and who made the best pignoli cookies, classic Italian treats that you have to taste to believe. George has always been secretive about his proprietary recipes, but he was kind enough to share this one with me. The cookie is the essence of simplicity: chewy and rich, it packs a big almond punch to complement the White Chocolate Ganache and toasted pine nuts.

Makes 24 cookies

Prep Time: 10 minutes
Baking Time: 22 to 24 minutes
Cooling Time: 30 minutes
Level: *

Preheat the oven to 325°F.

Break the marzipan into pieces and transfer to a medium mixing bowl. Add the almond flour, sugar, salt, and almond and lemon extracts and mix with a handheld electric mixture until crumbly. Add the egg white, beating just until the mixture is smooth. Add the White Chocolate Ganache and beat on medium speed until well blended.

Spread the pine nuts and sesame seeds in a shallow dish and stir gently to mix.

Using a kitchen tablespoon, a #40 scoop, or your lightly oiled or damp hands, drop 1-inch balls of dough into the dish with the pine nuts and sesame seeds. Roll the dough until evenly coated. Transfer to the prepared baking sheets, leaving 1 inch between each cookie. Bake for 22 to 24 minutes, or until lightly browned. Set the baking sheets on wire cooling racks and let the cookies cool on the pans.

When completely cool, remove the cookies from the pans. Serve immediately or store in a container with a tightly fitting lid or wrap them tightly in plastic wrap. You can freeze the baked cookies for up to three weeks.

 gluten free

special toolbox:

2 baking sheets lined with parchment paper or silicone baking mats

handheld electric mixer

kitchen tablespoon or #40 scoop

wire cooling racks

8 to 9 ounces marzipan (about 1 cup)

1/2 cup almond flour

1/4 cup granulated sugar

1/8 teaspoon salt

1/8 teaspoon pure almond extract

1/8 teaspoon lemon extract

1 large egg white

3 tablespoons White Chocolate Ganache (page 29), at room temperature

1 1/2 cups pine nuts (pignoli)

1/4 cup sesame seeds

Chocolate
Peanut Butter Ripples

Makes 24 cookies

Prep Time: 20 minutes
Baking Time: 15 minutes
Cooling Time: 30 minutes
Level: ***

special toolbox:

2 baking sheets lined with parchment paper or silicone baking mats

double boiler

electric stand mixer, bowl, and paddle

sifter

2 wire cooling racks

chocolate dough:

1/3 cup Dark Chocolate Ganache (page 28)

1 ounce unsweetened baking chocolate, coarsely chopped

10 tablespoons unsalted butter, at room temperature

3/4 cup granulated sugar

1 teaspoon pure vanilla extract

1/4 teaspoon salt

1 large egg

1 cup plus 1 tablespoon all-purpose flour, sifted

1/4 cup milk chocolate chips

Preheat the oven to 325°F. Adjust the racks to divide the oven into thirds.

For the chocolate dough: In the top of a double boiler set over barely simmering water on medium heat, melt the ganache and chocolate, stirring until smooth. Remove the top of the double boiler and set aside to cool the chocolate slightly.

In the bowl of an electric mixer fitted with the paddle attachment, beat the butter on medium-high speed until soft and creamy. Add the sugar, vanilla, and salt and beat until the dough is well mixed. Beat in the egg and then the melted chocolate. Scrape down the sides of the bowl with a rubber spatula several times during mixing.

With the mixer on low speed, gradually add the flour and beat just until incorporated and there are no streaks of white.

Divide the batter in half and place each half in a separate bowl. Set the mixing bowl aside. Stir in the chocolate chips to half the batter.

For the peanut butter dough: In the same mixing bowl using an electric mixer fitted with the paddle attachment, beat the peanut butter and butter on medium-high speed until smooth and creamy. Beat in the brown sugar until well mixed. Gradually beat in the flour until the batter is evenly colored.

To assemble the cookies, shape the chocolate chip dough into mounds using a teaspoon and place 2 inches apart on the baking sheets. Top each mound with a teaspoon of the peanut butter dough and then with a teaspoon of the chocolate dough. Using a fork dipped in granulated sugar (to prevent sticking), very lightly flatten the cookies to meld the three doughs.

Bake for 15 minutes or until the cookies darken a little around the edges and look set. About halfway through baking, rotate the baking sheets, so that the top sheet is now on the bottom shelf of the oven and the lower sheet on the top. This ensures even baking.

Let the cookies cool on the baking sheets for about 5 minutes before transferring to wire racks to cool completely.

Store the cookies in a container with a tightly fitting lid or wrap them tightly in plastic wrap for up to one week.

peanut butter dough:

$1/3$ cup smooth peanut butter, at room temperature

2 tablespoons unsalted butter, at room temperature

$1/2$ cup firmly packed light brown sugar

2 tablespoons sifted all-purpose flour

WHY DO YOU USE SO MUCH PARCHMENT PAPER?

Parchment paper is great to prevent cookies and other baked goods from sticking to the pan and drying out during baking. It also keeps the cookies from getting too dark on the bottom, and you won't have to scrub pans. This is no truer than in our own test kitchen and Chocolate Studios, where the guys hate to scrub dough-encrusted baking sheets. You can find parchment paper in rolls in most supermarkets, cookware shops, and similar venues. Restaurant supply stores sell it in individual sheets, which are very handy.

Double Chocolate Chunk Cookies

This is a classic! A big, bold cookie liberally studded with large chunks of chocolate so that with just about every bite, your teeth sink into a piece of soft, close-to-melted chocolate—particularly if the cookies are served warm from the oven. The crispy edges of these chunky chocolate cookies taste of caramel, and the centers are sweet, fudgy, soft, and chewy. Try a combination of bittersweet, semisweet, milk, or white chocolate chunks or even toffee pieces to give these cookies your personal stamp.

Makes 25 cookies

Prep Time: 15 minutes
Baking Time: 10 to 12 minutes
Cooling Time: 30 minutes
Level: *

special toolbox:

2 baking sheets lined with parchment paper or silicone baking mats

12 baking rings, 3½ inches in diameter and 1 inch high

electric stand mixer, bowl, and paddle

wire cooling racks

2⅓ cups all-purpose flour

½ teaspoon baking soda

¼ teaspoon salt

12 tablespoons (1½ sticks) unsalted butter, at room temperature

½ cup granulated sugar

½ cup packed light brown sugar

1 large egg

2 teaspoons pure vanilla extract

2 ounces semisweet or bittersweet chocolate, melted

1½ cups semisweet chocolate chunks

½ cup chopped walnuts (optional)

Preheat the oven to 350°F. Spray twelve 3½-inch baking rings with flavorless vegetable oil and arrange on two parchment paper–lined baking sheets.

In a medium mixing bowl, whisk together the flour, baking soda, and salt and set aside.

In the bowl of an electric mixer fitted with the paddle attachment, beat the butter and both sugars on medium speed until light and fluffy, about 1½ minutes.

Add the egg and vanilla and beat well, scraping down the sides of the bowl with a rubber spatula. Add the melted chocolate and mix for 15 seconds until incorporated. Gradually add the dry ingredients, beating on low speed to mix well. Fold in the chocolate chunks and walnuts, if using.

Between dampened palms, roll the dough into 2-inch balls. Place in the prepared baking rings. Gently press the cookies to flatten slightly, leaving 1 inch between each cookie. Bake for 10 to 12 minutes or until the edges darken and the cookies become firm.

Immediately remove the cookies from the baking rings and transfer to wire cooling racks. Let cool completely before serving.

Store the cooled cookies in a container with a tightly fitting lid or wrap them tightly with plastic wrap for up to one week.

Peanut Butter Chocolate Cookies

You don't have to wait for National Peanut Butter Week to make Peanut Butter Chocolate Cookies. Yaa-hoo! They're delicious any old time. Okay, maybe I'm a little overly enthusiastic about the whole thing, but I mean, come on; who doesn't love peanut butter and chocolate? You will quickly discover that these are the best-tasting and easiest peanut butter cookies you will ever make. And by the way, peanut butter has come a long way since its inception in the 1880s, when it was created as toothpaste!

Makes 24 cookies

Prep Time: 5 minutes
Baking Time: 10 minutes
Cooling Time: 30 minutes
Level: *

Preheat the oven to 350°F. Position two oven racks in the center of the oven.

In a large mixing bowl, stir together the peanut butter, both sugars, the Dark Chocolate Ganache, egg, and vanilla using a sturdy wooden spoon. Stir in the chocolate chips. Using 1 tablespoon of dough for each cookie, roll the dough between dampened hands to form smooth balls. Place 1 inch apart on two ungreased baking sheets. Flatten the dough with the back of a fork in two directions to form a cross-hatch pattern. Bake for 10 minutes or until lightly brown. Cool for 5 minutes on the baking sheet and then transfer to wire cooling racks to cool completely.

D dairy free

special toolbox:

2 baking sheets

wire cooling racks

1 cup creamy peanut butter

½ cup granulated sugar

½ cup firmly packed light brown sugar

¼ cup Dark Chocolate Ganache (page 28)

1 large egg, beaten

1 teaspoon pure vanilla extract

½ cup semisweet chocolate chips

ED'S BOX-TOP WISDOM
Home!

Home is where the hearth is. Life is where the larder is. Love is where the heart is. Destiny is knowing the difference and being able to share each to support the other.

Chocolate Ganache and Spice Cookies

A couple of years ago, we featured cinnamon ganache truffle hearts for Valentine's Day. We had a few boxes left over and thought these truffles would be a perfect ingredient for a new spice cookie. We added cloves and nutmeg along with cocoa powder to round out the flavor of these perfect, chewy spice cookies.

Makes about 24 cookies

Prep Time: 15 minutes
Baking Time: 10 to 12 minutes
Cooling Time: 30 minutes
Chilling Time: 3 hours 30 minutes
Level: *

Melt the Dark Chocolate Ganache in a bowl set over a saucepan of barely simmering water.

In a large bowl, whisk together the flour, cocoa powder, ground ginger, cinnamon, cloves, nutmeg, and salt.

In the bowl of an electric mixer fitted with the paddle attachment, beat together the butter and candied ginger on high speed until pale, about 4 minutes. Add the brown sugar and beat until smooth. Add the molasses and beat until mixed. In a small bowl, dissolve the baking soda in the boiling water.

With the mixer on low speed, beat half the dry ingredients into the dough. Add the baking soda mixture and then the remaining dry ingredients. Stir in the melted ganache.

Shape the dough into a ball and then flatten into a 1-inch-thick disk. Wrap the dough in plastic and refrigerate for at least 3 hours and up to 24 hours.

Preheat the oven to 325°F.

Remove the dough from the refrigerator and roll the dough into 1½-inch balls. Arrange the balls 2 inches apart on the prepared baking sheets. Refrigerate for at least 30 minutes. Spread the granulated sugar into a shallow bowl. Roll the balls in the sugar until evenly coated and return to the baking sheets. Bake for 10 to 12 minutes, until the surfaces crack slightly and the cookies are lightly browned. Cool on the baking sheets on wire cooling racks for about 5 minutes. Transfer the cookies to the racks to cool completely.

special toolbox:

saucepan

electric stand mixer, bowl, and paddle

2 baking sheets lined with parchment paper or silicone baking mats

2 wire cooling racks

metal spatula

1 cup Dark Chocolate Ganache (page 28)

1½ cups all-purpose flour

2 tablespoons unsweetened Dutch-processed cocoa powder

1 teaspoon ground ginger

1 teaspoon ground cinnamon

¼ teaspoon ground cloves

¼ teaspoon ground nutmeg

¼ teaspoon salt

¼ pound unsalted butter, at room temperature

1 tablespoon minced candied ginger

½ cup firmly packed dark brown sugar

½ cup molasses

1 teaspoon baking soda

2 teaspoons boiling water

¼ cup granulated sugar

Chocolate Madeleines

Madeleines are small, lighter-than-air, shell-shaped tea cakes that were all the rage in the French court in the eighteenth century—or was it the nineteenth century? It's hard to pinpoint, as there is debate about who first baked these small delicacies in their specially molded pans. Whatever their origin, madeleines are inexorably linked with France and were chosen to represent France on Europe Day in 2006 for the EU's Café Europe initiative. Whoopee!

My version incorporates a little chocolate ganache that makes them moister than the originals. You can take it one step further and dip half of the madeleine in melted Dark, Milk, or White Chocolate Ganache.

Makes 24 madeleines

Prep Time: 15 minutes
Resting Time: 15 minutes
Baking Time: 10 minutes
Cooling Time: 30 minutes
Level: *

Preheat the oven to 350°F. Spray the madeleine pans with vegetable oil spray and dust with flour, tapping out the excess flour from the pan.

In the top of a double boiler set over simmering water, melt the butter and chocolate ganache, stirring until smooth. Set aside.

In a mixing bowl, whisk together the eggs, sugar, and vanilla until well blended, about 2 minutes. Add the flour, baking powder, and cocoa powder to the batter. Whisk for 1 minute longer. Stir in the melted butter and ganache until fully incorporated. The batter will have the consistency of heavy cream.

Fill the molds of each madeleine pan with enough batter to nearly reach the top. Let rest for 15 minutes before baking. Bake for about 10 minutes, until the madeleines lightly spring back when touched in the center. Cool the pans on wire cooling racks.

special toolbox:

2 madeleine pans
double boiler
sifter
2 wire cooling racks

¼ pound (1 stick) unsalted butter
4 tablespoons Dark Chocolate Ganache (page 28), at room temperature
3 large eggs
¾ cup granulated sugar
1 teaspoon pure vanilla extract
1 cup all-purpose flour, sifted
½ teaspoon baking powder
1 tablespoon unsweetened Dutch-processed cocoa powder

Chocolate Curl Meringue Kisses

If you have time to let them cool in the oven for an hour or so, few cookies are easier than these little, light meringue kisses—and they are gluten free, which is an added bonus. We love them perked up with chocolate ganache and a touch of cinnamon and vanilla. Go for it!

Makes 4 dozen small kisses or 2 dozen large kisses

Prep Time: 30 minutes
Baking Time: 50 to 60 minutes
Cooling Time: 1 hour 30 minutes
Setting Time: 30 to 60 minutes
Level: **

Heat the oven to 250°F.

In the top of a double boiler set over barely simmering water, whisk together the egg whites and sugar until warm to the touch (warming the whites helps them incorporate more air into the foam as they are whipped).

Transfer the whites to the bowl of an electric mixer fitted with the whisk attachment and whip on medium-high speed until soft peaks form. Add the cocoa powder, cinnamon, and almond extract and continue whipping just until the whites are stiff and glossy.

Fold the dark chocolate curls into the whites. Gently spoon the meringue into a pastry bag fitted with a large (1½-inch) plain or star tip, taking care not to deflate the meringue. Pipe bite-size kisses onto the prepared baking sheets. Bake until crisp and dry to the touch and the color of milky coffee, 50 to 60 minutes.

To test for doneness, remove one meringue from the oven. Let cool for 1 minute and then taste. It should be dry and crisp all the way through. Turn off the oven and let the meringues cool on the pans in the oven with the door propped open for 1 hour.

Transfer the meringues to wire cooling racks to cool completely.

In the top of a double boiler over simmering water, or in a microwave oven, melt the Dark Chocolate Ganache.

Dip the tines of a fork into the warm Dark Chocolate Ganache and drizzle over the meringues. Let the meringues sit for 30 to 60 minutes for the chocolate to set.

Store in an airtight container for up to five days.

gluten free

special toolbox:

2 baking sheets lined with parchment paper or silicone baking mats

double boiler

electric stand mixer, bowl, and whisk

pastry bag fitted with a large plain or star tip

wire cooling racks

½ cup egg whites (about 4 large eggs)

¾ cup granulated sugar

¼ teaspoon unsweetened Dutch-processed cocoa powder

¼ teaspoon ground cinnamon

¼ teaspoon almond extract

½ cup small bittersweet or semi-sweet chocolate curls (page 35)

3 tablespoons Dark Chocolate Ganache (page 28), warmed

Chocolate Spritz Cookies

I spent a memorable Christmas in Aarhus, Denmark, with my friend Birget Jensen's family. Everyone seemed to cook and bake throughout the days leading up to the holiday. From the time we woke in the morning until we retired at night, it was *eat and drink*. I discovered two wonderful Danish specialties—Aalborg Jubilee Aquavit and Danish butter cookies—spritz.

These spritz cookies are made of butter and chocolate ganache and can be extruded from a cookie press, dropped onto the baking sheets, or rolled into a cylinder and sliced. You don't have to chill this dough before baking; it keeps its shape regardless.

Makes about 7 dozen small cookies

Prep Time: 10 minutes
Baking Time: 8 to 10 minutes
Cooling Time: 30 minutes
Level: *

special toolbox:

baking sheets

electric stand mixer, bowl, and paddle

sifter

cookie press

wire cooling racks

¾ pound (3 sticks) unsalted butter, at room temperature

1 cup granulated sugar

¾ cup Dark Chocolate Ganache (page 28), at room temperature

1 large egg

1 teaspoon pure vanilla extract

½ teaspoon almond extract

4 cups all-purpose flour

1 teaspoon baking powder

Preheat the oven to 400°F.

In the bowl of an electric mixer fitted with the paddle attachment, beat the butter and sugar together until light and fluffy, 3 to 4 minutes. Add the Dark Chocolate Ganache and continue to beat the mixture until creamy. Add the egg and vanilla and almond extracts and beat well.

Sift together the flour and baking powder. Stir the dry ingredients into the dough until well blended.

Spoon the dough into a cookie press and force it through the desired discs to make various shapes. Arrange the cookies 1 inch apart on ungreased baking sheets. (Alternatively, drop the dough by the tablespoonful onto the baking sheets or roll the dough into a log and cut into ½-inch-thick slices.)

Bake for 8 to 10 minutes or until the edges of the cookies just start to brown. Transfer the cookies to wire cooling racks to cool completely.

ChefSecret: For true Danish flavor, replace the American unsalted butter with Plugrá or another European butter. European-style butters are lower in moisture and higher in butterfat than our butters and impart a richer flavor and smoother texture to baked goods. They have long been preferred by chefs, bakers, confectioners—anyone who appreciates fine food.

Grandma Gray's Chocolate Cookies

I loved my childhood trips to the Big Apple. Grandmother Gray baked for days before we arrived for our summer visits, and I joyfully anticipated her sweet creations during those same days leading up to our vacation. I particularly remember a delicious double-baked German cookie called Mandelbread, almost like an Italian biscotti. It was a great chocolate cookie, soft when baked and laced with dark chocolate ganache, and toasted walnuts and I recall it fondly. When it was time for us to leave, my grandmother packed a big tin with the cookies for us to carry back all the way to Los Angeles.

Makes 24 cookies

Prep Time: 10 minutes
Baking Time: 12 minutes
Cooling Time: 30 minutes
Setting Time: 1 hour
Level: *

For the cookies: Preheat the oven to 350°F. Butter 2 baking sheets lined with parchment paper or silicone baking mats.

In the bowl of an electric mixer fitted with the paddle attachment, beat the sugars and butter on medium-high speed until light and fluffy, 3 to 4 minutes. Add the eggs and beat well.

In a separate bowl, whisk together the flour, baking soda, and salt.

With the mixer on low speed, add dry ingredients and the milk alternately in batches. Add the vanilla when the milk is added. Mix just until smooth.

Beat in the melted Dark Chocolate Ganache until the dough is smooth and evenly colored. Stir in the nuts by hand. Drop the cookies by tablespoonfuls onto the prepared baking sheets. Each cookie should weigh about 1 ounce. You will have about 24 cookies. Bake until crisp around the edges, about 12 minutes. Cool the cookies for 5 minutes on the baking sheets and then transfer to wire cooling racks to cool completely.

For the mocha frosting: In a large mixing bowl, stir together the confectioners' sugar, cocoa powder, and Hot Fudge Ganache. Add the coffee and vanilla and blend until smooth and spreadable. Add more sugar or coffee, or both, to achieve a spreadable consistency, if necessary.

Frost each cookie with about 1 tablespoon of frosting. Set aside for 1 hour to let the frosting set.

special toolbox:

electric stand mixer, bowl, and paddle

2 baking sheets lined with parchment paper or silicone baking mats

tablespoon or #30 scoop

wire cooling racks

offset spatula

cookies:

1 cup granulated sugar

1/2 cup firmly packed light brown sugar

4 tablespoons unsalted butter, at room temperature

2 large eggs

2 cups all-purpose flour

1 teaspoon baking soda

1/4 teaspoon salt

3/4 cup plus 2 tablespoons milk

1 teaspoon pure vanilla extract

5 tablespoons Dark Chocolate Ganache (page 28), melted

1/2 cup walnuts or pecans, lightly toasted and chopped

mocha frosting:

2 cups confectioners' sugar

3 tablespoons unsweetened Dutch-processed cocoa powder

3 tablespoons Hot Fudge Ganache (page 30), at room temperature

1 teaspoon instant coffee, dissolved in 1/4 cup hot water

1/2 teaspoon pure vanilla extract

New York Deli-Style Black and White Cookies

These are just like the original black-and-white cookies you find in New York delis— only better! When baked, they measure about four inches across and weigh in at a hefty three ounces. One side is topped with rich dark chocolate ganache icing and the other with white chocolate ganache icing. When I was a kid, I used to cut black-and-whites in half and eat the dark chocolate side one day and the white chocolate the next.

Makes 18 large cookies

Prep Time: 15 minutes
Baking Time: 20 to 30 minutes
Cooling Time: 30 minutes
Resting Time: 30 minutes
Level: **

For the cookies: Preheat the oven to 375°F. Butter two parchment paper–lined baking sheets and set aside.

In the bowl of an electric mixer fitted with the paddle attachment, beat the sugar and butter at medium-high speed until light and fluffy, 3 to 4 minutes. Add the eggs, milk, and vanilla and lemon extracts and beat until smooth.

Sift together the flours, baking powder, and salt. Add the dry ingredients to the dough in batches, mixing on low speed just to combine.

Using a soup spoon or a #12 scoop, drop the dough 2 inches apart onto the prepared baking sheets. Each spoonful should weigh 2¾ to 3 ounces. Bake until the edges begin to brown, about 20 to 30 minutes. Transfer the cookies to wire cooling racks to cool completely.

For the frosting: Put the confectioners' sugar in a large bowl. Gradually add enough boiling water to make a thick, spreadable consistency, stirring constantly. Divide the mixture between two bowls.

Add the White Chocolate Ganache to one-half of the mixture and the Dark Chocolate Ganache to the other half. Stir well until the ganaches melt and the frosting is smooth.

To frost, turn the cookies upside down so that the flat bottoms face up. Using an offset metal spatula, coat half the cookie with white chocolate frosting and the other half with dark chocolate frosting. Let the cookies rest at room temperature for 30 minutes so the frosting can set.

special toolbox:

2 baking sheets lined with parchment paper or silicone baking mats

sifter

electric stand mixer, bowl, and paddle

soup spoon or #12 scoop

wire cooling racks

offset spatula

cookies:

1¾ cups granulated sugar

½ pound (2 sticks) unsalted butter, at room temperature

4 large eggs

1 cup milk

½ teaspoon pure vanilla extract

¼ teaspoon lemon extract

2½ cups cake flour

2½ cups all-purpose flour

1 teaspoon baking powder

½ teaspoon salt

frosting:

4 cups confectioners' sugar

⅓ to ½ cup boiling water

2 tablespoons White Chocolate Ganache (page 29), at room temperature

4 tablespoons Dark Chocolate Ganache (page 28), at room temperature

Chocolate Chunkaholic Cookies

The crackled surface of this little cookie intrigues just about everyone—and few can resist reaching for one or two. But how do you make them? It looks as though it might be complicated. It's not! The secret is to roll the dough into balls and toss them in confectioners' sugar. They look great, but taste even better.

Makes 48 cookies

Prep Time: 10 minutes
Chilling Time: 2 hours
Baking Time: 8 to 10 minutes
Cooling Time: 30 minutes
Level: *

Preheat the oven to 350°F.

In the bowl of an electric mixer fitted with the paddle attachment, beat the eggs, granulated sugar, Dark Chocolate Ganache, oil, baking powder, and vanilla at medium-high speed until blended.

Beat in as much of the flour with the mixer as possible. Stir in the remaining flour and the chocolate chunks by hand.

Scrape down the sides of the bowl with a rubber spatula and cover with plastic wrap. Refrigerate for 2 hours.

Spread the confectioners' sugar into a shallow bowl. Shape the dough into 1-inch balls with dampened palms. Roll the balls in the sugar, coating well, and arrange 1 inch apart on the prepared baking sheets. Bake for 8 to 10 minutes, until they take on a crackled appearance. As soon as the cookies looked cracked, immediately transfer to wire cooling racks to cool completely.

ChefSecret: To keep these cookies pleasingly soft, store them in an airtight plastic container with a slice of bread on top. The dough freezes well for up to one week, well wrapped in plastic. They are as good as gold when baked.

dairy free

special toolbox:
2 baking sheets lined with parchment paper
electric stand mixer, bowl and paddle
sifter
kitchen tablespoon or #40 scoop
wire cooling racks

3 large eggs

1 1/2 cups granulated sugar

1/2 cup Dark Chocolate Ganache (page 28), melted and cooled

1/2 cup vegetable oil

2 teaspoons baking powder

2 teaspoons pure vanilla extract

2 cups all-purpose flour

1/2 cup semisweet or bittersweet chocolate chunks or large chocolate chips

1 cup sifted confectioners' sugar

White Chocolate and Macadamia Nut Cookies

Debbi Fields of cookie fame opened the first of her many stores in Palo Alto, California, just a few miles from where we were opening some restaurants in 1977. I stopped in and cannot deny I became a fan of Mrs. Fields cookies, along with the rest of America. Years later, when Debbi was a guest on my syndicated radio program, *The Food Show*, she revealed some deep, dark secrets for making the White Chocolate and Macadamia Nut cookies that were one of her signatures. To this day, the combination is popular everywhere, in part, I believe, because macadamia nuts sound exotic and white chocolate is decadent.

Makes 24 cookies

Prep Time: 10 minutes
Baking Time: 16 minutes
Cooling Time: 30 minutes
Level: *

Preheat the oven to 350°F. Butter the parchment paper–lined baking sheets.

In a medium bowl, sift together the flour, baking soda, and salt and set aside.

In the bowl of an electric stand mixer fitted with the paddle attachment, beat the butter and White Chocolate Ganache on medium-high speed until light and fluffy, 3 to 4 minutes. Add the sugars and beat until well blended and creamy. Add the eggs, one at a time, beating well after each addition. Beat in the vanilla. Add the dry ingredients all at once and beat on medium speed until just blended. Scrape down the sides of the bowl a few times with a rubber spatula. Stir in the white chocolate chips and nuts into the dough using a spatula.

Drop the dough by heaping tablespoonfuls 2½ inches apart onto the prepared baking sheets. Bake until just golden on top, about 16 minutes. Let the cookies cool on the baking sheets for about 5 minutes and then transfer to wire cooling racks to cool completely.

special toolbox:

2 baking sheets lined with parchment paper or silicone baking mats
sifter
electric stand mixer, bowl, and paddle
wire cooling racks

3 cups all purpose flour

1 teaspoon baking soda

¾ teaspoon salt

½ pound (2 sticks) unsalted butter, at room temperature

4 tablespoons White Chocolate Ganache (page 29), at room temperature

1 cup firmly packed light brown sugar

¾ cup granulated sugar

2 large eggs

1 tablespoon pure vanilla extract

1½ cups white chocolate chips (about 8 ounces)

1 cup roasted, chopped salted macadamia nuts (4 to 5 ounces)

Ed's Best "Got Milk" Brownies

This is a "break glass in case of emergency" brownie recipe for those times when you need a chocolate fix quickly. You'll find all of these ingredients in your home pantry or refrigerator and—best of all—you'll never need to buy one of those store-bought mixes again. This is all natural and tastes amazing with White Chocolate Ice Cream (page 200) or White Chocolate Whipped Cream (see variations on page 238) and Hot Fudge Sauce (see box on page 30).

Makes about 10 brownies

Prep Time: 10 minutes
Baking Time: 25 to 30 minutes
Cooling Time: 30 minutes
Level: *

special toolbox:

8-inch square baking pan

wire cooling rack

6 tablespoons butter

1/2 cup Dark Chocolate Ganache (page 28)

2 large eggs, beaten

1 1/3 cups granulated sugar, divided

3/4 cup all-purpose flour

1/2 cup crushed pecans or walnuts

Preheat the oven to 350°F. Butter an 8-inch square baking pan.

In a glass mixing bowl, melt the butter and Dark Chocolate Ganache in the microwave on high for 1 to 2 minutes or until the butter is just melted. Stir until the ganache is melted and the mixture is smooth. Set aside to cool slightly.

Add the eggs one at a time, stirring after each addition. Add 1 cup of the sugar and the flour. Using a wooden spoon, stir vigorously, being careful not to overmix. Stir in the nuts.

Pour the batter into the prepared pan. Sprinkle the remaining 1/3 cup sugar over the top and bake for 30 minutes or until crisp and light brown on the top. Cool in the pan set on a wire cooling rack before cutting into 10 squares.

THE ORIGIN OF THE BROWNIE

The brownie is one of America's favorite baked treats. It was born in the USA—we just aren't quite sure when and where—although evidence points to somewhere in Boston in the early twentieth century. The legend told is about a chef who mistakenly added melted chocolate to a batch of biscuits, or it may have been a cook who baked a cake without enough flour, or a New England housewife who forgot to add the baking powder to a chocolate cake. Regardless of how they came to be, the first chocolate brownie recipe was published in the *Fannie Farmer Cookbook* in 1906. Although it may be baked in a square cake pan, the brownie is classified as a bar. There are thousands of recipes, both "cake"-style and moister, richer "fudge-y" style. Either is perfectly acceptable depending on your preference, and more than delicious.

Double Chocolate Brownies

I made this brownie as the base for Chocolate Sludge, one of the most decadent desserts we ever served at the Custom House Restaurants, but it's totally delicious on its own. This brownie is a seductive blending of a dark chocolate ganache and liquid pools of milk chocolate. The result is a brownie that is twice as dark, twice as rich, twice as moist—and twice as delicious as any other brownie!

Makes about 24 brownies

Prep Time: 30 minutes
Baking Time: 25 to 30 minutes
Cooling Time: 30 minutes
Chilling Time: 15 minutes
Level: *

Preheat the oven to 350°F. Butter and flour a 13 x 9-inch baking pan. Line the bottom and sides with aluminum foil, leaving an overhang on two opposite sides.

Combine the butter and Dark Chocolate Ganache in a double boiler set over barely simmering water and stir until melted. Remove from the heat and set aside to cool.

In the bowl of an electric mixer fitted with the paddle attachment, beat the eggs, granulated sugar, and brown sugar on high speed until creamy, 2 to 3 minutes.

With mixer on low speed, beat in the salt and melted ganache, followed by the vanilla. Gradually beat in the flour just until no white streaks remain in the batter. Stir in the chopped milk chocolate.

Spoon the batter into the prepared pan, smoothing the surface with a spatula. Bake for 25 to 30 minutes or until the brownies are set in the middle and a cake tester inserted into the center comes out slightly moist with batter. Cool in the pan set on a wire cooling rack for 30 minutes.

Use the foil overhang to lift the brownies from the pan and transfer to a plate. Refrigerate for 15 minutes. Transfer to a cutting board and cut into 24 squares.

special toolbox:

13 x 9-inch pan

double boiler

electric stand, mixer, bowl, and paddle

wire cooling rack

cake tester

12 tablespoons (1$\frac{1}{2}$ sticks) unsalted butter

1 cup Dark Chocolate Ganache (page 28)

4 large eggs

1$\frac{1}{4}$ cups granulated sugar

$\frac{1}{2}$ cup firmly packed light brown sugar

$\frac{1}{4}$ teaspoon salt

1$\frac{1}{2}$ teaspoons pure vanilla extract

1 cup all-purpose flour

1 cup coarsely chopped milk chocolate

Rocky Road Brownies

This is one of my favorite recipes—a rich, fudgy he-man brownie for the guys' weekly poker game or Super Bowl Sunday. Aside from being absolutely failure-proof, these are easy and fast to make. There is nothing quite like them.

Makes 9 brownies

Prep Time: 20 to 25 minutes
Baking Time: 25 to 30 minutes
Cooling Time: 20 minutes
Level: *

1 cup Dark Chocolate Ganache (page 28)

¼ pound (1 stick) unsalted butter

1¼ cups granulated sugar

3 large eggs

½ teaspoon pure vanilla extract

1½ cups all-purpose flour

¼ teaspoon salt

2 cups miniature marshmallows

1 cup walnut or pecan pieces

½ cup Burnt Caramel Sauce (page 242) or Chocolate Sauce (see box on page 30)

Preheat the oven to 350°F. Spray an 8-inch square baking pan lightly with flavorless vegetable oil spray.

In a glass mixing bowl, melt the Dark Chocolate Ganache and butter together in the microwave on high for 1 to 2 minutes, or until the butter is just melted. Stir until the ganache is melted and the mixture is smooth. Let cool for 10 minutes.

Stir in the sugar until dissolved. Add the eggs, one at a time, beating well with a wooden spoon. Mix in the vanilla. Stir in the flour and salt until just combined.

Spread the batter evenly in the prepared pan. Bake for 25 to 30 minutes, or until cake tester inserted in the center comes out clean.

Turn on the broiler. Immediately sprinkle the marshmallows and nuts evenly over the hot brownies. Broil for 1 to 2 minutes, or until the marshmallows are light golden brown. Cool the brownies to room temperature in the pan set on a wire cooling rack. Drizzle the Caramel or Chocolate Sauce over the cooled brownies before cutting into 9 squares.

MY PRAYERS WERE ANSWERED
IN SWITZERLAND

The phone call came five minutes before we were going on the air. "How would you and Joan like to take an all-expense-paid wine, cheese, sausage, and chocolate tour of Switzerland?" This was the invitation we received from the Swiss Consulate to travel and experience Switzerland on our stomachs. Needless to say, as the hosts of *The Food Show*, we thought this was a great idea and one that would give us plenty to talk about on future shows.

The Swiss consul general asked us to call him back during the week to help plan our fifteen-day itinerary. We told him that we didn't want to travel with other journalists; we didn't want to go to museums or churches; and we didn't want to meet with public relations people or politicians. We wanted the trip to be solely about food, allowing us to experience the Swiss farm-to-table food chain from one end of the country to the other. Everything was agreed upon, and we were set to leave the first week of November, just in time for the beginning of the Christmas season. There is no better place to celebrate the holidays than Europe. Swiss Air was our magic flying carpet from Los Angeles to Zürich. Ten hours later we were in a stunningly beautiful city that sits astride the river Limmat. Its charming old town, comprising a substantial part of the city center, is full of beautifully restored historic buildings and narrow, hilly alleys. In the distance, snow-clad peaks overlook the waters of the lakes and the shores dominated by turn-of-the-century mansions.

Zürich is our kind of city. It is a mecca for foodies, with more than two thousand bars and restaurants to pamper guests' palates with culinary delicacies from all over the world. We quickly learned that whether you prefer trendy gourmet temples inside old factory walls or Zürich specialties served in a traditional guild-hall setting, Zürich had just the right ambiance.

Our first dinner was with the mayor of Zürich in his unpretentious riverfront home on the Limmat. We were treated to a great home-cooked meal prepared by his wife and mother-in-law and enjoyed it with their children and some local neighbors. The ladies prepared some traditional Swiss specialties made from potatoes and cheese—*Rösti* (a potato dish), fondue, and raclette—and, of course, some exquisite homemade desserts made from famous Swiss chocolate. We also imbibed some of grandpapa's homemade grappa.

Little did we know that there were battles under way in the basement of the mayor's house, where his hobby was making miniature lead soldiers in precise detail—soldiers from all countries, portraying all battles—nearly ten thousand in all, row after row in perfect formation.

Our host asked us to meet him in the morning for chocolate croissants, coffee, and a tour of the local

View of Lake Geneva, Veyvey, Switzerland.

church, and despite our earlier decision to bypass churches and museums, we agreed. He told us that there was a special place in the basement where all the locals prayed for good crops. We descended a winding stairway nearly five stories beneath the sanctuary floor. As he flicked on the light switch, we discovered we had found the wine warehouse for the entire local community. There were casks and casks of reds and whites. We got a good dose of Swiss religion as we sampled the fruits of the vine before the clock even struck nine. Our appreciation of the importance of the church and the Swiss people had reached a new understanding.

We traveled by train from city to city and town to town, impressed at every stop, but Vevey became our favorite destination. It is the home of the world headquarters of the food giant Nestlé. By coincidence, milk chocolate was invented in Vevey by Daniel Peter in 1857.

Most important for us, it is the home of the Alimentarium, a modern museum opened in 1985 by the Nestlé foundation, which features permanent exhibitions of cooking, eating, food purchasing, digesting, and a history of Nestlé S.A. The museum demonstrates the different stages of the path traveled by food as it moves from the producer to the consumer: production, processing, preparation, and consumption. The exhibits are innovative, lively, and dynamic, encompassing about four thousand square feet.

One of our last days involved a quick trip to the Cailler chocolate factory, about a thirty-minute drive up in the hills overlooking the lake. The plant was almost a museum in itself, with its turn-of-the-century equipment chugging out chocolate confections by the thousands every hour. We only wish today that we had just one of the wrapping machines to help us package our Choclatique chocolate ingots.

Christmas Morning Brownies

If you didn't eat the cookies left out for Santa the night before, you will still have room for Christmas Morning Brownies. This is a great-tasting brownie with or without the green-tinted holiday frosting.

Makes 18 to 24 brownies

Prep Time: 20 minutes
Baking Time: 30 to 35 minutes
Cooling Time: 30 minutes
Level: *

special toolbox:

13 x 9-inch pan

electric stand mixer, bowl, and paddle

offset metal spatula

instant-read thermometer

cake tester

wire cooling rack

4 tablespoons Milk Chocolate
 Ganache (page 26)

4 tablespoons unsalted butter

2$\frac{1}{4}$ cups granulated sugar

1$\frac{1}{4}$ cups unsweetened
 Dutch-processed cocoa powder

1 teaspoon salt

1 teaspoon baking powder

1 tablespoon pure vanilla extract

4 large eggs

1$\frac{1}{2}$ cups all-purpose flour

1 cup semisweet chocolate chips

1 cup White Chocolate Ganache
 (page 29), at room temperature

Green food coloring

Holiday sugar sprinkles
 (for decoration)

Preheat the oven to 350°F. Coat a 13 x 9-inch pan with butter and set aside.

In a glass mixing bowl, melt the Milk Chocolate Ganache and butter together in the microwave on high for 1 to 2 minutes, or until the butter is just melted. Stir until the ganache is melted and the mixture is smooth. Add the sugar and stir until nearly dissolved.

Return the mixture to the microwave and heat just until hot (110°F to 120°F), but not bubbling. Stir the mixture until it looks shiny. (A second heating will dissolve most of the sugar, which will result in a shiny, cracked, homemade-looking top crust. This is a plus if you choose not to ice the brownies.)

Stir in the cocoa powder, salt, baking powder, and vanilla. Whisk in the eggs, stirring until smooth. Stir in the flour until just combined. Fold in the chocolate chips.

Pour the batter into the prepared pan. Bake for 30 to 35 minutes, checking for doneness after 25 minutes. The brownies are done when a cake tester inserted into the center comes out slightly moist with batter. The edges of the brownies should be set, but the middle still a little soft. Cool the brownies in the pan set on a wire cooling rack.

In the bowl of an electric mixer fitted with the paddle attachment, place the White Chocolate Ganache. Add a few drops of green food coloring to the ganache and beat on medium-high speed until whipped and happily green. Spread the ganache over the brownies and then decorate with holiday sugar sprinkles. Cut the brownies into 18 to 24 squares.

ChefSecret: For Chanukah brownies, use a little blue food coloring and sprinkles. For Valentine's Day, use red food coloring, and for Easter, tint the ganache with yellow food coloring.

Peanutty Crispy Brownie Bars

We sponsored a holiday cookie recipe contest for ABC-TV a few years back, and this was an anonymous entry that arrived in the mail. It didn't make the cut for the contest because it was more of a brownie than a cookie (and because it arrived without a name attached), but I thought it sounded interesting and suggested we bake it in the test kitchen. Magnificent! And it includes two of our favorites—chocolate and peanuts.

Makes 12 brownies

Prep Time: 15 minutes
Baking Time: 20 to 25 minutes
Cooling Time: 20 minutes
Assembly Time: 10 minutes
Level: **

For the brownies: Preheat the oven to 350°F. Butter a 13 x 9-inch baking pan.

In the bowl of an electric mixer fitted with the paddle attachment, beat the sugar, butter, Dark Chocolate Ganache, eggs, and vanilla on medium-high speed until blended.

In a mixing bowl, whisk the flour with the baking soda. Reduce the mixer speed to medium low and add the flour to the batter. Mix just until no white streaks remain in the batter. Pour the batter into the prepared pan.

Bake for 20 to 25 minutes or until a cake tester inserted in the center comes out clean. Cool the brownies in the pan set on a wire cooling rack.

For the icing: In the bowl of an electric mixer fitted with the whisk attachment, whip the White Chocolate Ganache with the confectioners' sugar until smooth and creamy. With an offset metal spatula, spread the icing over the brownies.

For the topping: In a small microwave-safe bowl, heat the chocolate chips and peanut butter on high for about 1 minute. Stir until smooth. Microwave for 30 to 40 seconds longer, if necessary, to make the consistency of the sauce spreadable.

Sprinkle the peanuts and cereal over the icing. Pour the sauce over the nuts and cereal and let the topping cool and set before cutting the brownies into 12 squares.

special toolbox:

13 x 9-inch baking pan

electric stand mixer, bowl, paddle, and whisk

offset metal spatula

cake tester

wire cooling rack

brownies:

1 cup granulated sugar

¼ pound (1 stick) unsalted butter, at room temperature

½ cup Dark Chocolate Ganache (page 28), at room temperature

2 large eggs

1 teaspoon pure vanilla extract

⅔ cup all-purpose flour

¼ teaspoon baking soda

icing:

1 cup White Chocolate Ganache (page 29), at room temperature

1 cup confectioners' sugar

topping:

2 cups semisweet chocolate chips

1 cup creamy peanut butter

¾ cup chopped salted peanuts

3 cups chocolate crisp rice cereal, such as Cocoa Krispies

8-inch square pan

8-inch parchment paper square

electric stand mixer, bowl, and paddle

cake tester

wire cooling rack

brownies:

2 tablespoons unsalted butter

1 cup White Chocolate Ganache
(page 29), divided

2 large eggs

1/2 teaspoon salt

1/2 cup granulated sugar

1 1/2 teaspoons pure vanilla extract

1 cup all-purpose flour

1/2 cup white chocolate chips

1/2 cup bittersweet chocolate chips

Blushing White Chocolate Brownies

The executive chef at the Parkroyal Kuala Lumpur hotel in Malaysia asked me if I had a recipe for white chocolate brownies. White brownies are tricky because they are not made with cocoa powder and have a tendency to fall.

My "mission impossible" on this trip was to make white chocolate brownies for a blushing bride, to be served at her wedding rehearsal dinner at this five-star hotel. The ladies of Kuala Lumpur are thought by many to be the most beautiful women in Asia, and this bride was no exception. I was told that this very special dessert did the bride justice.

Makes 9 brownies

Prep Time: 15 minutes
Baking Time: 35 minutes
Cooling Time: 30 minutes
Level: *

For the brownies: Preheat the oven to 325°F. Lightly butter the sides and bottom of an 8-inch square baking pan. Line the bottom with parchment paper and butter the paper.

In a small saucepan, melt the butter over low heat. Remove from the heat and add 1/2 cup of the White Chocolate Ganache. Do not stir.

In the bowl of an electric mixer fitted with a paddle attachment, beat together the eggs and salt on high speed until frothy, about 30 seconds. Continue to beat for 2 to 3 minutes, gradually adding the sugar. Mix until all the sugar is incorporated and soft peaks form.

Add the ganache mixture, vanilla, and flour and beat just until smooth. Fold in the white chocolate chips and bittersweet chocolate chips. Spoon the batter into the prepared pan.

Bake for 35 minutes or until a cake tester inserted into the center comes out slightly moist with batter. The edges of the brownies should be set, but the middle still a little soft. Cool in the pan set on a wire cooling rack until completely cool.

For the sauce: In a saucepan, melt the Dark Chocolate Ganache and butter over medium heat, stirring until the ganache melts. Add the granulated sugar and brown sugar, stirring until dissolved. Whisk in the cocoa powder and salt until well mixed. Reduce the heat and add as much coffee as needed to make the consistency of the sauce pourable.

Using a biscuit cutter, cut the brownies into 2½-inch rounds. Coat the bottom of each serving plate with about 3 tablespoons of chocolate sauce. Put a brownie in the center of the plate on top of the sauce. Top each brownie with a scoop of vanilla ice cream and garnish with fresh berries.

sauce:

½ cup Dark Chocolate Ganache (page 28)

3 tablespoons unsalted butter, cut into pieces

⅓ cup granulated sugar

⅓ cup firmly packed dark brown sugar

2 tablespoons unsweetened Dutch-processed cocoa powder

Pinch of salt

Scant ¼ cup brewed strong coffee

garnish:

1½ pints vanilla ice cream

Assorted fresh berries

Chapter

8

CHOCOLATE PIES AND TARTS

MY MOTHER HAD A LIMITED REPERTOIRE OF THINGS SHE COULD COOK—
AND SHE DID NONE OF THEM VERY WELL. SHE BOILED THE GREEN OUT
OF THE BEANS AND BROILED THE MOO OUT OF MEAT. REGARDLESS OF
THESE FAILINGS, SHE WAS PROUD OF HER APPLE PIE AND TOLD ANYONE WHO WOULD
LISTEN THAT FOLKS LINED UP TO GET A PIECE. HA! NOT HARDLY, MOM!

WHEN I OPENED THE PALM GRILL IN BURLINGAME, CALIFORNIA, I WAS COM
PELLED TO PUT APPLE PIE ON THE MENU, AND I DIDN'T FORGET ABOUT MOM. LISTED
ON THE MENU WAS "APPLE PIE LIKE MOM USED TO MAKE – $1.95" . . . "APPLE PIE
LIKE MOM THOUGHT SHE MADE – $4.95." SHE ONLY VISITED THE RESTAURANT ONCE
AND DIDN'T ORDER THE APPLE PIE.

Chocolate, Chocolate Pecan Pie

The French created the pecan pie after settling in New Orleans and discovering the quad-lobed nut, introduced to them by the Quinipissa and Tangipahoa Indians. The pie was inspired by the traditional sugar pies and sweet nut confections of their homeland and quickly became a favorite of the American South, ranking alongside pralines, fudge, and other pecan-flavored foods.

In this recipe I add a measure of Dark Chocolate Ganache to tease out a fuller flavor from the praline-sweetened pecans. Topped with the White Chocolate Ganache Whipped Cream, it's a taste sensation not soon forgotten!

Makes 1 (9-inch) pie, serving 6 to 8

Prep Time: 30 minutes
Chilling Time: 1 hour or overnight (for the crust)
Cooking Time: 20 minutes
Baking Time: 60 to 65 minutes
Cooling Time: 45 to 60 minutes
Level: ***

special toolbox:

food processor fitted with a metal blade

parchment paper

rolling pin

scissors

pie weights or dry beans

9-Inch pie pan

wire cooling rack

piecrust:

1¼ cups all-purpose flour

4 tablespoons granulated sugar

¼ teaspoon salt

4 tablespoons chilled unsalted butter, cut into ½-inch cubes

2 tablespoons chilled vegetable shortening or lard, cut into ½-inch cubes (for an extra flaky piecrust use lard)

2 tablespoons Dark Chocolate Ganache (page 28), chilled

1 tablespoon fresh lemon juice

4 tablespoons (or more) ice water

For the piecrust: In the bowl of a food processor fitted with the metal blade, pulse the flour, sugar, and salt just to mix. Add the butter, shortening, and Dark Chocolate Ganache and pulse until coarse crumbs form, about 30 seconds. Add the lemon juice and water and pulse just until moist crumbs form. Gather the dough into a ball. If the mixture does not come together when gathered in your hand, add a bit more water. Gently shape into a disk about 4 or 5 inches in diameter. Wrap the disk in plastic wrap and refrigerate for at least 1 hour or overnight.

Remove the dough from the refrigerator and roll it out between 2 large sheets of lightly floured parchment paper into a circle that is ⅛ inch thick and 14 inches around. Remove the top sheet of the parchment paper. Gently roll the dough around the rolling pin and position the pin over a 9-inch pie pan. Unroll the dough, gently easing the dough into the pan and gently but firmly pressing the dough against the sides and bottom of the pan, taking care not to pull or stretch the dough.

With scissors, trim the dough, leaving a ¾-inch overhang. Tuck the edge under and pinch and crimp using your fingers or the tines of a fork. Transfer the pie pan to the freezer for at least 30 minutes and up to an hour.

When ready, position a rack in the middle of the oven and preheat to 350°F. Line the pie shell with foil and fill the bottom with pie weights or dried beans. Bake for about 12 minutes until the crust begins to get firm to the touch. This is called blind baking.

Remove the weights and foil and return the pie shell to the oven for about 8 minutes longer. If the pastry bubbles during baking, push the bubbles down with the back of a spoon. Let the piecrust cool on a wire cooling rack.

For the filling: In a large saucepan, heat the sugar, corn syrup, and butter over medium-high heat. When the mixture starts to bubble, whisk constantly. The mixture will bubble vigorously once it starts to boil. Cook until the mixture thickens, about 5 minutes, whisking to control the bubbling.

Remove the pan from heat and whisk the Dark Chocolate Ganache into the hot syrup until smooth. Set aside for 20 minutes to cool.

When the ganache mixture is cool, preheat the oven to 350°F. Whisk in the eggs, one at a time. Add the chocolate chips and rum and stir thoroughly. Pour the filling into the baked pie shell. Arrange the pecan halves randomly on top of the filling. Bake until the filling edges are puffed and the center jiggles slightly, 40 to 45 minutes. Cool on a wire cooling rack.

Serve at room temperature topped with a dollop of White Chocolate Ganache Whipped Cream.

ChefSecret: If using a glass or Pyrex pie pan, decrease the baking temperature to 325°F. To save a little time, blind bake a store-bought crust. It won't be as good but will do very nicely in a pinch.

To toast the pecans, spread them on a dry baking sheet and roast in a 350°F oven for 6 to 8 minutes, shaking the pan several times during toasting to ensure even toasting. The nuts are done when they darken a shade and are fragrant. Let cool before using.

filling:

¼ cup granulated sugar

1¼ cups light corn syrup

2 tablespoons unsalted butter, cut into chunks

⅓ cup Dark Chocolate Ganache (page 28)

3 large eggs

¼ cup semisweet chocolate chips

1 tablespoon dark rum, such as Myers Rum

1½ cups large pecan halves, lightly toasted (see ChefSecret)

1 cup White Chocolate Ganache Whipped Cream (page 238), for garnish

Upside-Down Chocolate-Pecan Meringue Pie

I use to work for Lawry's, the prime rib people in Beverly Hills, California. When we created this dessert for the restaurant, we turned a meringue pie on its head, which took a lot more time to bake and a little more care to plate than anything else we served. It was one of those desserts that no one liked to make but everyone loved to eat.

Don't be put off by this description. I have reworked the recipe so that it's very doable for the home cook. I'm not saying it's simple, but it's not too hard if you have a little time.

Makes 1 (9-inch) pie, serving 6 to 8

Prep Time: 30 minutes
Baking Time: 1 hour 45 minutes
Cooling Time: 1 hour
Chilling Time: 2 hours
Level: ***

For the meringue pie shell: Preheat the oven to 200°F. Butter a pie pan.

In the bowl of an electric mixer fitted with the whisk attachment, beat the egg whites on medium speed until frothy. Add the salt and cream of tartar and continue beating for 5 minutes or until soft peaks form.

Gradually add 3 tablespoons of the sugar and continue beating for 5 minutes longer. Add the remaining 3 tablespoons of sugar very gradually and continue beating for 15 minutes longer. (This is not a typo — 15 minutes, no less.) At this point the meringue will be firm and silky. Add the vanilla and blend well.

Remove the bowl from the mixer and, using a rubber spatula, fold the toasted pecans into the meringue.

Spoon the meringue into the pie pan. Using a rubber spatula, make an indentation in the center, forming the meringue into a nest, and gently press the meringue against the sides of the pan.

Set the pie pan inside a second pie pan and bake for 1 hour and 45 minutes or until light brown and crisp. Set the pie pans on a wire cooling rack to cool completely, at least 1 hour.

Ingredients and directions continued on page 136.

special toolbox:

2 heavy metal 9-inch pie tins
(for double panning)

electric stand mixer, bowl, and whisk

offset metal spatula

pastry bag fitted with a star tip

wire cooling rack

meringue pie shell:

2 large egg whites

Pinch of salt

Pinch of cream of tartar

6 tablespoons granulated sugar,
divided

1/4 teaspoon pure vanilla extract

1/4 cup coarsely chopped pecans,
lightly toasted

For the filling: Melt the Dark Chocolate Ganache in a microwave oven or in a bowl set over simmering water. When melted, stir in the hot water until smooth. Set aside to cool. When cool, stir in the vanilla.

In the bowl of an electric mixer fitted with the whisk attachment, whip the cream on medium speed. Slowly add the confectioners' sugar and continue beating, increasing the speed to medium high until stiff peaks form. Fold in the cooled ganache mixture with the rubber spatula.

Spoon the chocolate filling into the center of the meringue. Wrap the shell and filling in plastic so that it is as airtight as possible and refrigerate for at least 2 hours and up to 8 hours.

When ready to serve, remove the plastic wrap from the meringue. If the pie has been refrigerated for more than 3 hours, let sit at room temperature for 20 minutes before serving. Fill a pastry bag fitted with a star tip with the White Chocolate Ganache Whipped Cream. Pipe rosettes on the filling to garnish.

filling:

¾ cup Dark Chocolate Ganache (page 28)

1½ tablespoons hot water

1 teaspoon pure vanilla extract

1 cup heavy cream

¼ cup confectioners' sugar

1½ cups White Chocolate Ganache Whipped Cream (page 238), for garnish

HIT MAN

Pies were my first entrepreneurial business venture. I got the idea from the television show *Have Gun—Will Travel*. While in high school I opened a "syndicate" called Hit Man—We Deliver. For $25, anyone could put out a contract on someone, and we would throw a pie in that unsuspecting person's face. Don't laugh; the business helped me get through college. We were mere pranksters taking target at politicians and others to make social statements. Pies were our sweet weapons in the '60s.

We never dreamed of going after other kids and targeted only business moguls, politicians, and entertainers. As the godfather of the group, I had about twenty others in the syndicate. The ladies were the most daring and usually were able to get the closest to the unsuspecting targets. When I think of those days now, I am surprised we didn't end up in jail, especially when we nailed Los Angeles Mayor Sam Yorty. It was a different time. Nowadays we would be labeled terrorists and thrown in Gitmo.

Chocolate French Silk Pie

This quick, creamy chocolate dessert was one of the melt-in-your-mouth recipes that I originally developed for T. R.'s Restaurants in Wichita, Kansas. I doubt old Teddy ever tasted anything as good as this. I still make it for friends and family when a light, chocolate dessert is on the menu. This goes to prove that a good chocolate recipe can even outlive the life of a presidential restaurant.

Makes 1 (9-inch) pie, serving 6 to 8

Prep Time: 10 minutes
Baking Time: 13 minutes
Cooling Time: 30 minutes
Chilling Time: 1 hour
Level: *

special toolbox:

9-inch pie pan

heavy-duty aluminum foil

pie weights or dry beans

electric stand mixer, bowl, and whisk

wire cooling rack

pastry bag fitted with a plain tip
(optional)

Piecrust dough for a 9-inch pie
(page 228)

3 cups Milk Chocolate Ganache
(page 26), at room temperature

3 cups White Chocolate Ganache
Whipped Cream (page 238),
at room temperature, divided

¼ cup shaved chocolate curls
(page 35) (optional)

Preheat the oven to 450°F. On a lightly floured surface with a floured rolling pin, roll the dough into a circle. Gently roll the dough around the rolling pin and position the pin over a 9-inch pie pan. Unroll the dough, gently easing the dough into the pan and gently but firmly pressing the dough against the side and bottom of the pan, taking care not to pull or stretch the dough. Line the pie shell with two pieces of heavy-duty foil and fill with pie weights or dry beans. Bake for 8 minutes. Remove the foil and weights and bake for about 5 minutes longer, until lightly brown. Cool on a wire cooling rack.

While the crust is cooling, make the filling. In the bowl of an electric mixer fitted with the whisk attachment, whip the Milk Chocolate Ganache on medium speed for 2 minutes until light and fluffy. Using a rubber spatula, fold 1½ cups of the White Chocolate Ganache Whipped Cream into the ganache.

Spoon the filling into the cooled crust and smooth the surface. Refrigerate for at least 1 hour and up to 10 hours to chill.

Just before serving, top the pie with dollops of the remaining White Chocolate Whipped Cream. (Alternatively, spoon the whipped cream into a pastry bag fitted with a plain tip and pipe florets around the edge of the pie.) Garnish with chocolate curls, if desired.

THE PLEASURES OF BALI HA'I

Bali is a beautiful island paradise, one of the seventeen thousand islands of Indonesia. Like the island itself, the Balinese people are very welcoming and accommodating. The weather, however, is far less hospitable, especially if you are a chocolatier. There are only three seasons in Bali—hot, very hot, and very, very hot and humid.

In 2001 I held a chocolate workshop at the Grand Hyatt in Bali. When I first arrived, the weather concerned me. But before I worried about presenting failed desserts in front of a paying audience, I wanted to experience Bali. The first thing in the morning I took a tour of the central island going from Denpasar up to the craft city of Ubud, which is a remarkable little town in the middle of the island and for more than a hundred years has been the island's preeminent center for fine art, mask making, dance, music, and food. While many of the visitors are actively involved in art, nature, anthropology, music, dance, architecture, and environmentalism, Ubud is also the place for romance, food, and chocolate.

It was at the Maya Ubud Resort and Spa where I first met Ariani, a mask-maker who had worked at the spa for six years. She was a little difficult to understand at first, but when she mentioned chocolate, my ears perked up and I paid close attention to her every word. It seems that she was hawking chocolate for a purpose other than eating; chocolate body masks are the spa's specialty at Maya Ubud Resort. After a relaxing thirty-minute plunge in the soothing waters of a floral bath, they cover your body in a soft, smooth, unctuous, warm, great-smelling chocolate body mask.

In the early evening hours I discovered the real magic of Ubud, hidden away in the backstreets, backwaters, courtyards, and cafés and in people's hearts, minds, and dreams. That was when I found local chocolatiers who specialized in cacao from the small plantations in Sulawesi and sampled their wares. I met up with Janet De Neefe, owner of Casa Luna Restaurant, hands-down my favorite restaurant in Ubud. Janet offers mind-blowing chocolate desserts—chocolate mousse, chocolate decadence, flourless chocolate cake—you name it, she makes it. Janet's chocolate desserts, along with the ambiance of Ubud, brings all the magic of Bali to life!

It was also in Ubud that I further refined many of my own hybrid standards for selecting, growing, harvesting, fermenting, drying, buying, and producing chocolate for Choclatique.

I took all that I learned, along with fifteen kilos of Indonesian chocolate, back to the Grand Hyatt to prepare for the next day's chocolate class. I was amazed at how different everything tasted now, and how I was better able to teach my budding chocolatiers to have deep respect for the chocolate and all the other local ingredients as they began to make their ganaches. But the true adventure for me was going behind the tourist façade to experience the local culture and discover the real people of the island, the real Bali, and real Indonesian chocolate.

Bittersweet Chocolate Tart

I asked my friend Vitor, the executive chef at Pingo Doce in Lisbon, Portugal, for a recipe for the national dessert—Portuguese Chocolate Tart. He didn't have a clue what I was talking about! The national dessert is an egg custard tart, he told me. We corresponded back and forth, and I showed him pictures of what I was searching for. Finally, the two of us came up with this wonderful Portuguese-style recipe.

This incomparable chocolate tart is nothing short of a bewitching combination of the dark and sultry that stops just shy of complete and utter perfection.

Makes 1 (9-inch) tart, serving 6 to 8

Prep Time: 20 minutes
Baking Time: 35 to 40 minutes
Cooling Time: 1 hour
Chill Time: 2 hours
Cooling Time: 20 minutes
Level: ***

For the pastry shell: Scrape the seeds from the vanilla bean into a small bowl. Add the egg yolk and stir to blend. Add the vanilla and almond extracts and stir to blend.

In the bowl of a food processor fitted with the metal blade, mix together the confectioners' sugar and almonds and process until the nuts are finely ground. Add the flour and salt and pulse to blend. Add the butter and pulse until the mixture resembles coarse crumbs.

Add the egg yolk mixture and pulse just until the dough begins to hold together. Do not over process; the dough should not form a ball.

Turn out the dough onto a lightly floured surface and very gently pat the dough into a disk, handling it as little as possible. Wrap the dough in plastic wrap and refrigerate for at least 1 hour or until well chilled.

Butter the bottom and sides of a 9-inch fluted tart pan with a removable bottom. Roll out the chilled dough on a lightly floured surface into an 11-inch round. If the dough sticks to the rolling pin, rub some flour on the pin. Transfer the dough to the prepared pan and gently press against the sides, allowing for ½-inch overhang. With a fork, prick the bottom of the dough all over and refrigerate the crust again for at least 1 hour.

Ingredients and directions continued on page 141.

special toolbox:

food processor fitted with a metal blade

9-inch fluted tart pan with removable bottom

rolling pin

wire cooling rack

sifter

pastry shell:

1 vanilla bean, split lengthwise

1 large egg yolk, at room temperature

1 teaspoon pure vanilla extract

½ teaspoon almond extract

½ cup confectioners' sugar, sifted

2 tablespoons toasted whole blanched almonds

¾ cup all-purpose flour, sifted

Pinch of salt

5 tablespoons unsalted butter, cut into pieces, at room temperature

Preheat the oven to 350°F.

Set the tart pan on a baking sheet and bake in the middle of the oven for about 5 minutes, until the pastry just begins to firm up. Remove from the oven and, with a sharp knife, carefully trim and discard the overhanging pastry to make a smooth, even edge. Return the pan to the oven and bake for about 15 minutes longer, until the pastry is nicely browned. Transfer to a cooling rack and let the crust cool completely before filling.

Do not turn off the oven.

For the filling: In a medium saucepan, bring the cream, milk, and sugar to a simmer over medium-low heat. Remove from the heat, add the Dark Chocolate Ganache and stir until melted. Let the mixture cool to lukewarm and then whisk in the egg until thoroughly blended.

Pour the custard into the pastry shell and bake in the middle of the oven until the filling is almost set but still trembles in the center, 12 to 15 minutes. Transfer the pie to a wire rack to cool. Sift the cocoa powder over the tart and serve warm or at room temperature.

ChefSecret: You can add another level of flavor by drizzling the tart with a little Red Raspberry Sauce (page 243)—which might seem like gilding the lily, but why not?

filling:

¾ cup heavy cream

⅓ cup milk

¼ cup granulated sugar

1 cup Dark Chocolate Ganache (page 28), at room temperature

1 large egg, lightly beaten

½ teaspoon unsweetened Dutch-processed cocoa powder, for sifting

ED'S BOX-TOP WISDOM
Integrity

We embrace integrity in the ingredients we use, which allows the crispness of texture, the vibrancy of flavor, and the spectrum of color.

Chocolate Ganache Puddin' Pie

This is an all-American recipe with its roots in the Deep South. Even Yankees won't be able to resist this semisweet, sumptuous creation, with its ribboned layers of rich chocolate puddin' topped with White Chocolate Ganache Whipped Cream nestled on a chocolate cookie crumb crust. It is best garnished with chocolate shavings and served chilled.

Makes 1 (9-inch) pie, serving 6 to 8

Prep Time: 15 minutes
Baking Time: 10 minutes
Cooling Time: 15 minutes
Chilling Time: 4 hours
Level: **

For the piecrust: Preheat the oven to 325°F. Spray the bottom and sides of a 9-inch pie pan with vegetable oil spray.

In the bowl of a food processor fitted with the metal blade, mix together the cookie crumbs, butter, and sugar and process until moist crumbs form.

Press the crumb mixture over the bottom and up the sides of the pie pan and bake until set, about 10 minutes. Remove from the oven and cool on a wire cooling rack.

For the filling: In a heavy saucepan over low heat, whisk together the milk and Hot Fudge Ganache over medium-low heat until the ganache is melted. Set aside to cool for at least 15 minutes.

In a mixing bowl, whisk together the egg yolks and sugar until pale yellow. Whisk in the cornstarch and salt and then the vanilla until well blended. Slowly pour the warm chocolate mixture into the yolks, whisking constantly until well blended.

Special Toolbox

food processor fitted with a metal blade

9-inch glass pie pan

wire cooling rack

heavy, non-aluminum saucepan

pastry bag fitted with a star tip

piecrust:

2 cups chocolate sandwich cookie crumbs, such as Oreos

¼ pound (1 stick) cold unsalted butter, cut into pieces

3 tablespoons granulated sugar

filling:

2½ cups milk

¾ cup Hot Fudge Ganache (page 30)

8 large egg yolks

¾ cup granulated sugar

3 tablespoons cornstarch

¼ teaspoon salt

1½ teaspoons pure vanilla extract

Return the filling to the saucepan and cook over medium heat until thickened and slowly bubbling, 6 to 8 minutes. Remove from the heat and continue to stir until smooth, about 1 minute. Pour the filling into the cooled crumb crust and smooth the surface with a spatula.

Cover with plastic wrap, gently pressing the plastic directly onto the surface of the filling, and refrigerate until completely cold and firm, 4 hours.

For the topping: Spoon the White Chocolate Ganache Whipped Cream into a pastry bag fitted with a star tip and pipe rosettes over the top of the pie. Garnish with chocolate curls and refrigerate until ready to serve. Before serving, let the pie stand at room temperature for 15 minutes.

ChefSecret: To make decorative chocolate curls, wrap a medium-size chunk (3- to 6-ounce bar) of semisweet chocolate in plastic wrap. Rub the wrapped chocolate between your palms for 1 or 2 minutes to warm it, the chocolate should not melt. (For larger chunks, microwave on low power for about 5 seconds.)

Unwrap the chocolate and, using a vegetable peeler, slowly and evenly scrape the edge of the chunk until very small curls form. If the chocolate is cold, the peeler will make ragged shavings rather than curls; repeat warming the chocolate between your palms as necessary.

topping:

1 cup White Chocolate Ganache Whipped Cream (page 238)

2 tablespoons small chocolate curls (page 35), for garnish

White Chocolate Cream with Tropical Fruit Tart

Barcelona is one of the most beautiful cities in Europe, largely because of the Catalan people, the Gaudi architecture, Picasso art, flamenco music, and, of course, the fantastic food. Joan and I spent a week exploring the city before driving down to Marbella in the south of Spain to work with clients at the Hotel Los Monteros Costa del Sol. It had been cold and rainy in Barcelona, but in Marbella it was a sunny eighty degrees. We ate al fresco at the hotel's new patio restaurant overlooking the Mediterranean. For dessert we discovered a white custard mousse tarte laced with spring berries and topped with delicate white chocolate curls. This tart is best eaten the day it is made.

Makes 1 (12-inch) tart, serving 6 to 8

Prep Time: 20 minutes
Baking Time: 20 to 25 minutes
Cooling Time: 30 minutes
Chilling Time: 1 hour
Level: **

special toolbox:

electric stand mixer, bowl, and whisk

12-inch round tart pan with a removable bottom

offset spatula

pastry brush

crust:

12 tablespoons (1½ sticks) unsalted butter, softened

½ cup confectioners' sugar

1½ cups all-purpose flour

¼ cup Dark Chocolate Ganache (page 28), melted

filling:

¼ cup heavy whipping cream

1 cup White Chocolate Ganache (page 29), at room temperature

1 (8-ounce) package cream cheese, softened

glaze:

¼ cup apricot preserves

1 tablespoon water

2 cups chopped or sliced assorted fruit, such as kiwi, mango, papaya, berries, peaches, plums, or nectarines

For the crust: Heat the oven to 300°F.

In the bowl of an electric mixer fitted with the paddle attachment, beat the butter and confectioners' sugar on medium speed until light and fluffy, 3 to 5 minutes. Reduce the speed to low and mix in the flour until the dough comes together.

Press the dough over the bottom and up the sides of a 12-inch tart pan with a removable bottom. Bake for 20 to 25 minutes or until just lightly brown. Let the piecrust cool completely on a wire cooling rack.

When the crust is cool, brush the melted Dark Chocolate Ganache over the bottom and sides of the piecrust.

For the filling: In the bowl of an electric mixer fitted with the whisk attachment, whip the cream until stiff peaks form. Beat in the White Chocolate Ganache and cream cheese. Spread the filling evenly over the baked crust. Cover with plastic wrap and chill for at least 1 hour or overnight until ready to serve.

For the glaze: In a small saucepan, heat the preserves and water over medium-high heat until boiling. Remove from the heat and let cool.

Arrange the fruit of your choice decoratively over the top of the tart. Brush the cooled glaze over the fruit for shine.

Frozen Chocolate Mousse
Meringue Pot Pie

No place on earth is farther from the world's cares than the island of Saint John and its Caneel Bay, where the clear, sapphire Caribbean waters kiss the golden sands. Here you can relax as cool ocean breezes whisper through the plantation shutters, but the warm, humid weather makes working with chocolate taxing and the delivery of a traditional mousse nearly impossible. As a guest chef, I created this frozen pot pie scented with dark rum to overcome these challenges. This is an incredibly rich and easy-to-make frozen chocolate dessert that rivals the best chocolate ice cream.

Makes 1 (9-inch) pie, serving 6 to 8

Prep Time: 20 minutes
Baking Time: 20 minutes
Freezing Time: 3 hours or overnight
Level: *

Roll out the dough into a circle. Gently roll the dough around the rolling pin and position the pin over a 9-inch deep-dish pie pan. Unroll the dough, gently easing the dough into the pan and gently but firmly pressing the dough over the bottom and against the sides of the pan, taking care not to pull or stretch the dough.

With scissors, trim the dough to leave a ¾-inch overhang. Tuck the edge under the rim, pinch and crimp using your fingers or the tines of a fork. Transfer pie pan to the freezer for at least 30 minutes and up to a few hours.

Meanwhile, position a rack in the middle of the oven and preheat it to 350°F.

Line the piecrust with foil and fill the bottom with pie weights or dried beans. Bake for about 12 minutes until the dough begins to get firm to the touch.

Remove the foil and weights and return the piecrust to the oven for about 8 minutes longer. If the pastry bubbles during baking, push the bubbles down with the back of a spoon. Let the piecrust cool on a wire cooling rack.

special toolbox:

9-inch deep-dish pie pan

pie weights or dry beans

wire cooling rack

electric stand mixer, bowl, paddle, and whisk

butane kitchen torch

Piecrust dough for a 9-inch pie (page 228)

mousse:

2 cups Milk Chocolate Ganache (page 26), at room temperature

3 tablespoons plus 1 quart heavy cream, divided

1 tablespoon dark rum, such as Myers, or brandy

1 teaspoon pure vanilla extract

3 cups confectioners' sugar

For the mousse: In the bowl of an electric stand mixer fitted with the paddle attachment, beat the Milk Chocolate Ganache, 3 tablespoons of the cream, the rum, and vanilla on medium-high speed until smooth, about 5 minutes.

In a clean, dry bowl of an electric mixer fitted with the whisk attachment, whip the remaining 1 quart of cream on medium-high speed until soft peaks form. With the mixer going, gradually add the confectioners' sugar and continue to beat until stiff peaks form. Fold in the ganache mixture. Pour the mousse into the pie shell and wrap in plastic. Freeze for at least 3 hours and up to 12 hours.

For the meringue: In the bowl of an electric mixer fitted with the whisk attachment, beat the egg whites on medium speed until frothy. Add the salt and cream of tartar and continue beating until soft peaks form, about 5 minutes. With the mixer running, gradually add 3 tablespoons of the sugar and continue beating for 5 minutes longer. Add the remaining 3 tablespoons sugar very gradually and continue beating for another 15 minutes, no less. At this point the meringue will be firm and silky. Blend the vanilla into the meringue. Remove the plastic wrap from the pie and pile the meringue on top.

For the topping: Put the brown sugar in a coffee grinder or small food processor and grind to a fine powder. Sprinkle the sugar over the meringue and, using a butane torch (or under a hot broiler), caramelize the sugar.

Sprinkle chocolate curls on top of the pie to garnish.

meringue:

2 large egg whites

Pinch of salt

Pinch of cream of tartar

6 tablespoons granulated
   sugar, divided

1/4 teaspoon pure vanilla extract

topping:

3 tablespoons light or
   dark brown sugar

1 tablespoons small semisweet
   chocolate curls, for garnish
   (page 35)

Salted Caramel Chocolate Tart

While salt is a flavor enhancer for chocolate, I never really appreciated the salted caramels that so many of the nation's chocolatiers have been making. I was asked to make a chocolate-caramel tart with salted peanuts for the National Peanut Board, and of course, "salted" peanuts were the important ingredient. I discovered I really liked the added flavor element of the salt with the caramel and chocolate, but the next time I made the tart, I dispensed with the peanuts and simply dusted the top with *fleur de sel*. You can also make this delicious dessert tart with toasted pecans and walnuts; just don't forget the salt.

Makes 1 (9-inch) tart, serving 8 to 10

Prep Time: 45 minutes
Baking Time: 20 minutes
Freezing Time: 15 minutes
Chilling Time: 20 minutes + 1 hour
Level: ***

For the crust: In the bowl of a food processor fitted with a metal blade, process the flour, sugar, lemon zest, and salt for 5 seconds. Add the butter, egg yolk, and vanilla and almond extracts and process until large moist clumps form. Gather the dough into a ball and knead briefly to combine. Flatten the dough into a disk, wrap in plastic, and chill until firm enough to roll, about 30 minutes.

Preheat the oven to 400°F.

Roll the dough between sheets of parchment paper into an 11- to 12-inch round. Remove the top sheet of the parchment paper. Turn the dough over and press over the bottom and up the sides of a 9-inch tart pan with removable bottom. Remove the bottom sheet of parchment paper. Fold any overhanging dough back over the edge of the tart pan to form double-thick sides. Using a fork, pierce the crust all over. Freeze for 15 minutes.

special toolbox:

food processor fitted with a metal blade

parchment paper

rolling pin

9-inch tart pan with a removable bottom

offset spatula

wire cooling rack

pastry brush

crust:

1 cup all-purpose flour

3 tablespoons granulated sugar

1 teaspoon grated lemon zest

1/8 teaspoon salt

1/4 pound (1 stick) cold unsalted butter, cut into 1/2-inch pieces

1 large egg yolk

1/2 teaspoon pure vanilla extract

1/4 teaspoon almond extract

Bake the crust for 10 minutes. Use the back of a fork to press the crust flat if the bottom bubbles during baking. Continue to bake until golden brown, about 10 minutes longer (the sides of the crust may shrink slightly.) Transfer the baked piecrust to a wire cooling rack to cool.

For the chocolate filling: In a medium heavy saucepan, melt the Milk Chocolate Ganache over medium heat, whisking until smooth. Spread 1 cup of the chocolate filling into the prepared crust. Reserve any excess chocolate filling in the saucepan. Refrigerate the filled pie until firm, about 45 minutes.

For the caramel filling: In a medium heavy saucepan, heat the sugar and water over low heat, stirring, until the sugar dissolves. Cover and raise the heat to high. Bring the syrup to a boil and cook until amber, 8 to 10 minutes. Remove the lid and brush down the sides of the pan with a wet pastry brush to prevent the caramel from crystallizing. Remove from heat.

Carefully add the cream, butter, vanilla, and salt to the caramel. The mixture will bubble up. Return the pan to very low heat and stir until the caramel is smooth and the color deepens, about 5 minutes. Refrigerate the caramel, uncovered, until chilled but not firm, about 20 minutes.

Spoon the caramel filling over the chocolate filling, spreading to cover the chocolate. Drizzle the reserved chocolate filling over the caramel. If the chocolate is too firm to pour, warm it slightly over low heat. Cover the tart with plastic wrap and refrigerate until the caramel is firm, at least 1 hour and up to 12 hours.

Just before serving, sprinkle the top with a dusting of sea salt to taste.

chocolate filling:

$1\frac{1}{2}$ cups Milk Chocolate Ganache (page 26)

caramel filling:

$\frac{3}{4}$ cup granulated sugar

$\frac{1}{3}$ cup water

$\frac{1}{3}$ cup heavy cream

5 tablespoons unsalted butter, cut in $\frac{1}{2}$-inch pieces

$\frac{1}{2}$ teaspoon pure vanilla extract

Pinch of salt

1 teaspoon specialty sea salt, for garnish

Cherry Chocolate Pie

George Washington got it right when he planted cherry trees at Mount Vernon. Cherries are a good source of potassium and melatonin; they have anti-inflammatory properties and are rich in antioxidants. So it was only natural that we decided to bring healthful chocolate and healthful cherries together for this pie. Plus, it's a flavor combination much desired throughout the chocolate-loving world!

I've added graham cracker crumbs to a traditional piecrust for a unique texture and honey graham flavor. This is one of those desserts you find yourself making over and over again, and as such, it will become a summertime family favorite.

Makes 1 (9-inch) pie, serving 8 to 10

Prep Time: 45 minutes
Chilling Time: 20 minutes
Baking Time: 50 minutes
Cooling Time: 1 hour
Level: **

For the crust: Preheat the oven to 400°F.

Sift together the flour and salt.

In the bowl of a food processor fitted with the metal blade, mix the flour and salt with the graham cracker crumbs until the mixture resembles fine meal. Add the frozen butter and shortening to the food processor, one piece at a time, and pulse after each addition. Once the butter and shortening are incorporated, add the water, 1 tablespoon at a time, pulsing after each addition, until the dough looks like coarse breadcrumbs. Only add as much water as you need; you do not want the dough to be too wet or the crust will not be flaky. The dough will come together when you pinch it between your fingers. It should not form a ball in the food processor.

Remove the dough from the bowl and form into a ball. Divide in half and wrap each half in plastic wrap. Freeze for 20 minutes.

special toolbox:

food processor fitted
with a metal blade

rolling pin

9-inch pie pan

pastry brush

wire cooling rack

crust:

1½ cups chilled all-purpose flour

1 teaspoon salt

½ cup finely ground honey
graham cracker crumbs (about
4 whole crackers)

¼ pound (1 stick) unsalted butter,
frozen and cut into ¼-inch cubes

6 tablespoons vegetable shortening
or lard, frozen, cut into pieces

1 cup ice water

1 egg, lightly beaten

2 tablespoons water

On a lightly floured work surface and with floured hands and a floured rolling pin, roll out one-half of the dough until it is large enough to fit into a 9-inch pie pan. Carefully roll the dough over the rolling pin and unroll it in the pie dish, pressing the dough into the bottom and up the sides of the pan. Trim any overhanging dough.

Combine the egg and water in a small bowl to make an egg wash; set aside.

For the cherry filling: In a large mixing bowl, toss the cherries with the sugar and cornstarch. Add the melted Hot Fudge Ganache and gently toss until the cherries are well coated. Spoon the cherry filling into the piecrust.

Roll out the remaining half of the dough and drape it over the rolling pin. Using the rolling pin as a guide, lay the dough over the top of the pie. Pinch the sides closed using your thumb and forefinger. Use a small, sharp knife to cut steam vents in the top of the crust.

Brush the crust with the egg wash and bake in the middle of the oven for 25 minutes. Reduce the oven heat to 350°F and bake for about 25 minutes longer, until the crust is golden brown and the cherries are bubbling. Cool the pie on a wire cooling rack for 1 hour before serving.

ChefSecret: If cherries aren't in season, in a pinch you use frozen cherries or canned cherry pie filling. If you use canned fruit, omit the step where you toss the cherries with sugar and cornstarch.

cherry filling:

$2\frac{1}{2}$ pounds fresh sweet cherries, stemmed and pitted (about 2 pounds pitted)

$\frac{1}{2}$ cup granulated sugar

3 tablespoons cornstarch

$\frac{1}{2}$ cup Hot Fudge Ganache (page 30), melted

Chapter

9

CHOCOLATE PUDDINGS, CUSTARDS, MOUSSES, AND TRIFLES

CHOCOLATE PUDDINGS AND CUSTARDS RANK HIGH AMONG MY FAVORITE COMFORT FOODS, AND CLEARLY I AM NOT ALONE. CHOCOLATE PUDDING WAS POPULARIZED IN THE UNITED STATES BY GENERAL FOODS WITH THEIR JELL-O BRAND IN 1936, AND IT'S BEEN ON THE SHELVES EVER SINCE.

IF YOU'RE A FAN OF COOKED, INSTANT, OR EVEN THE READY-MADE STUFF IN THE DELI SECTION OF THE SUPERMARKET, GIVE YOURSELF A TREAT AND TAKE A FEW MINUTES TO TRY ONE OF MY RECIPES. GOOD HOMEMADE PUDDINGS ARE MADE WITH FRESH MILK, CANE SUGAR, FRESH EGGS, PURE VANILLA, AND GREAT CHOCOLATE GANACHE. IT TAKES ONLY A FEW MINUTES AND JUST A SINGLE POT TO MAKE A DEEP, DARK, ULTIMATELY SATISFYING, TRADITIONAL, HOMEMADE AMERICAN-STYLE CHOCOLATE PUDDING.

Authentically American Chocolate Pudding

In the early days of the last century, chocolate pudding was considered "good-for-you" food, perfect for invalids and growing children. The soft consistency made it easy to eat and digest, and the calories were beneficial for "active youngsters." In modern terms, pudding would never be considered healthful—much less health food—but my recipe has been known to cure incurable diseases, make men out of boys, and even bring back the spirits of the dead! Okay, maybe that's a little exaggeration, but this dessert is very easy to make and it's just damn good puddin'.

Makes 4 servings

Prep Time: 20 to 25 minutes
Cooking Time: 35 minutes
Cooling Time: 30 minutes
Chilling Time: 2 hours
Level: *

In the bowl of an electric mixer fitted with the paddle attachment, beat the egg yolks and sugar on medium speed until light yellow and thick, 4 to 5 minutes. Add the cornstarch, cocoa powder, and salt and beat until mixed.

In a medium saucepan, bring the milk to a boil over low heat. Temper the egg mixture with the milk (see ChefSecret below) and then slowly pour the tempered milk into the remainder of the egg mixture and beat to mix well.

Return the custard to the saucepan and cook over low heat, whisking or stirring constantly, for about 3 minutes or until thickened to the consistency of heavy cream.

Remove the pan from the heat and stir in the Dark Chocolate Ganache, vanilla, and cream with a spoon until the ganache melts and the ingredients are thoroughly incorporated.

Divide the pudding among four 6-ounce ramekins or custard cups. Cover the surface of each with plastic wrap to prevent a skin from forming. Set the pudding aside for 30 minutes to cool, then refrigerate for 2 hours or until chilled. The pudding will keep for up to two days if properly covered and refrigerated. Serve with White Chocolate Ganache Whipped Cream and Hot Fudge Ganache.

ChefSecret: The technique used to blend uncooked eggs into a hot liquid or sauce is called tempering (not to be confused with tempering chocolate). A little of the hot liquid (in this case, milk) is whisked into the beaten eggs just until the eggs are warm, or tempered. Tempering slowly raises the temperature of eggs without curdling them. This prevents the eggs from scrambling or the milk from curdling.

G gluten free

special toolbox:
4 (6-ounce) ramekins
electric stand mixer, bowl, and paddle

6 large egg yolks

½ cup granulated sugar

¼ cup cornstarch

3 tablespoons unsweetened Dutch-processed cocoa powder

Pinch of salt

2 cups whole milk

⅓ cup Dark Chocolate Ganache (page 28)

1½ teaspoons pure vanilla extract

2 tablespoons heavy cream

White Chocolate Ganache Whipped Cream (page 238), for serving

Hot Fudge Ganache (page 30), melted, for serving

Scan for Ed's ChefSecret

Dark Chocolate
French Crème Caramel

Crème caramel is a wonderful classic bistro dessert. It is usually the first dessert that a French cook-in-training learns to make. It is light, sophisticated, and easy to prepare, and can be made up to a day in advance.

Crème Caramel is also versatile and reliable enough to stand up to the high humidity and temperatures of tropical climates. I always turn to this classic in warm weather, as it is the essence of simplicity, and It needs no garnish othor than an attractive plate.

Makes 8 servings

Prep Time: 5 minutes
Cooking Time: 45 minutes
Cooling Time: 20 minutes
Chilling Time: 1 to 8 hours
Level: *

In a medium saucepan, heat 1 cup of the sugar over medium-low heat until melted and caramelized. Shake the pan occasionally to distribute the sugar in the pan so that it will color evenly. The sugar is caramelized when it has turned a uniform light brown color and is syrupy.

Evenly divide the syrup among eight 4- to 6-ounce ovenproof ramekins. Swirl the caramel inside each ramekin to coat the bottom and sides completely. Put the ramekins in a deep roasting pan large enough to hold them without crowding and with a little space between them.

Preheat the oven to 325°F.

G gluten free

special toolbox:

8 ovenproof ramekins

roasting pan

wire cooling rack

2 cups granulated sugar, divided

2 cups whole milk

2 cups heavy cream

1 teaspoon Tahitian vanilla bean paste or $1/2$ teaspoon pure vanilla extract

1 cup Dark Chocolate Ganache (page 28)

8 large eggs, beaten

$1/4$ teaspoon salt

$1^1/2$ teaspoons pure vanilla extract

In a separate saucepan, stir together the milk, cream, and vanilla bean paste over medium heat and cook just until it begins to scald, about 5 to 7 minutes. Do not allow the liquid to simmer or boil at any time. Remove the pan from the heat and stir in the Dark Chocolate Ganache.

In a medium bowl, whisk together the remaining 1 cup of sugar and the eggs. Set aside for 5 minutes.

Slowly pour about ⅔ cup of the hot cream mixture into the eggs to temper, whisking constantly. Still whisking, return the mixture to the saucepan with the eggs. Stir in the salt and vanilla extract. When well mixed, carefully divide the custard among the ramekins.

Set the roasting pan on the center rack of the oven. Very carefully pour enough boiling water into the pan to come halfway up the sides of the ramekins. Bake the custards just until set, being careful not to overcook, 30 to 35 minutes. Remove the roasting pan from the oven and allow the ramekins to cool in the water bath for 5 minutes.

Lift the ramekins from the water and set on a wire cooling rack for 20 minutes. Refrigerate for at least 1 hour or for up to 8 hours.

When ready to serve, run a dull knife around the edge of each ramekin to loosen the custard and invert onto serving plates. Let the caramel in the bottom of the ramekins drizzle over the top and down the sides of the custards.

White Chocolate and Strawberry Creamy Custard

If you like homemade vanilla bean ice cream with a strawberry swirl, then you'll love this recipe. It's made in half the time of traditional ice cream and tastes divine. All great ice cream recipes begin with basic vanilla custard, and this recipe begins with vanilla cream and white chocolate custard, in which we swirl the strawberries. You can use store-bought strawberry preserves or change up the flavor and use Red Raspberry Sauce (page 243). Either way you are in for a real cool summertime treat.

Makes 8 servings

Prep Time: 10 minutes
Cooking Time: 5 minutes
Cooling Time: 10 minutes
Chilling Time: 3 to 8 hours
Level: *

In a saucepan, heat the milk over medium heat until it simmers. Do not let it boil. Set aside.

In the bowl of an electric mixer fitted with the paddle attachment, beat the egg yolks and sugar on medium-high speed until pale and doubled in volume, 4 to 5 minutes. Add the cornstarch and beat until thoroughly combined. Remove the bowl from the mixer.

Pour about 1/2 cup of the hot milk into the bowl with the eggs, whisking constantly until the eggs are well incorporated. Return the mixture to the saucepan with the hot milk. Cook the custard over high heat, stirring constantly with a wooden spoon, until the custard is thick enough to coat the back of the spoon and your finger leaves a trace in the custard when run along the back of the spoon. Add the White Chocolate Ganache and stir until melted.

Pour the custard into a clean bowl and let sit for about 10 minutes to cool slightly.

Spoon the strawberry preserves into the custard, swirling with a rubber spatula to distribute and make a pleasing pattern.

Cover the surface of the custard with plastic wrap to prevent a skin from forming. Refrigerate for at least 3 hours and up to 8 hours or until the custard is the consistency of sour cream.

To serve, spoon the custard into serving dishes and garnish with fresh strawberries.

G gluten free

special toolbox:
electric stand mixer, bowl, and paddle

2 1/4 cups whole milk

5 large egg yolks

2 tablespoons granulated sugar

1 tablespoon cornstarch

1/2 cup White Chocolate Ganache (page 29)

1/4 cup strawberry preserves

Fresh strawberries, for garnish

Grand Marnier
Dark Chocolate Crème

The Grand Marnier truffle is one of our most popular. It is made with the quintessential luxurious orange liqueur that is made by blending real Cognacs with the essence of the bigaradia orange. The oranges are harvested at their aromatic peak at the Marnier-Lapostolle plantation in the Caribbean. The famous and award-winning liqueur was created in 1880 and is still produced using the original recipe.

This custard is pure indulgence, designed to stir the senses and awaken your palate. The Cognac allures, the orange excites, and the sweetness blends it all together into a creamy, dark chocolate masterpiece.

Makes 6 servings

Prep Time: 15 minutes
Cooking Time: 10 minutes
Chilling Time: 3 to 8 hours
Level: *

Place the chocolate ganache in a large bowl and set aside.

In the bowl of an electric mixer fitted with the paddle attachment, beat the egg yolks and ⅓ cup of the sugar on high speed until pale and creamy, 3 to 4 minutes.

In a saucepan, bring the cream, milk, and remaining sugar to a boil over medium heat, stirring to melt the sugar. When the mixture boils, remove from the heat and let sit for 1 minute.

Pour half the hot milk into the bowl with the eggs, whisking continuously. Return the mixture to the saucepan with the hot milk and return to the heat. Stir constantly until it begins to thicken or coats the back of a wooden or metal spoon.

Pour the custard over the Dark Chocolate Ganache. Add the Grand Marnier and stir until the ganache melts and the custard is thick and smooth.

Cover the surface of the custard with a piece of plastic wrap directly to prevent a skin from forming and refrigerate for about 3 hours and up to 8 hours before serving.

To serve, spoon into serving bowls and garnish with candied orange peel.

 gluten free

special toolbox:

electric stand mixer, bowl, and paddle

1 cup Dark Chocolate Ganache
  (page 28)

8 large egg yolks

¾ cup granulated sugar, divided

1 cup heavy cream

1 cup milk

2 tablespoons Grand Marnier

Candied orange peel, for garnish

Cold-Processed
Chocolate Custard Cups

special toolbox:

medium mixing bowl

electric hand mixer and beaters

6 to 8 (3-½ inch, 5-ounce) ramekins or fluted parfait glasses

⅓ cup Dark Chocolate Ganache (page 28), at room temperature

1 (14-ounce) can sweetened condensed milk

1 cup cold plain yogurt

¼ cup freshly squeezed lemon juice

Down in New Orleans, Cajun and Creole chefs, even in the finest restaurants, keep a few cans of Borden's Sweetened Condensed Milk on hand. It goes into the coffee instead of cream and sugar and is a crucial ingredient in the handmade fudge and pralines. Due to its reaction with lemon juice, it's my secret and valuable "Wizard of Oz magic elixir," great in many recipes.

These pudding cups, which need no cooking, can be whipped up in no time flat to serve surprise visitors. The custard is very rich and is best served in small quantities.

Makes 6 to 8 servings

Prep Time: 10 minutes
Chilling Time: 20 minutes to 12 hours
Level: *

In a mixing bowl using a handheld electric mixer, beat the Dark Chocolate Ganache until creamy. Add the condensed milk and yogurt and blend well.

Add the lemon juice and mix thoroughly. The custard will begin to thicken immediately.

Spoon the custard into ramekins and cover the surface of each one with a piece of plastic wrap to prevent a skin from forming. Refrigerate for at least 20 minutes and up to 12 hours.

ChefSecret: For a more elaborate dessert, layer the custard with drained canned fruit in parfait glasses.

DID YOU KNOW? Americans consumed more than 3.9 billion pounds of chocolate in 2009—almost half of the total world's production! That's an average of thirteen pounds of chocolate per person.

DISCOVERING THE SERENGETI

Even today Africa is an amazing continent that attracts both novice and experienced travelers from across the globe looking to add another impressive stamp to their passports. In 1982, it was almost like visiting another planet. There was an unspoken and unwritten pact between the animals and the land itself, an understanding that human beings had not yet earned the right to be here.

I set out alone from Nairobi, driving south in my Rover over the defoliated, parched plains that traverse the border between Kenya into Tanzania. After several hours, the green outlines of tall trees on the other side of the Mara River came into sight. I had come upon the Garden of Eden, and I opted to walk the last two miles to camp so as not to miss a detail. It was my own personal discovery . . . the Serengeti. To me, it felt as if no man had been there before. I met up with my friends from Kenya and Australia and with our safari guides. We found a clearing and set up our own wood-floored tents. I volunteered to be the official chef for our very small, private safari. For dinner we had a dish called bobotie, a cross between meat loaf and shepherd's pie with a custardlike topping, often eaten on the continent. I served it with freshly baked African-style breads—rich in molasses and sharp with chocolate—that I baked in our campfire oven. I even steamed a chocolate pudding cake over an open flame.

During the cooler days, our fearless group drove for hours, munching on beef biltong, an addictive, well-seasoned, cured African meat similar to beef jerky. We encountered a very protective baboon standing guard over his family in a tree, and lithe, sleek cheetahs whose beauty literally took our breath away. There were scores of well-fed rhinos, sepia-toned zebras, and massive herds of giant buffalo, any one of which might later become dinner for a nearby pride of snoozing lions.

The night drives were always spectacular, and wild animal sounds created an eerie symphony of pleasure and pain. We came across prides of lions savoring their kills, while hyenas lurked in the shadows, hoping to steal a portion for themselves. Our own days ended with a similar carnivorous spirit—a dinner of barbecued ostrich or kudu (a kind of antelope), and if we were lucky, a spoonable dessert of chocolate pudding or tapioca.

For me, the Serengeti will always be a fascinating and exclusive experience. I felt a part of the human history of the endless plains, but from the hunter-gatherers of the distant past to those who today preserve the Serengeti as a prime travel destination, we are all but trespassers in this infinite animal kingdom.

Faultless Chocolate Soufflé

Chocolate soufflés must be the true ambrosia. Nothing ends a meal better than a gloriously poofed, light-as-air, hot-from-the-oven chocolate soufflé. Often temperamental but not as demanding as you might think, this intense, semisweet version is close to foolproof. If you follow my directions to the letter, it should not fail. If these little soufflés are not rich enough for your tastes, top them with a warm chocolate ganache sauce, crème Anglaise, or whipped cream, chocolate or not.

Makes 8 individual soufflés

Prep Time: 30 minutes
Cooking Time: 15 minutes
Cooling Time: 5 minutes
Baking Time: 12 to 15 minutes
Level: *

special toolbox:

electric stand mixer, bowl, and whisk

8 (4 to 6-ounce) individual soufflé dishes

baking sheet

2 tablespoons unsalted butter

2 tablespoons granulated sugar

¾ cup Dark Chocolate Ganache (page 28), softened

½ cup heavy cream

3 tablespoons unsweetened Dutch-processed cocoa powder

5 large eggs, separated

½ cup confectioners' sugar

1 teaspoon pure vanilla extract

Preheat the oven to 400°F. Brush the bottom and sides of eight (4 to 6-ounce) soufflé dishes with melted butter and sprinkle with granulated sugar, tilting to lightly coat the dishes. Tap out the loose sugar. Arrange the prepared dishes on a baking sheet.

Melt the Dark Chocolate Ganache in a metal bowl set over boiling water on medium-high heat.

In another saucepan, bring the cream to a boil over medium-high heat. As soon as the cream boils, remove the pan from the heat. Add the melted ganache and cocoa powder and stir well. The batter should be about the consistency of buttermilk. Set aside to cool to lukewarm.

In the bowl of an electric mixer fitted with the whisk attachment, beat the egg whites until firm peaks form, 8 to 10 minutes. Add the confectioners' sugar and vanilla and beat for about 1 minute longer to fully incorporate. Set aside.

Add the egg yolks to the cooled chocolate mixture and whisk well. When fully incorporated, gently fold in the egg whites about ½ cup at a time. Immediately fill the soufflé dishes to the rim and level the surface with a metal spatula.

Bake the soufflés on the baking sheet for 12 to 15 minutes. Resist the urge to open the oven door for the first 12 minutes before checking to make sure they have risen nicely. When you open the oven door, do so slowly and just peek inside. Close it quickly but as gently as you can. Serve immediately.

White-On-Black Chocolate
Crème Brûlée

G gluten free

special toolbox:

double boiler

fine mesh sieve

8 (4-ounce) ramekins or custard cups

shallow roasting pan

wire cooling rack

butane kitchen torch

1 vanilla bean, split lengthwise or
   1 teaspoon pure vanilla extract

2 cups heavy cream

3 tablespoons plus 8 teaspoons
   granulated sugar, divided

6 large egg yolks

3 tablespoons White Chocolate
   Ganache (page 29)

6 tablespoons Dark Chocolate
   Ganache (page 28)

4 teaspoons small dark chocolate
   curls (page 35), for garnish

I worked at a Chinese restaurant in Hong Kong while learning to make dim sum pastries. This gigantic restaurant prepared thousands of meals a day, and the most popular desserts were don tarts, a delicate pastry shell filled with custard. When we were asked to prepare a dessert for an event for the *Standard*, the local English-language newspaper, I thought serving a black-and-white dessert, rather than the more expected yellow-custard tart, would be appropriate. After all, newspapers are black and white. We prepared two custards—one made with White Chocolate Ganache and the other with Dark Chocolate Ganache. After they were baked, we topped them with caramelized sugar.

Makes 8 servings

Prep Time: 20 to 25 minutes
Cooking Time: 5 to 10 minutes
Baking Time: 30 minutes
Cooling Time: 30 minutes
Chilling Time: 6 to 24 hours
Level ***

In a saucepan, scrape the seeds from the vanilla bean into the cream. Heat over medium high until boiling. Remove from the heat and set aside.

In a double boiler or metal bowl, whisk together 3 tablespoons of the sugar and egg yolks until smooth. Set over a saucepan filled with about 1 inch of water and set over low heat. The water should not touch the bottom of the bowl. Whisk the mixture until thick enough to form a ribbon when the whisk is lifted from the pan.

Set two clean, empty saucepans over medium heat and heat until warm. Turn off the heat and then divide the cream evenly between them.

Add the White Chocolate Ganache to one of the pans and the Dark Chocolate Ganache to the other. Whisk until incorporated. Set aside to cool, stirring occasionally.

Preheat the oven to 325°F. Arrange eight (4-ounce) ramekins in a shallow roasting pan.

Strain the dark chocolate mixture though a fine-mesh sieve or chinois. Pour the strained chocolate into each ramekin to cover the bottoms. Strain the white chocolate mixture. Pour over the chocolate without splattering by holding a spoon, bowl-side down, over the dark chocolate so that the white chocolate lands gently on top of it. Gently run the tines of a fork through the chocolate to create an artistic, lacy effect.

Put the pan on the middle rack of the oven. Very carefully, add enough hot water to the pan to come halfway up the sides of the ramekins. Bake for about 30 minutes or until just set in the center. The water in the pan should just barely simmer during cooking; adjust the oven temperature accordingly.

Transfer the ramekins to a wire cooling rack and cool for 30 minutes. When cool, refrigerate for at least 6 hours or up to 24 hours until well chilled.

When ready to serve, sprinkle each ramekin with 1 teaspoon of sugar. Using a butane kitchen torch, caramelize the sugar. Garnish each ramekin with ½ teaspoon of dark chocolate curls and serve.

Chocolate Crème Brûlée

I've been eating a lot of egg white omelets in an attempt to keep my girth in check ever since I started writing this cookbook. Between the low-cal omelets and meringue in the book, I have enough egg yolks in the refrigerator to whip up everything from aioli to zabaglione.

One great way to make a dent in the yolks is to make crème brûlée, but not just any crème brûlée, Chocolate Crème Brûlée. What else? This recipe marries three of my all-time favorite flavors: chocolate, vanilla, and caramel.

Makes 6 servings

Prep Time: 15 minutes
Baking Time: 30 minutes
Cooling Time: 30 minutes
Chilling Time: 3 to 24 hours
Level **

Preheat the oven to 325°F.

Melt the Dark Chocolate Ganache in a microwave oven or in a bowl set over hot water; set aside.

In a mixing bowl using a handheld electric mixer, beat the egg yolks and granulated sugar until pale yellow, 3 to 4 minutes.

With the mixer on medium speed, add the melted ganache, cream, and the seeds from the vanilla bean. Increase the speed and beat until smooth and well mixed.

Pour the custard into six 6-ounce ramekins, filling them nearly to the top.

Set the ramekins in a shallow roasting pan and put the pan on the middle rack of the oven. Very carefully, add enough hot water to the pan to come halfway up the sides of the ramekins. Bake for 30 minutes or until just set. The water in the pan should just barely simmer during cooking; adjust the oven temperature accordingly.

Transfer the ramekins to a wire cooling rack and cool for 30 minutes. When cool, refrigerate for at least 3 hours or up to 24 hours until well chilled.

When ready to serve, sprinkle each ramekin with 1 teaspoon of sugar. Using a butane kitchen torch, caramelize the sugar.

ChefSecret: Use wide, shallow dishes to give the brûlée the optimum ratio of burnt sugar to custard.

G *gluten free*

special toolbox:

electric hand mixer and beaters

6 (6-ounce) shallow ramekins or custard cups

shallow roasting pan

wire cooling rack

butane kitchen torch

½ cup Dark Chocolate Ganache (page 28)

7 large egg yolks

¼ cup granulated sugar plus 6 teaspoons, divided

2½ cups heavy cream

1 vanilla bean, split lengthwise

No Bake—Quick and Easy— Chocolate Crème Brûlée

When you make this recipe, you don't have to bake the crème brûlées in a water bath, which can be a little cumbersome, because the custard essentially is replaced with chocolate ganache. The ganache cools differently from the more traditional custard, rendering the water bath unnecessary. You couldn't make a classic crème brûlée this way without it tasting like an overcooked flan, but as long as you've got the solidifying power of chocolate ganache, there's no need for more complicated oven maneuvers. Just get the eggs properly cooked and you're good to go.

Makes 6 servings

Prep Time: 15 minutes
Cooking Time: 30 minutes
Cooling Time: 20 minutes
Chilling Time: 1 to 6 hours
Level: *

In the bowl of a stand mixer fitted with the paddle attachment, beat the egg yolks and ½ cup of sugar on high speed until pale and creamy, about 5 minutes.

In a medium saucepan, bring the cream to a boil over medium heat. When it boils, remove the pan from the heat. Whisk about ½ cup of the warm cream vigorously into the egg mixture to temper the eggs so they won't curdle. Return to the remaining cream in the saucepan and bring to a low simmer over low heat, stirring continuously until thick. Do not let the custard boil.

Place the Dark Chocolate Ganache in a large bowl and pour the custard over it, stirring until melted and smooth. Pour the ganache mixture into six 5-ounce ramekins. Let the ganache cool for about 20 minutes and then transfer to the refrigerator for at least 1 hour (and up to 6 hours) or until set.

When ready to serve, sprinkle each ramekin with 1 teaspoon of sugar. Using a butane kitchen torch, caramelize the sugar.

ChefSecret: If you don't have a kitchen torch, put the ramekins under a hot broiler for a few minutes, turning them around a few times so that the sugar melts and caramelizes evenly.

special toolbox:

electric stand mixer, bowl, and paddle
6 (3-½ inch, 5-ounce) ramekins
butane kitchen torch

8 large egg yolks
½ cup granulated sugar
　plus 6 teaspoons, divided
2 cups heavy cream
12 ounces Dark Chocolate Ganache
　(page 28), at room temperature

ED'S BOX-TOP WISDOM
Simplicity
We subscribe to simplicity when it allows mankind to spend valuable time improving humanity, inspiring youth, preserving the family, and raising our consciousness for the foods provided by the Creator.

The Mousse Is Loose

I seem to have an unnatural passion for soufflés and mousses—especially when it comes to making them with White Chocolate Ganache. For a recent office birthday celebration, the birthday boy requested a mousse of a different color, so I made it with white chocolate. "It's the best darn dessert I've ever tasted," said Victor. This mousse is snowy white and creamy, with a wonderful whipped texture and intense white chocolate and vanilla flavor. Who can dispute Victor's proclamation?

Makes 6 servings

Prep Time: 40 minutes
Chilling Time: 3 to 6 hours
Level: *

In a bowl set over a pan of boiling water and using an electric hand mixer, beat the egg yolks, sugar, and 3 tablespoons of cold water for about 15 minutes or until the mixture is thick and airy. Remove the bowl from the hot water and beat for about 10 minutes longer while the mousse cools.

Scrape the seeds of the vanilla bean into a small bowl. Add the butter and stir to mix. Fold into the mousse.

In a clean, chilled bowl, beat the cream with the handheld electric mixer fitted with clean beaters on medium-high speed until stiff peaks form.

Fold the whipped cream into the mousse and spoon into six (6-ounce) ramekins or a large serving bowl. Cover and refrigerate until chilled and firm, for at least 3 hours and up to 6 hours. Serve topped with Milk Chocolate Ganache Whipped Cream and fresh berries for garnish.

G **gluten free**

special toolbox:

electric hand mixer and beaters

6 (6-ounce) individual soufflé dishes

4 large egg yolks

2 tablespoons granulated sugar

3 tablespoons cold water

2 cups White Chocolate Ganache (page 29), softened

1 vanilla bean, split lengthwise or 1 teaspoon pure vanilla extract

2 tablespoons unsalted butter, melted and warm

2 cups heavy cream, chilled

Milk Chocolate Ganache Whipped Cream (page 238)

Fresh berries, for garnish

Traditional Chocolate Mousse

The most delicious sweets are sometimes the easiest to make. That is the case with Traditional Chocolate Mousse. Reportedly, chocolate mousse was a great favorite of Julia Child's, and it certainly is of mine. It is a wonderful dessert that is mouthwatering and decadent and will be a hit whether you are serving it for a party of thirty or at an intimate dinner for two.

As Julia used to say, "We wish you bon appétit!"

Makes 12 servings

Prep Time: 20 minutes
Cooking Time: 8 to 10 minutes
Chilling Time: 1 to 8 hours
Level: *

In the bowl of an electric mixer fitted with the whisk attachment, whip the Dark Chocolate Ganache until creamy, about 5 minutes. Using a spatula, fold the White Chocolate Ganache Whipped Cream into the ganache and refrigerate.

In the top of a double boiler set over simmering water, whisk together the egg whites, sugar, and cream of tartar until the mixture registers 160°F on a thermometer. Remove from the heat. Using a handheld electric mixer set on medium-high speed, beat the warm egg white mixture until stiff peaks form. (Alternatively, heat the egg white mixture in a mixing bowl of a stand mixer set over a large saucepan. Remove from the heat and beat the warm egg whites in the bowl using the stand mixer.) Fold half the egg whites into the chocolate, taking care not to overmix and deflate the egg whites. Refrigerate the remaining egg whites.

Evenly divide the mousse among twelve (4-ounce) ramekins and refrigerate for at least 1 hour and up to 8 hours.

When ready to serve, spoon the remaining egg whites into a pastry bag fitted with a medium star tip. Top each ramekin with a meringue floret. Using a kitchen torch, carefully brown the tops of the meringue floret until just barely light golden brown.

 gluten free

special toolbox:

electric stand mixer, bowl, and whisk

double boiler

instant-read temperature probe or candy thermometer

12 (4-ounce) ramekins or custard cups

pastry bag fitted with a medium star tip

butane kitchen torch

2 cups Dark Chocolate Ganache (page 28), at room temperature

3 cups White Chocolate Ganache Whipped Cream (page 238), at room temperature

6 large egg whites

1 cup granulated sugar

1 teaspoon cream of tartar

White Chocolate Brioche Pudding

My friend's eight-year old son, Byron, wouldn't eat anything red or brown—no tomatoes, no watermelons, no gravy, and no CHOCOLATE. No matter how hard I tried, I couldn't get him to even taste a single square. It's hard for me to believe there's anyone who doesn't like chocolate, but I had a minor victory with Byron when I discovered he ate white chocolate.

There are lots of options for delicious desserts using the ivory-colored bar. My personal favorite is this bread pudding made with slightly stale brioche. It's simple, warm, comforting, and scrumptiously sweet.

Makes 12 to 16 servings

Prep Time: 40 minutes
Cooking Time: 8 to 10 minutes
Sitting Time: 20 minutes
Baking Time: 1 hour 20 minutes
Cooling Time: 20 minutes
Level: **

For the bread pudding: Preheat the oven to 275°F.

Lay the bread slices on a baking sheet and bake for about 15 minutes or until dry but not browned. This "stales" the bread a little. (Alternatively, use day-old bread that has been left on the countertop to turn slightly stale.) Arrange the bread slices in a 13 x 9-inch baking dish in an even layer to cover the bottom. Increase the oven temperature to 350°F.

In a large saucepan, heat the cream, milk, and sugar over medium heat until hot but not steaming. Remove from the heat and add the White Chocolate Ganache. Stir until melted.

In a large mixing bowl, whisk the eggs with the egg yolks. In a slow, thin, steady stream, whisk the hot cream into the eggs until smooth. Pour the custard mixture over the bread and let sit until soggy, about 20 minutes, occasionally pressing the bread into the custard mixture.

special toolbox:

serrated bread knife

baking sheet

13 x 9-inch baking dish

bread pudding:

1 standard-size loaf brioche, challah. or egg bread, crusts trimmed, bread cut into 1-inch-thick slices

4½ cups heavy cream

1½ cups milk

¾ cup granulated sugar

2 cups White Chocolate Ganache (page 29), at room temperature

3 large eggs

12 large egg yolks

white chocolate sauce:

½ cup heavy cream

¼ cup Grand Marnier or other orange-flavored liqueur

1 cup White Chocolate Ganache, (page 29), at room temperature

Put the baking dish on a baking sheet and cover the pudding with aluminum foil. Bake for 1 hour. Remove the foil and bake until golden and puffed, about 20 minutes. Let the pudding cool on a wire cooling rack for at least 20 minutes.

For the white chocolate sauce: In a small saucepan, bring the cream to a boil over medium-high heat. Remove from the heat and stir in the Grand Marnier and White Chocolate Ganache until completely smooth. Cut the bread pudding into squares and serve warm with the white chocolate sauce.

THE TRIFLE

The Brits claim to have invented the English trifle, which sounds reasonable. They serve it at Christmastime but also all through the year, so most of us have no reason to doubt this claim. The Parisians have Le Diplomate, so the French naturally take credit for coming up with trifles. The Italians argue that their zuppa inglese (English soup), a dessert similar to both that was created during the reign of Caesar, should get the credit. Whatever the case, I know for a fact that I served the first Hot Fudge Nut Trifle aboard the original *Pacific Princess* somewhere off the coast of Alaska.

Trifles are not to be trifled with, but to be enjoyed. Classically, they are layers of custardy pastry cream and leftover cake that is soaked in sherry, Madeira, or even Grand Marnier. They are topped off with plenty of fresh fruit and berries and ample billows of whipped cream. When you have cake on hand, they are among the easiest of show-stopping desserts and can be presented in a large glass punch or trifle bowl, a sundae glass, a teacup, or individually wrapped in baker's acetate.

Hot Fudge Nut Trifle

This is my original and still favorite trifle dessert. I love the confluence of flavors and textures that by themselves are simple and when assembled together are so delightfully complex. The other thing that you will love is that you can't make a mistake; be as careful and artsy or as casual as you like.

The assembly instructions given here are for individual trifles. I like to use baker's acetate as a collar to hold all the ingredients together until I am ready to serve.

Makes 4 servings

Prep Time: 30 minutes
Chilling Time: 4 hours or overnight
Level ***

special toolbox:

4 clear baker's acetate sheets for trifle collars (cut into 14 x 4$\frac{1}{2}$-inch strips)

3$\frac{1}{2}$-inch cake ring

serrated knife

2 pastry bags fitted with star tips

6 (1-inch-thick) Dark Chocolate Cake Layers (page 50), cut into 3$\frac{1}{2}$-inch diameter rounds

$\frac{1}{2}$ cup dry or sweet sherry

1$\frac{1}{3}$ cups Red Raspberry Sauce (page 243)

4 cups fresh raspberries, divided

2 cups toasted chopped pecans (see ChefSecret)

$\frac{1}{2}$ cup Dark Chocolate Ganache Pastry Cream (page 237)

$\frac{1}{2}$ cup White Chocolate Ganache Pastry Cream (page 237)

1 cup Hot Fudge Ganache (page 30), melted

1 cup White Chocolate Ganache Whipped Cream (page 238)

Using a 3$\frac{1}{2}$-inch round cake ring, form a 4$\frac{1}{2}$-inch tall acetate collar around the ring. Tape the ends together and pull gently off the ring. Repeat, making 3 more collars.

Set each acetate collar over a cake round and drizzle with 1 tablespoon of sherry over to soak. Drizzle each round with 1 tablespoon of Red Raspberry Sauce.

Halve 2 cups of the raspberries; set the whole raspberries aside. Top each cake round with 3 tablespoons of halved berries. Sprinkle 1 tablespoon of chopped pecans over the raspberries. Using the pastry bag fitted with a star tip, pipe a layer (about 2 tablespoons) of Dark Chocolate Ganache Pastry Cream over the pecans. Repeat to make 3 more trifles.

Using a serrated knife, slice the remaining 2 cake rounds in half horizontally to yield four $\frac{1}{2}$-inch-thick layers. Place one layer on top of the dark chocolate pastry cream and drizzle with 1 tablespoon of sherry and 1 tablespoon of Red Raspberry Sauce. Top with 1 tablespoon of halved raspberries and 1 tablespoon of pecans. Using a separate pastry bag fitted with a star tip, pipe a layer (about 2 tablespoons) of White Chocolate Ganache Pastry Cream over the pecans. Repeat to complete all 4 trifles.

Arrange a layer of whole raspberries over each trifle. Cover each trifle with plastic wrap and refrigerate for at least 4 hours or overnight.

When ready to serve, arrange each trifle on a serving plate and remove the plastic wrap and acetate ring. Pour the Hot Fudge Ganache over the trifle and garnish with a dollop of White Chocolate Ganache Whipped Cream. Top each trifle with a whole raspberry and a sprinkling of chopped pecans.

ChefSecret: To toast the pecans, spread on a dry baking sheet and roast in a 350°F oven for 6 to 8 minutes, shaking the pan several times during toasting to ensure even toasting.

White Chocolate and Strawberry Cream Trifle

"Razzle-dazzle" your guests with this yummy showstopper dessert! I have made thousands of trifles in my lifetime, but this one has to be the fastest and most fun. My only caveat is: allow enough time for the trifle to properly chill.

The ingredients listed are mere suggestions. Feel free to use any leftover cake you have available (fresh or stale), or even cookies you may have on hand. Use white and dark cakes and soft and crisp cookies too. It's hard to make a mistake when you assemble a trifle.

Makes 6 to 8 servings

Prep Time: 30 minutes
Chill Time: 4 hours or overnight
Level: ^^

Using a wooden spoon or a gloved hand, smear ½ cup of the Strawberry Sauce on the bottom and around the side of a 3-quart glass serving bowl or trifle dish.

Fill the bottom of the bowl with 1½ cups of cake cubes. Drizzle ¼ cup of sherry over the cake and let soak. Drizzle with ¼ cup of strawberry sauce and then top with ½ cup of sliced strawberries.

Using a pastry bag fitted with a round plain tip, pipe ⅓ cup of White Chocolate Ganache Pastry Cream over the strawberries in an even layer. Layer 2½ cups of cake cubes over the pastry cream. Drizzle with ¼ cup of sherry and ¼ cup of the strawberry sauce. Top with ½ cup sliced strawberries.

Pipe ⅓ cup of the pastry cream over the strawberries in an even layer. Layer the remaining 2½ cups cake cubes over the pastry cream. Drizzle with the remaining ¼ cup sherry and the remaining ¼ cup strawberry sauce. Top with the remaining ½ cup sliced strawberries. Pipe the remaining ⅓ cup of White Chocolate Ganache Pastry Cream over the strawberries in an even layer.

Using a separate pastry bag fitted with a star tip, pipe florets of White Chocolate Ganache Whipped Cream (about 2 cups) over the pastry cream, covering the entire top of the trifle. Cover with plastic wrap and refrigerate for at least 4 hours or overnight.

When ready to serve, scoop a large spoonful (about 1 cup) onto a dessert plate and garnish with a whole strawberry.

special toolbox:

3-quart glass serving bowl or trifle dish

serrated knife

2 pastry bags fitted with a round plain tip and a star tip

1¼ cups Strawberry Sauce (page 243), divided

6½ cups Classic White Chocolate Génoise (page 52), cut into 1-inch cubes

¾ cup dry or sweet sherry

1½ cups sliced fresh strawberries

1 cup White Chocolate Ganache Pastry Cream (page 237)

2 cups White Chocolate Ganache Whipped Cream (page 238)

6 to 8 whole strawberries, for garnish

Chapter

10

CHOCOLATE DRINKS

Chocolate has been enjoyed as a beverage for thousands of years. Archaeologists tell us that the Olmecs, the oldest civilization of the Americas (1500–400 BC), were probably the first users of cacao, followed by the Maya. The Maya consumed cacao-based drinks by the gallon, all made with beans from their plantations in the Chontalpa region of what is now eastern Tabasco in Mexico. The original cocoa (*choco-latl*) recipe was a mixture of ground cocoa beans, water, wine, and peppers. It didn't take long for Spaniards, who carried the beans back to the Old World, to begin heating the mixture and sweetening it with sugar. After being introduced in England, milk was added to the after-dinner treat.

As you will discover in this chapter, there is a difference between the taste of hot cocoa and hot chocolate. Sometimes the terms are used interchangeably, but technically they are as different as milk chocolate and bittersweet (or dark) chocolate. Hot cocoa is made from cocoa powder, which is chocolate pressed free of all its richness, meaning the fat of cocoa butter has been reduced. Hot chocolate is made from melted bar chocolate, which may be mixed with milk or cream—usually cream, which makes this a sinfully rich and decadent beverage.

DID YOU KNOW?

In 2010 the annual world consumption of cacao beans was approximately 3.6 million tons, reflecting an average annual increase of 2.1 percent from 2.8 million tons from the base period of 2001.

Hot Dark Chocolate

special toolbox:

2 (8-ounce) mugs

1 cup whole milk

½ cup heavy cream

4 tablespoons Dark Chocolate
Ganache (page 28)

½ teaspoon pure vanilla extract
or the seeds from 1 vanilla bean,
split lengthwise

2 tablespoons White Chocolate
Ganache Whipped Cream
(page 238), for garnish

2 teaspoons small chocolate curls
(page 35), for garnish

Scan for Ed's ChefSecret

The ancient Maya and Aztec cultures paid particular attention to the ceremony around making their drinking chocolate. By all accounts, it was an expressive ritual not too dissimilar from the earliest tea ceremonies of China and Japan. You can celebrate your adventures in chocolate by purchasing a hot chocolate pitcher and frother to create your own sacred memories. And when you garnish the cups, you may opt to skip the whipped cream and chocolate curls and top the hot chocolate with a Homemade Chocolate Marshmallow (page 236).

Makes 2 (8-ounce) servings

Prep Time: 3 minutes
Cooking Time: 2 to 3 minutes
Level: *

In a saucepan, heat the milk, cream, Dark Chocolate Ganache, and vanilla over medium heat, blending with a whisk, until the ganache is melted and the hot chocolate is hot and a bit frothy.

Pour the hot chocolate into two warm serving cups, top with a dollop of White Chocolate Whipped Cream, and garnish with a sprinkle of chocolate curls.

ChefSecret: If you want a little sizzle and a little show, combine the ingredients in a 20-ounce frothing pitcher and steam using the wand of your espresso maker, being careful not to scorch the chocolate ganache.

Variations:

Substitute any flavor ganache (pages 26–33) for the Dark Chocolate Ganache to make your favorite hot chocolate.

Chocolate Espresso

This creamy hot drink is not for the worried weight watcher; it is pure indulgence. I can't think of a more perfect drink after an afternoon of ice fishing, ice skating, snowboarding, or sledding on a cold wintry day.

You don't need much coffee to improve on this already excellent hot chocolate. For garnish, homemade White Chocolate Ganache Whipped Cream is always best, if you have the time to make it.

Makes 1 (12-ounce) serving

Prep Time: 2 minutes
Level: *

Using an espresso machine steamer, steam the milk with the Milk Chocolate Ganache in a frothing pitcher.

Pour the hot chocolate milk into a 12-ounce serving cup. Pour the espresso into the cup over the hot chocolate. Top with the Chocolate Marshmallow. Garnish with a dollop of whipped cream and then drizzle the chocolate sauce over the cream in a back and forth motion. Sprinkle with chocolate curls and serve at once.

G gluten free

special toolbox:

espresso machine with steamer

frothing pitcher

12-ounce mug

1 cup milk

4 tablespoons Milk Chocolate Ganache (page 26)

4 tablespoons espresso or freshly brewed very strong coffee

1 Chocolate Marshmallow (page 47)

1 heaping tablespoon White Chocolate Ganache Whipped Cream (page 238), for garnish

1 tablespoon Dark Chocolate Sauce (see box on page 30), for garnish

1 teaspoon small bittersweet or semisweet chocolate curls (page 35), for garnish

gluten free

special toolbox:

blender

2 tall glasses

¼ cup Dark Chocolate Ganache
    (page 28), at room temperature

¼ cup White Chocolate Ganache
    (page 29), at room temperature

2 cups very cold whole milk

Go-for-the-Gold
Chocolate Milk

The Olympic Games were flooded by controversies over steroids and supplements, but American swimmer Michael Phelps, who won fourteen career Olympic gold medals—the most of any Olympian—played it safe drinking chocolate milk between races in Beijing.

Chocolate milk may be as good, or even better, than sports drinks at helping athletes recover from strenuous exercise. It has the optimal ratio of carbohydrates to protein, which helps refuel tired muscles. And let's face it: it tastes much better than those sugary-sweet sports beverages.

Makes 2 servings

Prep Time: 5 minutes
Level: *

In a microwave-safe bowl, heat the Dark and White Chocolate Ganaches in a microwave on medium power until soft and pourable, about 15 seconds, stirring until smooth.

Transfer the melted ganache to a blender. Add the milk and blend until well combined and frothy. Divide the milk between two tall glasses.

Variations:

Peanutty Chocolate Milk: Add 2 tablespoons creamy peanut butter or peanut flour to the blender and process until combined and frothy.

Dark Chocolate-Raspberry Smoothie Float

This gourmet shake is an extravagant blend of fresh milk, yogurt, chocolate ganache, chocolate ice cream, and raspberry sorbet. One sip and you'll think you are drinking a raspberry crème truffle.

Makes 2 servings

Prep Time: 10 minutes
Level: *

In a blender, combine the milk, frozen yogurt, and Dark Chocolate Ganache and blend until smooth.

Put 1 scoop of chocolate ice cream in each of two tall glasses. Top with 1 scoop of raspberry sorbet. Pour the frozen yogurt mixture over the ice cream and top with generous spoonfuls of White Chocolate Ganache Whipped Cream. Garnish with chocolate curls. Serve right away.

G gluten free

special toolbox:
ice cream scoop
blender
2 tall glasses

1 cup whole milk

1 cup vanilla frozen yogurt, softened

4 tablespoons Dark Chocolate Ganache (page 28), at room temperature

2 scoops (about 1/2 cup) chocolate ice cream

2 scoops (about 1/2 cup) raspberry sorbet

1/2 cup White Chocolate Ganache 238), for garnish

1 teaspoon small bittersweet or semi-sweet chocolate curls (page 35)

special toolbox:

blender

ice cream scoop

4 (16-ounce) glasses

2 cups milk

4 tablespoons Azteca Chocolate
   Ganache (page 33),
   at room temperature

1/2 teaspoon chili powder

1/4 teaspoon cayenne pepper

1/4 teaspoon ground nutmeg

1/4 teaspoon ground cinnamon

4 scoops chocolate ice cream

4 cups ice cubes

1/2 cup Azteca Chocolate Ganache
   Whipped Cream (page 238)

4 teaspoons small bittersweet
   or semisweet chocolate curls
   (page 35)

1/4 teaspoon ground cinnamon

Spiced Brazilian Chocolate on the "Rocks"

We first discovered this zesty and refreshing chocolate treat in a little café in Bahia, Brazil, during Carnival Bahia. This is not for the nubile women in feathers high up on floats à la Carnival Rio. It's for YOU, out there on the streets, doing it 'til you drop. To get your strength back, you need a tall glass of Spiced Brazilian Chocolate. It never fails. No doubt, this drink will become the rage beverage of the 2016 Olympic Games.

Makes 4 servings

Prep Time: 10 minutes
Level: *

In a blender, combine the milk, Azteca Chocolate Ganache, chili powder, cayenne pepper, nutmeg, and cinnamon and blend until combined. Add the ice cream and purée until smooth.

Fill four 16-ounce glasses with ice cubes. Divide the drink among the glasses. Top each serving with generous spoonfuls of Azteca Chocolate Ganache Whipped Cream and garnish with chocolate curls and a sprinkle of cinnamon.

Chocolate
Ice Blended Float

I love this recipe because it is a cross between a hot fudge sundae and a chocolate shake. It takes just a few minutes to make, and it never disappoints either, as a dessert or a beverage. I like to add a little coffee flavor and drink it in the morning in place of a cup of joe. You can use frozen coffee ice cubes or just a teaspoon of instant coffee.

Makes 1 serving

Prep Time: 5 minutes
Level: *

Fill a 20-ounce glass with ice cubes just to chill the glass. As soon as the glass is full, transfer 1 cup of the ice to a blender and discard the rest.

Add the milk, Hot Fudge Ganache, and 1 scoop of the ice cream and blend until smooth.

Place the remaining scoop of ice cream in the chilled glass and pour the blended beverage over it. Top with the White Chocolate Whipped Cream and a sprinkle of cocoa powder.

G gluten free

special toolbox:

blender

#24 scoop or kitchen tablespoon

20-ounce serving glass

1 cup ice cubes, plus more
   for chilling the glass

1 cup cold milk

¼ cup Hot Fudge Ganache
   (page 30)

2 scoops vanilla ice cream, divided

4 tablespoons White Chocolate
   Ganache Whipped Cream
   (page 238)

Unsweetened Dutch-processed
   cocoa powder, for garnish

electric stand mixer, bowl, and whisk

blender

4 long-handled iced-tea spoons

butane kitchen torch

fluff stuff:

$1/2$ cup very cold heavy cream

$1/4$ cup Marshmallow Fluff

1 tablespoon White Chocolate
   Ganache (page 29)

milkshake:

1 cup cold whole milk

$1/4$ cup Milk Chocolate Ganache
   (page 26), at room temperature

3 extra-large scoops Chocolate Ice
   Cream, (page 192 or 195) or
   store-bought

1 cup Hot Fudge Ganache (page 30),
   melted

4 large marshmallows

1 tablespoon grated bittersweet
   chocolate or small bittersweet
   chocolate curls (page 35)

Chocolate Ganache
Marshmallow Milkshake

If you're an only child and have never learned how to share, this is one of those recipes you'll want to make and then hide in the dark closet so you can indulge all by yourself. It is that good.

Makes 4 servings

Prep Time: 15 minutes
Level: *

For the fluff stuff: In the bowl of an electric mixer fitted with the whisk attachment, whisk together the cream, Marshmallow Fluff, and White Chocolate Ganache until stiff peaks form. Set aside.

For the milkshake: In a blender, mix together the milk, Milk Chocolate Ganache, and ice cream and blend until smooth and thick.

Layer the ingredients in each of four glasses, starting with the milkshake followed by the fluff stuff, the Hot Fudge Ganache, and then more milkshake. This should fill about one-fourth to one-third of the glass. Repeat the process two more times to fill the glasses.

Top each drink with 1 marshmallow. Using a butane torch, lightly brown the marsh-mallows and then garnish with the grated chocolate or chocolate curls. Serve with a straw and a long spoon.

Frozen Hot Cappuccino

When I first got into the restaurant business, my good friend and colleague Leo Dardarian taught me many tricks of the trade. He showed me how to change the table linens in thirty seconds, how to dice an onion in an instant, how to bone a chicken by turning it inside out—and how to make frozen cappuccino.

Well, actually together, we made the first frozen cappuccinos at Tonio's Restaurant in Pasadena. They were easy. Mix the ingredients with ice in a blender and top the outcome with White Chocolate Ganache Whipped Cream, garnished with chocolate curls, decoratifs, or a shake of cocoa powder.

Makes 2 servings

Prep Time: 5 minutes
Cooling Time: 30 minutes
Level: *

special toolbox:

double boiler

blender

2 large margarita glasses

¹/₂ cup Milk Chocolate Ganache
(page 26)

2 tablespoons unsweetened
Dutch-processed cocoa powder

2 tablespoons granulated sugar

1¹/₂ cups milk or plain soy milk,
divided

3 cups ice cubes

1 tablespoon instant coffee granules

White Chocolate Ganache Whipped
Cream (page 238), for garnish

Choclatique decoratifs or chocolate
shavings, for garnish

In the top of a double boiler set over simmering water, mix together the Milk Chocolate Ganache, cocoa powder, and sugar, stirring occasionally until melted and well blended. Remove from the heat and slowly add ¹/₂ cup of the milk, stirring until smooth. Cool to room temperature.

In a blender, blend together the remaining 1 cup milk, the chocolate mixture, and the ice on high speed until smooth and the consistency of a frozen margarita. Add the instant coffee and blend to mix.

Pour the frozen cappuccino into two large margarita glasses and top with White Chocolate Ganache Whipped Cream and Choclatique decoratifs or shavings.

Variations:

For a different flavor treat, add 2 tablespoons of the liquor of your choice. You can also substitute Milk Chocolate Ganache with Chocolate Peanut Butter Ganache or Spiced Azteca Chocolate Ganache.

Peanut Butter and Jelly Milkshake

Here's a crazy idea that came from one of our most popular and my personal favorite Choclatique truffle flavors: peanut butter and jelly. The Peanut Butter and Jelly Chocolate Milkshake was first served as a bar drink at my Customs House Restaurant in Foster City, California, in 1976. This famous milkshake was the creation of two of our creative mixologists who added shots of framboise and vodka. Once you try it, you'll be back for seconds! Without a doubt, this is more than just a PB&J sandwich!

Makes 2 servings

Prep Time: 10 minutes
Level: *

In a blender, blend the ice cream, Dark Chocolate Ganache, milk, and peanut butter until smooth. Add the framboise and vodka, if using, and blend again.

Divide between two glasses and serve garnished with the White Chocolate Ganache Whipped Cream and a drizzle of grape jelly.

G gluten free

special toolbox:

blender

#16 scoop or kitchen tablespoon

2 (16-ounce) glasses

4 scoops vanilla ice cream

1/3 cup Dark Chocolate Ganache (page 28), at room temperature

1 cup milk

2 tablespoons creamy peanut butter

2 (1-ounce) shots framboise, optional

2 (1-ounce) shots vodka, optional

White Chocolate Ganache Whipped Cream (page 238), for garnish

2 tablespoons grape jelly, warmed until liquid

Cappuccino Ciocolatta

On the coldest day of winter, I discovered Baratti & Milano in Torino, Italy. Baratti & Milano, who has been making chocolate since 1858, sells candy and chocolate in addition to having an elegant *pasticceria* (bakery), which is adjacent to the Piazza Castello. We were there shortly after the Winter Olympics ended, and the local entrepreneurs found ways to get attention by showcasing the remarkable food and beverages of the region. On this trip we discovered Espesso—a chilled, spoonable form of espresso and Cappuccino Ciocolatta.

Makes 4 servings

Prep Time: 15 minutes
Cooking Time: 5 minutes
Level: *

In a heavy-bottomed saucepan, bring the milk to a simmer over medium heat, whisking continuously. Remove from the heat and add the coffee liqueur and the White Chocolate Ganache. Stir until the ganache has melted.

Pour the cappuccino into four warmed bowls or mugs and top with the Milk Chocolate Ganache Whipped Cream. Dust with cinnamon and serve immediately.

Variations:

Use any of the base ganaches to make Dark, Milk, Hot Fudge, or Azteca Cappuccino Ciocolatta.

G gluten free

special toolbox:

4 cappuccino bowls or mugs, warmed

3 cups milk

1/4 cup coffee liqueur

1 cup White Chocolate Ganache (page 29)

1/2 cup Milk Chocolate Ganache Whipped Cream (page 238)

Ground cinnamon, for dusting

Drunken Chocolate Cow

Two cows went into a bar, a brown cow, a black cow, and a white cow. Wait a minute; that's one too many. Someone has been hanging around the cow bar, drinking a mixture of chocolate, rum, and a touch of mint. If you drink enough of these, you'll be able to see cows, too.

Makes 1 serving

Prep Time: 5 minutes
Level: *

In a blender, mix the White Chocolate Ganache, rum, crème de cacao, and crème de menthe for a few seconds on low speed. Add the Dark Chocolate Ganache Ice Cream and blend for about 1 minute on low speed until smooth and well mixed.

Pour the drink into a Champagne flute. Dust with the cocoa powder and decorate with the white chocolate curls. Serve immediately.

G gluten free

special toolbox:
blender
Champagne flute

2 tablespoons White Chocolate Ganache (page 29)
2 tablespoons white rum
1 tablespoon dark crème de cacao
1½ teaspoons crème de menthe
1 scoop Dark Chocolate Ganache Ice Cream (page 192)
½ teaspoon unsweetened Dutch-processed cocoa powder
½ teaspoon small white chocolate curls (page 35)

special toolbox:

6 Irish coffee glasses

2 cups milk

¹/₂ cup heavy cream

¹/₂ cup Hot Fudge Ganache (page 30)

¹/₄ cup Irish whiskey

¹/₂ cup White Chocolate Ganache
   Whipped Cream (page 238)

2 teaspoons small bittersweet
   or semisweet chocolate curls
   (page 35)

Hot Irish Chocolate

"By gosh and by golly," said in my best Irish brogue. Oh, sure, it sounds a bit crazy: the idea that chocolate makes the world a nicer place to be, but that's what we heard at Butlers Chocolates in Dublin. When you order a cup of joe at Butlers, you get a chocolate ganache truffle to eat or drop in the coffee. I believe when in Ireland, do what the Irish do—drink Irish. And by that, I mean Irish whiskey! Whenever we dropped into Irish cafés, we enhanced our coffee with a drop of chocolate and a dram or two of real Irish whiskey.

Makes 6 servings

Prep Time: 10 minutes
Cooking Time: 5 to 7 minutes
Level: *

In a heavy-bottomed saucepan, bring the milk and cream to a boil over medium heat. Reduce the heat to low, add the ganache, and stir until melted. Stir in the whiskey and pour into four warmed Irish coffee glasses. Top with White Chocolate Ganache Whipped Cream and garnish with chocolate curls. Serve immediately.

11

CHOCOLATE ICE CREAMS

Chocolate is the number-two ice cream flavor purchased in the United States. It's topped by vanilla, which outsells chocolate three to one. At first I didn't get it. Why does chocolate lag behind? But finally I realized that it's the fault of commercially made ice cream, and has nothing to do with the glories of chocolate. The ice cream you buy in the market—regardless of how "premium" it might be—doesn't taste like mine.

TIPS FOR MAKING GREAT ICE CREAM

It's easy to make good ice cream. It takes a little more care and attention to make truly fantastic ice cream every single time. Follow these tips and superb ice cream will be yours!

- Always start with clean, sanitized equipment. Follow the manufacturer's instructions for taking care of the equipment.

- Take care to make sure that the dairy mixture and flavors are well incorporated and fully chilled before you freeze the ice cream.

- Ingredients, i.e., nuts, chocolates, cookies, candies, and so on, should always be frozen before they are added to the ice cream maker. They also need to be frozen if the recipe instructs you to stir them into the frozen ice cream after it has been churned in the ice cream maker.

- When specified, layer the frozen ingredients as the ice cream is being spooned from the canister. Reserve some ingredients for topping the ice cream. This makes it easier to identify the flavor variety.

- Protect your ice cream by monitoring temperatures to make sure ice crystals do not develop in your perfectly made ice creams:

    1. Harden and store ice cream in the freezer. For best results, it should be stored at 0°F.

    2. When ready to scoop ice cream, let it sit out for about 10 minutes to bring it up to 10°F.

- Scrape down the sides of all ice cream containers, and lay a piece of plastic wrap directly onto the surface of the ice cream. Using more plastic wrap, enfold the entire container(s) to further reduce the amount of exposed surfaces, which cause oxidation and ice crystal formation.

- Clean utensils and equipment as you go; that's the sign of a pro.

Dark Chocolate Ganache Ice Cream

Rich, deep, and dark. Ben & Jerry and Messrs. Baskin and Robbins would be proud to make this chocolate ganache ice cream. It is made with eight all-natural ingredients—everything you might commonly find in your kitchen pantry, including dark chocolate. We add the Dark Chocolate Ganache on page 28 to enrich the ice cream with chocolate flavor and creaminess you can feel on the tongue. As you will gleefully discover, it is like no other chocolate ice cream you have ever tasted!

This ice cream is used as a base for other ice creams or served just as it is. See page 194 for the variations.

Makes 2 quarts

Prep Time: 5 minutes
Cooking Time: 15 minutes
Chilling Time: 4 hours
Freezing Time: 4 hours 20 minutes
Level: **

In a medium saucepan, heat the cream and cocoa powder over medium heat, whisking to ensure the cocoa is fully absorbed. When the cream bubbles around the edges, remove the pan from the heat and add the Dark Chocolate Ganache. Wait for 30 seconds and then stir until smooth and blended. Add 1 cup of the milk and stir to combine.

Return the saucepan to the stove and stir in the remaining 1½ cups milk, the sugar, and salt. Heat the mixture over medium heat, keeping the milk at a simmer; do not let it boil over the sides of the pan.

Meanwhile, in a medium bowl, whisk the egg yolks together. Slowly drizzle about ¼ cup of the warm milk into the egg yolks, whisking constantly until combined.

Pour the egg yolks into the saucepan and cook for 3 to 5 minutes, stirring constantly with a wooden spoon to prevent the eggs from cooking. Cook until the custard is thick enough to coat the back of the spoon and your finger leaves a trace in the custard when run along the back of the spoon.

Pour the custard through a fine-mesh sieve or strainer into a bowl. Add the vanilla and stir to combine.

Cover the surface of the custard with plastic wrap to prevent a skin from forming. Refrigerate the custard for at least 4 hours. Transfer to an ice cream maker and freeze according to the manufacturer's instructions.

Directions continued on page 194.

gluten free

special toolbox:

wooden spoon

fine-mesh sieve

electric ice cream maker

1½ cups heavy cream

2 tablespoons unsweetened ultra Dutch-processed cocoa powder or another high-quality cocoa powder

1 cup Dark Chocolate Ganache (page 28)

2½ cups whole milk, divided

½ cup granulated sugar

¼ teaspoon salt

4 large egg yolks

½ teaspoon pure vanilla extract

Dark Chocolate Raspberry Swirl Ice Cream

Transfer the ice cream to an airtight container and freeze for at least 4 hours to harden. Remove the ice cream from the freezer 10 to 15 minutes before serving to let soften.

Variations:

Dark Chocolate-Chip Ice Cream: When you transfer the churned ice cream from the ice cream maker to the freezer-safe container, stir in 2 cups of frozen semisweet chocolate chips, a third at a time. Reserve a handful of chocolate chips to sprinkle on top of the ice cream. Let the ice cream freeze for at least 4 hours before serving. Makes about 2¼ quarts.

Dark Chocolate Rocky Road Ice Cream: When you transfer the churned ice cream from the ice cream maker to the freezer-safe container, stir in ¾ cup of frozen, roughly chopped, toasted cashews, ¼ cup of frozen semisweet mini chocolate chips, and ½ cup of frozen, coarsely chopped mini marshmallows, a third at a time. Reserve a handful of the mixture to sprinkle on top of the ice cream. Finally, swirl ½ cup of Marshmallow Fluff through the ice cream. Let the ice cream freeze for at least 4 hours before serving. Makes about 2½ quarts.

Dark Chocolate Turtle Ice Cream: When you transfer the churned ice cream from the ice cream maker to the freezer-safe container, stir in 1 cup Burnt Caramel Sauce (page 242) and 1½ cups of frozen toasted, chopped pecans, a third at a time. Reserve a handful of the nuts to sprinkle on top of the ice cream. Let the ice cream freeze for at least 4 hours before serving. Makes about 2½ quarts.

Dark Chocolate Black Cherry Ice Cream: Spread ¼ cup of dried black cherries and ½ cup of chopped and drained canned black cherries on a baking sheet and freeze until solid. When you transfer the churned ice cream from the ice cream maker to the freezer-safe container, stir in the frozen cherries, a third at a time. Reserve a handful of the cherries to sprinkle on top of the ice cream. Let the ice cream freeze for at least 4 hours before serving. Makes about 2½ quarts.

Dark Chocolate Raspberry Swirl Ice Cream: When you transfer the churned ice cream from the ice cream maker to the freezer-safe container, swirl in 1 cup of room temperature Red Raspberry Sauce (page 243). It should marble through the ice cream. Let the ice cream freeze for at least 4 hours before serving. Makes about 2¼ quarts.

Milk Chocolate Ganache Ice Cream

I used to live a bike ride's distance from the old Adohr Farms Dairy in West Los Angeles. Right inside the dairy's front door was a cooler stocked with products that little kids were always welcome to sample.

My buddies and I made a habit of stopping at the dairy late on Friday afternoons, right before it closed for the weekend, when they were getting ready to toss out what was left in the display case. We took everything they were about to discard.

Once, there were two half gallons of chocolate milk up for grabs that I took home. My family was not big on chocolate milk and so my father thought perhaps a good use for my find would be homemade milk chocolate ice cream. It worked deliciously well.

Makes 2 quarts

Prep Time: 5 minutes
Cooking Time: 15 minutes
Cooling Time: 4 hours
Freezing Time: 4 hours
Level: **

In a medium saucepan, heat the cream and cocoa powder over medium heat, whisking to ensure the cocoa is fully absorbed. When the cream bubbles around the edges, remove the pan from the heat and add the Milk Chocolate Ganache. Wait for 30 seconds and then stir until smooth and blended. Add 1 cup of the milk and stir to combine.

Return the saucepan to the stove and stir in the remaining 1 cup milk, the sugar, and salt. Heat the mixture over medium heat, keeping the milk at a simmer; do not let it boil over the sides of the pan.

Meanwhile, in a medium bowl, whisk the egg yolks together. Slowly drizzle about ¼ cup of the warm milk into the egg yolks, whisking the entire time until combined.

Pour the egg yolks into the saucepan and cook the custard for 3 to 5 minutes, stirring constantly with a wooden spoon to prevent the eggs from cooking. Cook until the custard is thick enough to coat the back of the spoon and your finger leaves a trace in the custard when run along the back of the spoon.

Directions continued on page 196.

gluten free

special toolbox:
wooden spoon
fine-mesh sieve
electric ice cream maker

1 cup heavy cream
4 tablespoons natural cocoa powder
¾ cup Milk Chocolate Ganache (page 26)
2 cups chocolate milk, divided
½ cup granulated sugar
¼ teaspoon salt
5 large egg yolks
½ teaspoon pure vanilla extract

Pour the custard through a fine-mesh sieve or strainer into a bowl. Add the vanilla and stir to combine.

Cover the surface of the custard with plastic wrap to prevent a skin forming. Refrigerate the custard for at least 4 hours. Transfer to an ice cream maker and freeze according to the manufacturer's instructions.

Transfer the ice cream to an airtight container and freeze for at least 4 hours to harden.

Remove the ice cream from the freezer 10 to 15 minutes before serving to let soften.

Variations:

Some variations are not gluten free.

Milk Chocolate Mocha Chip Ice Cream: Just before transferring the ice cream to the ice cream maker, stir in 1 cup of chilled, strong brewed coffee. When you transfer the churned ice cream from the ice cream maker to the freezer-safe container, stir in 2 cups of frozen mocha or semisweet chocolate chips, a third at a time. Reserve a handful of the chocolate chips to sprinkle on top of the ice cream. Let the ice cream freeze for at least 4 hours before serving. Makes about 2½ quarts.

Milk Chocolate-Almond Bark Ice Cream: When you transfer the churned ice cream from the ice cream maker to the freezer-safe container, stir in 2 cups of frozen small, milk-chocolate-coated almonds, a third at a time. Reserve a handful of the almonds to sprinkle on top of the ice cream. Let the ice cream freeze for at least 4 hours before serving. Makes about 2½ quarts.

Milk Chocolate-Peanut Butter Ice Cream: When you transfer the churned ice cream from the ice cream maker to the freezer-safe container, swirl in 2 cups of room temperature Chocolate Peanut Butter Ganache (page 26), a third at a time. It should marble through the ice cream. Freeze the ice cream for at least 4 hours. Makes about 2½ quarts.

Milk Chocolate Birthday Cake Ice Cream: Just before transferring the chilled ice cream to the ice cream maker, transfer 1 quart of the custard to a blender and add half of a package of chocolate cake mix (half of the contents will weigh just more than 9 ounces). Blend until well mixed. Transfer to the ice cream maker with the remaining chilled custard and process according to the manufacturer's instructions. When you transfer the churned ice cream from the ice cream maker to the freezer-safe container, stir in ¼ cup of frozen decorative colored confetti candy disks, a third at a time. Reserve some to sprinkle over the ice cream. Let the ice cream freeze for about 4 hours. Makes about 2½ quarts.

Santa Fe "Hot" Milk Chocolate Ice Cream: Just before transferring the chilled ice cream to the ice cream maker, transfer 1 quart of the custard to a blender and add ½ cup of room temperature Azteca Chocolate Ganache (page 33), ¼ teaspoon of ground cinnamon, and ¼ teaspoon of cayenne pepper and mix well. Transfer to the ice cream maker with the remaining chilled custard and process according to the manufacturer's instructions. When you transfer the churned ice cream from the ice cream maker to the freezer-safe container, swirl in 1 cup of frozen chopped marshmallows and 1 cup of Marshmallow Fluff. Swirl the marshmallows and fluff through the ice cream with a metal spoon. Freeze for at least 4 hours. Makes about 2½ quarts.

THE SPY WHO CAME IN
FROM THE COLD

The 1980 Moscow Olympics were a flop, and I was there.

Six years earlier, Vladimir Promyslov, mayor of Moscow, retained my company, Perspectives/The Consulting Group, to teach the Soviet Olympic hosts how to welcome and show hospitality to foreign visitors, American-style. For the next six years, our team traveled to the Soviet Union every six weeks or so and became very familiar with Moscow and those old Soviet ways.

This job, as it turned out, would be a bigger challenge than anything portrayed in TV's *Mission Impossible*.

We were housed in the Rossiya Hotel, a large, cold, poorly constructed building built in 1967. At the time, the Rossiya was, according to the *Guinness Book of World Records*, the largest hotel in the world. It is also noted in "Ed's Book of Records" as the ugliest, most unfriendly hotel in Russia.

The Rossiya had 3,200 single rooms, most of them only 118 square feet in size—about twice the size of an American prison cell. Its only redeeming feature was the view from its twenty-one-story tower, from which we could see the Kremlin, Saint Basil's Cathedral, and Red Square.

A funny thing happened on the way to the Olympics: the USSR invaded Afghanistan. President Jimmy Carter politicized the games by demanding a boycott, resulting in more than sixty countries refusing to participate in the games. The Russians were angry, and their suspicion of foreigners was on heightened alert.

Even though we were cleared through KGB security, we were still Americans, and were followed wherever we went during every visit throughout the six years leading up to the Olympics. The Soviets were so wary of Americans in their country that they suspected every one of being a spy. It was not unusual to have a creepy, no-name government "guide" assigned to you when you arrived at the airport, who followed your every step throughout your visit. "Igor" (not his real name) was my personal "bodyguard." He was a short, chain-smoking, dumpy-looking soul who physically resembled a fire hydrant. In true undercover style, he avoided eye contact and would turn in the opposite direction every time I walked toward him, which I did quite often just for fun.

As an avid reader of James Bond novels, I saw a Russian secret agent behind every lamppost, and I became nearly as paranoid as my hosts. I lightly dusted my dresser drawer knobs with talcum powder when I left my room, to see if anyone opened them; I placed a strand of hair in the doorjamb to see if anyone entered—just like 007.

On returning to my room one evening, I found that all my secret countermeasures had been disturbed and my camera was missing. I went down to speak to the hotel manager, who told me that my camera was, in fact, not missing; I had just misplaced it. There was no use arguing, as nothing good ever comes from that in Moscow. Miraculously, my camera reappeared two days later—minus the film. Once again, I complained to the manager, who again blew me off. My film was not stolen, he said; most likely I had forgotten I had sent it to be developed. Later that evening, an envelope slid under my door, containing twenty-four eight-by-tens and a loop of negatives. I guess whoever took the film didn't find what they were looking for. And so it went, year after year, during our sojourns to Moscow.

One of my clearest recollections of those days was Christmas Eve 1979, one of the coldest nights of the year in Moscow, -38°F. It's always difficult to be away from your family during the holidays, but freezing in Moscow at the ugly Rossiya made it twice as bad. We wound up in a hotel's breakfast restaurant that was opened for dinner on Christmas Eve for foreign guests only. They had no turkey, and goose was definitely out of the question, but we were able to order a "Charlie Brown" duck (overstewed and stringy) and boiled potatoes. We loaded up on pickles, blintzes, smoked fish, black bread, caviar, and other delicacies to prepare our stomachs for a bottle of great Ukrainian vodka. We toasted Lenin, Stalin, Nixon, Carter, and Mickey Mouse. We lit up brandy-soaked Cuban cigars, plentiful in the Soviet Union, while enjoying a snifter of French Cognac and a heaping portion of chocolate mousse prepared with Georgian-made chocolate.

As we looked out the hotel windows on the frigid scene outside, we saw old Igor chain-smoking and pacing back and forth in a vain attempt to keep warm. Feeling sorry for the poor guy, I slipped into my coat and went outside. I asked if he spoke any English—he did. I told him we knew he was assigned to "guard" us, and then asked, "How better can you protect us than by joining us inside this nice, warm restaurant?"

Igor reluctantly joined us, and after his third vodka, got into the swing of the holidays. We toasted Khrushchev, Beria, Kaganovich, Bulganin, Molotov, Lysenko, all of the members of the Presidium, and the ministers of the Politburo. A final toast was given to both Leonid Ilyich Brezhnev and Czar Nicholas II. With that, we called the holiday festivities to a close.

We never saw Igor again, and never learned his real name. Yet, for one brief, cold Christmas Eve, there was one barely noticeable break in the Iron Curtain—when we invited the spy to come in from the cold.

White Chocolate Ganache Ice Cream

I love ice cream for breakfast. When I developed this terrific recipe for White Chocolate Ganache Ice Cream, I had in mind to use it in place of milk for my morning cereal. Give your tired old fruit and cereal a facelift tomorrow morning with White Chocolate Ganache Ice Cream. Joan even discovered it was great stirred into her daily bowl of hot oatmeal. This ice cream is used as a base for other ice creams or served just as it is.

Makes 2 quarts

Prep Time: 5 minutes
Cooking Time: 15 minutes
Cooling Time: 4 hours
Freezing Time: 4 hours 20 minutes
Level: **

In a medium saucepan, scrape the seeds from the vanilla bean into the cream. Heat over medium heat, whisking to blend the flavors. When the cream bubbles around the edges, remove the pan from the heat and add the White Chocolate Ganache. Wait for 30 seconds and then stir until smooth and blended. Add 1 cup of the milk to the pan and stir to combine.

Return the saucepan to the stove and stir in the remaining 1 cup milk, the sugar, and salt. Heat the mixture over medium heat, keeping the milk at a simmer; do not let it boil over the sides of the pan.

Meanwhile, in a medium bowl, whisk the egg yolks together. Slowly drizzle about ¼ cup of the warm milk into the egg yolks, whisking constantly until combined.

Pour the egg yolks into the saucepan and cook for 3 to 5 minutes, stirring constantly with a wooden spoon to prevent the eggs from cooking. Cook until the custard is thick enough to coat the back of the spoon and your finger leaves a trace in the custard when run along the back of the spoon.

Pour the custard through a fine-mesh sieve into a bowl. Discard the vanilla bean. Stir in the vanilla.

Cover the surface of the custard with plastic wrap to prevent a skin from forming. Refrigerate the custard for at least 4 hours. Transfer to an ice cream maker and freeze according to the manufacturer's instructions.

Transfer the ice cream to an airtight container and freeze for at least 4 hours.

Remove the ice cream from the freezer 10 to 15 minutes before serving to soften.

Variations on page 202.

---

gluten free

special toolbox:

medium-size glass bowl

fine-mesh sieve

whisk

electric ice cream maker

1 vanilla bean, split lengthwise

2 cups heavy cream

¾ cup White Chocolate Ganache (page 29)

2 cups whole milk, divided

½ cup granulated sugar

¼ teaspoon salt

5 large egg yolks

1 teaspoon pure vanilla extract

ED'S BOX-TOP WISDOM

Land of Kings

When the tombs of the pharaohs' last retreat was opened, all that remained viable were kernels of ancient corn, nuggets of spilled wheat and grains of long-lost rice; Not much you say? But enough to start another great civilization on unparched lands.

White Chocolate Fresh Strawberry Ice Cream

Variations:

White Chocolate Mixed Chip Ice Cream: Just before transferring the churned ice cream from the ice cream maker to a freezer-safe container, stir in ½ cup of frozen milk chocolate chips and ½ cup of frozen semisweet chocolate chips, a third at a time. Reserve a handful of chocolate chips to sprinkle over the ice cream. Let the ice cream freeze for at least 4 hours before serving. Makes about 2½ quarts.

White Chocolate Fresh Strawberry Ice Cream: Just before transferring the ice cream to the ice cream maker, stir in 1 pint of stemmed, hulled, coarsely chopped frozen strawberries (it's best to chop the frozen berries in a food processor fitted with a metal blade after they're frozen), a third at a time. Swirl the berries through the ice cream and process according to the manufacturer's instructions. Makes about 2½ quarts.

White Chocolate Toffee Pecan Ice Cream: After transferring the ice cream to the ice cream maker, watch it carefully. When the ice cream begins to freeze, pour 4 ounces of melted milk chocolate into the ice cream machine to create uneven shards of chocolate in the ice cream. When you transfer the churned ice cream from the ice cream maker to a freezer-safe container, stir in 1 cup of chopped, frozen Heath Toffee Bars (6 bars) and ½ cup of frozen roughly chopped toasted pecans, a third at a time. Let the ice cream freeze for at least 4 hours. Makes about 2½ quarts.

White Chocolate Hawaiian Macadamia Nut Ice Cream: After transferring the ice cream to the ice cream maker, watch it carefully. When the ice cream begins to freeze, pour 4 ounces of melted white chocolate into the ice cream machine to create uneven shards of chocolate in the ice cream. When you transfer the churned ice cream from the ice cream maker to a freezer-safe container, stir in 1 cup of roughly chopped, frozen macadamia nuts, ½ cup of frozen, toasted sweetened coconut (optional) and ½ cup of frozen candied pineapple (optional), a third at a time. Reserve a handful of the nut mixture to sprinkle over the ice cream. Let the ice cream freeze for at least 4 hours. Makes about 2½ quarts.

White Chocolate "White-Out" Ice Cream: After transferring the ice cream to the ice cream maker, watch it carefully. When the ice cream begins to freeze, pour 4 ounces of melted white chocolate into the ice cream machine to create uneven shards of chocolate in the ice cream. When you transfer the churned ice cream from the ice cream maker to a freezer-safe container, stir in ½ cup of frozen white chocolate chips and ½ cup of frozen mini marshmallows, a third at a time. Stir in ½ cup of Marshmallow Fluff, swirling it through the ice cream. Reserve a handful of the chocolate chip-marshmallow mixture to sprinkle over the ice cream. Let the ice cream freeze for at least 4 hours. Makes about 2½ quarts.

Chapter

12

CHOCOLATE CANDIES

A T CHOCLATIQUE, I MAKE BEAUTIFUL MOLDED CHOCOLATE CANDIES. THIS IS ONE OF THE MOST FULFILLING THINGS I HAVE EVER DONE. IT IS MORE REWARDING THAN RUNNING A CHAIN OF RESTAURANTS OR DEALING WITH CLIENTS IN MY CONSULTING BUSINESS. IT GIVES ME THE OPPORTUNITY TO CHALLENGE MY EDUCATION AND LIFE EXPERIENCES WHILE DEVELOPING NEW SOLUTIONS FOR AN EVER-CHANGING MARKET.

Working with chocolate is both demanding and gratifying. You just can't stop what you're doing and put the chocolate on hold. We have all kinds of expensive, fancy molds, tempering machines, and every hand tool imaginable (including some that most chocolatiers would never consider part of their professional chocolate toolbox). Most important, I work with a group of wonderfully talented people every day.

With only modest equipment, "can I make good chocolate candy at home?" you ask? Of course you can! Inexpensive molds are available online and at hobby and craft stores across the country. You can purchase chocolate compounds instead of real chocolate, which make candy-making tasks easier than ever. True, compounds don't have the same great texture or luscious flavor of real chocolate, but you only need melting skills—no tempering required.

Do not fear; you don't have to settle for compounds or cheap molds to make some of the recipes in this chapter—all are made with my basic ganaches. You'll find recipes for making indulgences ranging from fancy truffles to county fair fudge. I have included recipes for making your own California Chews and toffee crunch. Once you start making candies, you might come to love it as much as I do.

Fabulous Fudge

The state fair in Texas is packed with some of the greatest "circus food" you can find anywhere in the world: giant cinnamon rolls, Hawaiian shaved ice, and chocolate fudge. I usually pass on the fudge, as it tends to be grainy and tasteless, but a few years back I met Peg and Gordon Rhymes—the fudge people. Their fudge tasted as I always thought fudge should taste: dense, rich, creamy, and packed with chocolate flavor. The secret is a form of tempering and whipping that allows the fudge to set without forming those pesky sugar crystals. This recipe is quite simple and starts with Dark Chocolate Ganache as a base.

Makes 24 fudge squares

Prep Time: 15 minutes
Cooking Time: 20 minutes
Chilling Time: 2 hours or overnight
Level: *

Line the bottom and sides of an 8 or 9-inch square pan with foil, leaving an overhang on two opposite sides.

In a heavy saucepan, melt the chocolate chips, Dark Chocolate Ganache, condensed milk, and salt over low heat. Stir with wooden spoon until smooth. Remove from the heat and stir in the nuts, if using, and the vanilla.

Using a handheld electric mixer, beat the mixture for 5 minutes or until as smooth as possible. Spread the fudge in the prepared pan and refrigerate for at least 2 hours or until firm.

G gluten free

special toolbox:

electric hand mixer and beaters

8 or 9-inch-square pan

wooden spoon

French knife

2 cups semisweet chocolate chips

1 cup Dark Chocolate Ganache (page 28)

1 (14-ounce) can sweetened condensed milk

Dash of salt

1/2 to 1 cup roasted chopped nuts, such as walnuts, pecans, or almonds (optional)

1 1/2 teaspoons pure vanilla extract

DID YOU KNOW?

In the United States, chocolate outsells all other types of candy combined by two to one.

Use the foil overhang to lift the fudge from the pan and transfer to a cutting board. Cut into 24 squares for serving.

Variations:

To make the fudge in the microwave, mix the chocolate chips, ganache, condensed milk, and salt in 1-quart glass measuring cup. Microwave on high power for 1½ minutes or until the chocolate chips are soft and shiny. Remove from the microwave and stir until smooth. Return to the microwave and heat on high for 1½ minutes longer. Remove from the microwave and stir in the remaining ingredients. Follow the instructions above for chilling and serving the fudge.

Creamy Dark Chocolate Fudge: Melt 2 cups miniature marshmallows with the chocolate chips and sweetened condensed milk. Proceed as above.

Milk Chocolate Fudge: Substitute 1 cup milk chocolate chips for the semisweet chocolate chips. Proceed as above.

Chocolate Peanut Butter Chip Glazed Fudge: Follow the recipe but replace the nuts with ¾ cup peanut butter chips. Make a glaze by melting ½ cup peanut butter chips with ½ cup cream and stir until thick and smooth. Spread the glaze over the chilled fudge.

Chocolate-Cherry Cordials

No matter what anyone tries to tell you, candy making is an enviable science that requires a certain amount of skill and a good candy thermometer. If you're lacking either but still want to impress your friends and try your hand at becoming a candymeister, consider mastering the art of making chocolate-covered cherries. But not the ninety-nine-cents-a-box chocolate-covered cherries that you find in every drugstore. We're talking about really outstanding chocolate candy—plump red cherries with liquid cordial centers and a rich chocolate coating. You must allow the candies to "ripen" for at least a month in order for the center to soften and liquefy.

Makes: 60 cordials

Time: 2 hours
Chilling Time: 3 to 4 weeks
Level: ****

Special Toolbox:

2 baking sheets lined with parchment paper or waxed paper

60 maraschino cherries with stems (there are about 30 cherries in a 10-ounce jar)

3 tablespoons White Chocolate Ganache (page 29), softened

3 tablespoons light corn syrup

2 cups sifted confectioners' sugar

1 pound dipping chocolate, couverture or confectioners' compound coating

Drain the cherries thoroughly, with their stems intact, on sheets of paper towels, 8 to 12 hours.

In a small bowl, stir together the softened ganache and corn syrup.

Stir in the sifted confectioners' sugar and, using your hand, knead until smooth. If the mixture is too soft to handle, put it in the refrigerator to chill.

Shape about ½ teaspoon of the confectioners' sugar mixture around each cherry. The stem will protrude from the coating. Put the coated cherries upright on a prepared baking sheet and refrigerate until firm, about 1 hour.

Melt the chocolate or confectioners' compound coating according to the package directions. Holding cherries by their stems, dip them, one at a time, into the chocolate. Spoon the chocolate over the cherries to coat completely. Be sure to seal the cherries with the coating to prevent cherry juice from leaking after the chocolate has set. Let any excess chocolate drip off the cherries.

Place the dipped cherries, stems up, on the second baking sheet and refrigerate until chocolate is firm, about 3 hours.

Transfer the cherries to a container with a tight lid. Refrigerate for about 4 weeks before serving. Taste one every day after 3 weeks, to determine when they are ready. Okay, you really don't need to taste them every day, but it's more fun that way. After a month, store any leftover cherries in a tightly lidded container in a cool, dry place.

Variations:

Liquour Cherries: Reserve 1¼ cups of drained cherry liquid. Bring the liquid to a boil in a medium-sized saucepan set over high heat. Remove from the heat and stir in ½ cup of amaretto or crème de cacao. Add the cherries and stir gently to coat. Let the saucepan stand at room temperature for 12 hours at room temperature.

Drain the cherries, discard the liquid and follow the recipe instructions above.

ChefsNote: For a nontraditional look, use white chocolate instead of bittersweet or semisweet chocolate.

Chocolate-Cherry Cordials

Ed's Easy Soft
Dark Chocolate Truffles

Ganache is the building block of every recipe in this book—a heavenly marriage of solid chocolate (bittersweet, semisweet, milk, or white) and cream. When cooked at just the right temperature and then cooled, the two ingredients transform into a rich, firm paste with intense chocolate flavor.

A truffle is a confection made with a ganache center (often flavored) that can be dipped into molten chocolate so it is covered with a thin, shiny shell of tempered bittersweet, semisweet, milk, or white chocolate. Truffles are often coated with cocoa powder, too, and various forms of decoratifs, sugar, or finely chopped nuts.

Makes 48 (½-ounce) truffles

Prep Time: 5 minutes
Cooking Time: 10 minutes
Cooling Time: 15 minutes
Chilling Time: 30 to 45 minutes
Level: *

Spoon the Dark Chocolate Ganache into a mixing bowl; set aside.

In a medium, heavy saucepan, bring the cream to a boil over medium-high heat. Reduce the heat and simmer for 5 minutes. Remove from the heat and slowly whisk into the ganache until smooth. Whisk in the liqueur, stirring until smooth. Whisk in the softened butter until incorporated and nearly smooth. Let the mixture cool for about 15 minutes, occasionally stirring to make the ganache smooth and silken. Cover the mixing bowl and refrigerate the ganache until set, 30 to 45 minutes.

Put the confectioners' sugar, cocoa powder, or decoratifs in separate bowls.

Using a melon baller or #40 scoop, scoop 1-ounce balls from the chilled ganache. Wearing latex gloves, roll the mounds into balls, then coat in the desired garnish. Place on a serving tray lined with parchment paper or directly into fluted paper or foil candy cups.

ChefSecret: Some people have "hot hands," making it difficult to roll chocolate ganache without it melting. For those people, soak your hands in a bowl of cold water with an ice cube or two and allow your hand to cool down before putting on the gloves. You may have to repeat this a couple of times during the rolling process.

G gluten free

special toolbox:

melon baller, small #40 scoop, or 2 tablespoons

latex gloves or allergen-free rubber gloves

serving tray

2 cups Dark Chocolate Ganache (page 28)

¾ cup heavy cream

3 tablespoons Grand Marnier or liqueur of your choice, warmed

6 tablespoons unsalted butter, softened

Confectioners' sugar, cocoa powder, or chocolate decoratifs, for rolling

Scan for Ed's ChefSecret

Chocolate-Almond Butter Toffee Crunch

My Grandmother Fanny was a wonderful cook, baker, and candy maker who made the most delicious butter toffee crunch for the holidays. Nobody could do it better. It seemed as if she could squeeze five pounds of butter into a one-pound slab of "crunch." The way the candy crunched between your teeth and melted in your mouth was a thing of beauty. The candy is great by itself, but even better with a spread of our Dark Chocolate Ganache and topped with toasted, crushed almonds.

Makes 2½ pounds

Prep Time: 10 minutes
Cooking Time: 15 minutes
Cooling Time: 30 minutes
Chilling Time: 20 minutes
Level: *

In a large saucepan, heat the butter, sugars, Cinnamon Water, and salt over medium-high heat until it boils. Reduce the heat to medium and cook until a candy thermometer registers 305°F. Remove the pan from the heat. Carefully stir in the vanilla and baking soda. The mixture may expand.

Pour the mixture on a baking sheet and spread into a thin layer with an offset metal spatula. While the toffee is still warm, cut into 1-inch squares and set aside to cool. When the toffee is at room temperature, break apart into squares.

In the top of a double boiler set over barely simmering water, melt the Dark Chocolate Ganache and stir until smooth. (Alternatively, melt the ganache in the microwave.) Set aside and let cool to warm.

Using a dipping fork, dip each square of toffee into the melted chocolate and set on the other baking sheet. Sprinkle with the crushed almonds. Refrigerate for about 20 minutes to cool.

Store the brittle in a rigid plastic container with a tight-fitting lid for up to one month.

ChefSecret: For a special "flavor thrill" to what would already be a great confection Cinnamon Water can be used in place of plain water in most chocolate confection and baked goods.

• In a saucepan, bring 2 cups of water and 1 cinnamon stick to a boil over medium-high heat and boil for 5 minutes.

• Strain the cinnamon water through a fine-mesh sieve. Store the cinnamon water in a rigid plastic container with a tight-fitting lid. The cinnamon water will keep in the refrigerator for up to four weeks.

 gluten free

special toolbox:

2 parchment paper–lined baking sheets

candy thermometer

offset metal spatula

double boiler

dipping fork

1 pound (4 sticks) unsalted butter, at room temperature

1¼ cups granulated sugar

⅔ cup light brown sugar

4 tablespoons Cinnamon Water (see ChefSecret)

½ teaspoon salt

1 teaspoon pure vanilla extract

1 teaspoon baking soda

1½ cups Dark Chocolate Ganache (page 28)

½ cup almonds, toasted and crushed

Chocolate-Covered Peanut Brittle Bites

This recipe dates back to the 1880s, when my Grandpa Max first perfected his real peanut "packin'" stuffed peanut brittle, featured in the *New York Times*. Max's "secret" recipe combines an abundance of Spanish red-skin peanuts in a perfectly cooked buttery sugar brittle. The result is a brittle with a much lighter "bite" than other brittles. It leaves a long-lasting, wonderful flavor you'll never forget.

We have made this brittle for years and have found that heating it to a temperature of 307°F results in the best texture. It may sound strange, but I don't like to meddle with a sure thing!

Makes 2½ pounds

Prep Time: 10 minutes
Cooking Time: 20 minutes
Cooling Time: 30 minutes
Chilling Time: 20 minutes
Level: **

In a large saucepan, heat the sugar, corn syrup, and water over medium-high heat and cook until the sugar dissolves and the syrup is clear. Continue to heat until a candy thermometer registers 255°F. Do not stir.

Reduce the heat to medium and stir in the peanuts and salt. Cook until the temperature reaches 307°F, stirring occasionally to prevent the peanuts from scorching. Remove the pan from the heat and set aside. The hot mixture will continue cooking.

Carefully and quickly stir in the baking soda, butter, and vanilla and stir for about 1 minute until thoroughly incorporated (the mixture will foam up).

Pour the brittle mixture onto one of the baking sheets. Place a large silicone baking mat on top of the brittle and, using a rolling pin flatten and spread the brittle to a thickness of ¼ inch. While the brittle is still warm, cut into 1-inch squares. Set aside to cool. When the brittle is at room temperature, break apart into squares.

In the top of a double boiler set over barely simmering water, melt the chocolate chips and Milk Chocolate Ganache and stir until smooth. (Alternatively, melt the chocolate in the microwave.) Set aside and let cool to warm.

Using a dipping fork, dip each square of brittle into the melted chocolate and set on the other baking sheet. Refrigerate for about 20 minutes to cool.

Store the brittle in a rigid plastic container with a tight-fitting lid for up to one month.

ChefSecret: Be sure to use a large saucepan or pot, as the mixture will expand enormously when the baking powder is added.

 gluten free

special toolbox:

candy thermometer

2 baking sheets lined with parchment paper

rolling pin

1 large silicone baking mat

chocolate dipping fork

2½ cups granulated sugar

½ cup light corn syrup

½ cup cold water

4 cups raw Spanish peanuts

1 tablespoon kosher salt

1 tablespoon baking soda

5 tablespoons unsalted butter, at room temperature

1 tablespoon pure vanilla extract

1 cup semisweet chocolate chips

½ cup Milk Chocolate Ganache (page 26)

Chocolate
Butter Finger Bars

gluten free

special toolbox:

candy thermometer

2 baking sheets

parchment paper

1/3 cup light corn syrup

1 cup granulated sugar

1/3 cup water

3/4 cup creamy peanut butter, at room
temperature

1 pound milk chocolate, coarsely
chopped and melted

The first commercial I directed was for the Curtiss Candy Company of Chicago—the inventors of Butterfinger and Baby Ruth candy bars. We spent several hours talking about how to interplay the live actors with the animated old candy maker before we shot the film. When I was ready to leave, they gave me a "swag bag" filled with products, which I polished off before the plane landed in Los Angeles.

My favorite was and still is a Butterfinger. Butterfinger is a combination of crispy, crunchy, peanut buttery tastes and textures. The original recipe called for freshly roasted peanuts to be chopped and made into a creamy peanut butter that was blended with a sugary candy, then kneaded, rolled, cut, and covered in a chocolaty coating. Try my version and see how it compares.

Makes 1 dozen bars

Prep Time: 5 minutes
Cooking Time: 20 minutes
Cooling Time: 30 to 40 minutes
Level: *

In a heavy saucepan, combine the corn syrup, sugar, and water over medium-high heat until it registers 330°F on a candy thermometer. Remove the pan from the heat and stir in the peanut butter until blended.

Pour the mixture onto a baking sheet that has been sprayed with flavorless vegetable oil spray. Score with a knife into the desired size bars.

When cool, dip the bars in the melted chocolate to coat. Place the dipped bars onto a baking sheet lined with parchment or waxed paper and set aside until the chocolate has completely set, about 20 to 30 minutes.

Chapter

13

MORNING CHOCOLATE

I LOVE THE SMELL OF CHOCOLATE IN THE MORNING, AND PERSONALLY I CAN'T START THE DAY WITH-
OUT A HIT OF THE DARK STUFF. THE THEOBROMINE IN CHOCOLATE MAKES ME FEEL GOOD AND
MILDLY STIMULATED. THAT'S JUST ABOUT PERFECT FOR ME IN THE MORNINGS.

I NEVER GOT HOOKED ON COFFEE; I HEAR IT CAN DO UGLY THINGS TO YOUR NERVOUS SYSTEM
BEYOND THE EFFECTS OF CAFFEINE. ICED TEA AND DIET COKE STILL SHOW UP IN MY DIET, SO I CANNOT
CLAIM TO BE CAFFEINE-FREE, BUT COMPARED TO OTHERS, MY EARLY-MORNING VICES ARE RELATIVELY
MILD AND MOSTLY REVOLVE AROUND MY ADDICTION TO CHOCOLATE.

FOR YEARS I HAVE BEEN THINKING THERE MUST BE A WAY TO MARRY CHOCOLATE OR COCOA WITH
BREAKFAST EGG DISHES, BUT SO FAR I'M STUMPED. I'VE TRIED EGGS BENEDICT WITH A WHITE CHOCO-
LATE GANACHE HOLLANDAISE SAUCE, AND THAT WAS PRETTY BAD. I ONCE MADE A SWEET MILK CHOCO-
LATE EGG FRITTATA WITH CHOCOLATE CHIPS, WHICH WAS NO BARGAIN EITHER. I TRIED A COUPLE OF
SCRAMBLES WITH CHOCOLATE CHUNKS AND, WELL, THAT DIDN'T RATE TOO HIGH ON THE OLD CHOCO-
METER. OTHER THAN CHOCOLATE IN PANCAKES, WAFFLES, FRITTERS, AND MUFFINS OR BAKED EGG AND
FLOUR COMBINATIONS (THINK BROWNIES), I'M PERPLEXED. SO, I HAVE DECIDED TO STICK WITH WHAT I
KNOW AND MAKE WONDERFUL, EARLY MORNING CHOCOLATE GOODIES OF THE FAMILIAR AND FAVORITE
KIND. I THINK YOU WILL FIND THERE IS ENOUGH VARIETY ON THE FOLLOWING PAGES TO MAKE ANY
MORNING A SPECIAL CHOCOLATE TREAT.

BUT SHOULD YOU HAVE ANY SUGGESTIONS FOR EGGS AND CHOCOLATES, DON'T KEEP THEM A SECRET
. . . DROP ME A LINE, AND IF THEY'RE AS GREAT AS YOU THINK, I WILL INCLUDE THEM IN THE NEXT
PRINTING.

3-D Chocolate-Filled Pancakes

In Denmark, these glorious pancakes are called ebelskivers; in the United States we call them 3-D pancakes. In any language, I call them delicious. I tasted my first ebelskiver at the food pavilion in Copenhagen's Tivoli Gardens, and it was love at first bite. In Europe, they fill or top the little pancakes with a cinnamon-apple mixture, but I have taken it two steps further and fill them with dark chocolate ganache and then top them with white chocolate whipped cream. No dark chocolate ganache on hand? Use bittersweet chocolate pastilles, chips, or chunks.

Makes about 25 pancakes, serving 8 to 10

Prep Time: 30 minutes
Resting Time: 20 to 30 minutes
Cooking Time: 2 to 3 minutes
Level: ***

In a medium mixing bowl, whisk together the flour, granulated sugar, baking powder, baking soda, and salt.

In a separate mixing bowl, lightly whisk the egg yolks. Add the buttermilk and sour cream and whisk until blended. Add the dry ingredients and whisk until well combined; the batter will be slightly lumpy. Allow the batter to rest for 20 to 30 minutes.

Meanwhile, in a small bowl, whisk together the confectioners' sugar and cinnamon and set aside.

In a clean, dry bowl of an electric mixer fitted with the whisk attachment, beat the egg whites on high speed for 2 to 3 minutes until stiff but not dry peaks form. Using a rubber spatula, gently fold the whites into the batter in 2 batches.

Brush the wells of an ebelskiver with melted butter. Heat the pan over medium heat until the butter is hot and small bubbles appear. Spoon about 1 tablespoon of batter into each well and cook for 3 to 4 minutes over medium heat or until the sides of the pancakes are golden brown and crispy. Add 1 teaspoon of Dark Chocolate Ganache to each well. Using 2 wooden skewers or large toothpicks, flip the pancakes over and cook about 3 minutes longer or until the sides are golden and crispy.

Transfer the pancakes to a heated plate and sprinkle with the sugar-cinnamon mixture while still hot. Continue to make more pancakes with the remaining batter.

Serve with the White Chocolate Ganache Whipped Cream, if desired.

ChefSecret: An ebelskiver pan looks like a frying pan with seven small muffin cups molded into its surface. These are easy to find online or in cookware stores for about $25. Once you have one, you will want to make these pancakes over and over again.

special toolbox:

electric stand mixer, bowl, and whisk

sifter

pastry brush

Danish ebelskiver pan

skewers

ladle

1¾ cups all-purpose flour

1½ tablespoons granulated sugar

1 teaspoon baking powder

¾ teaspoon baking soda

½ teaspoon salt

3 large egg yolks

1⅓ cups buttermilk

½ cup sour cream

1 tablespoon confectioners' sugar

¼ teaspoon ground cinnamon

5 large egg whites

5 tablespoons unsalted butter, melted

¾ cup Dark Chocolate Ganache (page 28)

White Chocolate Ganache Whipped Cream (page 238), for garnish (optional)

Scan for Ed's ChefSecret

GIVE ME CHOCOLATE OF
GIVE ME DEATH

I t was nearly midnight when we landed at Port Charleston, South Carolina, just before Christmas 1966. We transferred to a nuclear-powered submarine, rushed below deck, and were confined to the officers' mess until the ship slipped past its moorings into the moonless night. In the middle of the Cold War, the movements of navy ships, especially ballistic missile submarines, were highly classified and considered national security secrets.

We were a civilian film crew of six moviemakers among a crew of twelve career officers and one hundred men. Our production company had been contracted to produce a recruiting film called *Silent Service*, for submarine duty, and as such would be out to sea for the duration of this sub's deployment.

We quickly learned that being a submariner has its pluses and minuses. On the downside, when you set out on a cruise, you could be at sea for six long months. You are one of a hundred men—at least back then; there were no women, and no personal contact with the outside world. Plus, it is very dangerous work.

On the upside, the submarine service is blessed with the best cooks and the best food of any of the military branches. Meals were the highlight of the cruise, and chocolate was definitely the favorite flavor for dessert. Cookie, our well-trained navy chef, really knew his way around a galley and knew that chocolate was the key to the men's morale (in the King's Navy, it had been grog, or rum). Cookie's repertoire ranged from Almond Chocolate Crème Brûlée to Zebra Iced Chocolate Cupcakes. Every meal had freshly baked bread and a chocolate-something dessert. Even breakfast was often punctuated with terrific chocolate chip–cinnamon rolls or chocolate chip muffins.

At the end of the sixth week, we were asked to pack up our gear and prepare to leave the ship. She was taking on a complement of missiles and fresh food from the USS *Proteus* (AS-19)—a Fulton-class submarine tender—while at sea. As fresh lettuce was lowered down, we were hoisted up like sacks of potatoes dangling above the foaming sea.

The *Patrick Henry* was decommissioned on May 25, 1984, and struck from the Naval Vessel Register on December 16, 1985. She lives on in my memory, as she no doubt does for all those who proudly served aboard her.

Aunt Waffle's Chocolate Waffles

When I was a kid, we often visited a gregarious family friend whom we nicknamed "Aunt Waffle." Whenever we stopped by, she ran to the corner store for fresh milk and eggs and whipped up her wondrous waffles. The hard part was waiting the 30 minutes for the batter to rest before she could ladle it onto the hot waffle iron. Not surprisingly, I have expanded on Aunt Waffle's recipe by adding chocolate. What could be better? Here's to you, Aunt Waffle!

Makes 6 to 8 waffles

Prep Time: 30 minutes
Cooking Time: 2 to 3 minutes
Resting Time: 30 minutes
Level: **

In a small saucepan, warm $\frac{1}{2}$ cup of the milk over medium heat until lukewarm (about 110°F). Remove from the heat. Add 1 teaspoon of the sugar and sprinkle the yeast over the milk. Mix lightly and set aside while preparing the batter. The milk will bubble and foam when the yeast activates.

In another saucepan, melt the butter and Milk Chocolate Ganache over low heat until smooth. Whisk gently until blended. Set aside to cool slightly. Scrape the vanilla bean seeds into the saucepan.

In the bowl of an electric mixer fitted with the paddle attachment, beat the remaining sugar and the eggs on medium-high speed until well mixed.

In another bowl, sift together the flour, cocoa powder, and baking powder. With the mixer on low speed, add the dry ingredients to the mixing bowl in three batches until incorporated. Pour the yeast mixture into the bowl and beat just until mixed.

Slowly add the remaining $1\frac{1}{2}$ cups milk to the batter, beating on medium speed just until mixed. The batter will be fairly fluid. Finally, add the cooled ganache mixture to the batter and beat until well blended.

Let the batter rest at room temperature for about 30 minutes. This will allow the flour to completely hydrate and make a fluffier waffle.

Heat a waffle iron. Brush the hot iron with butter and ladle about 1 cup of batter onto the hot waffle iron. Close the lid and cook for about 4 minutes. The amount of batter and cooking time will vary depending on your waffle iron. When done, the waffles will be light and crisp.

Garnish with maple syrup, confectioners' sugar, cocoa powder, Chocolate Butter, White Chocolate Ganache Whipped Cream, and/or fresh berries, if desired.

ChefSecret: Use butter for greasing the waffle iron to add another layer of fresh, brown, buttery flavor to your chocolate waffles.

special toolbox:

electric stand mixer, bowl, and paddle

sifter

pastry brush

waffle iron

ladle

2 cups whole milk, divided

$\frac{1}{3}$ cup granulated sugar, divided

1 package dry, instant yeast ($\frac{1}{4}$ ounce)

$\frac{1}{4}$ pound (1 stick) unsalted butter

$\frac{1}{4}$ cup Milk Chocolate Ganache (page 26)

1 vanilla bean, split lengthwise or 1 teaspoon pure vanilla extract or 1 teaspoon chocolate extract

2 large eggs

$2\frac{1}{2}$ cups all-purpose flour

2 teaspoons unsweetened Dutch-processed cocoa powder

$\frac{1}{4}$ teaspoon baking powder

optional garnishes:

8 tablespoons pure maple syrup

3 tablespoons confectioners' sugar

1 tablespoon unsweetened Dutch-processed cocoa powder

Chocolate Whipped Butter (page 247)

White Chocolate Ganache Whipped Cream (page 238)

Fresh berries

Chocolate-Filled Chocolate Beignets
(New Orleans Doughnuts)

I love the food in New Orleans, and I love beignets! What are beignets? Beignets (ben-yays) are those delicious rectangular doughnuts served fresh and hot around the clock in French Quarter coffeehouses in New Orleans—perhaps most famously at Café du Monde on Decatur Street—and also at the newly restored French Market in that lovely old city. They are easy to prepare and make delightful breakfast bread, a delicious snack at any hour of the day, or a wonderful dessert. The yeast dough must be prepared in advance and refrigerated overnight. The dough keeps beautifully under refrigeration for almost a week.

Makes 5 dozen

Prep Time: 30 minutes
Chilling Time: 8 hours or overnight
Frying Time: 2 to 3 minutes
Level: **

Pour the warm water into a large bowl. Sprinkle with the yeast and stir until thoroughly dissolved. Add the eggs, evaporated milk, sugar, and salt and stir to mix. Gradually stir in 4 cups of the flour and the cocoa powder. Beat with a wooden spoon until smooth and thoroughly blended.

Stir in the Milk Chocolate Ganache. Add the remaining 3 cups flour, about ⅓ cup at a time, beating with a spoon until the batter becomes too stiff to stir. Work the rest in with your hands. Cover the bowl with plastic wrap and refrigerate for at least 8 hours or overnight.

Remove the dough from the refrigerator and roll out the dough on a lightly floured surface to a thickness of ⅛ inch. With a sharp knife, cut the dough into 2½ x 3½-inch rectangles.

Pour enough oil into a deep-fryer or a large, heavy pot to reach a depth of about 3 inches and heat until it reaches 360°F on a deep-fat frying thermometer. Preheat the oven to 200°F.

Fry the beignets, eight to ten at a time, in the hot oil until puffed and golden brown on both sides, 2 to 3 minutes, turning them once or twice with tongs. The beignets will rise to the surface of the oil as soon as they begin to puff. Remove the beignets with tongs and drain on a platter lined with several layers of paper towels. Keep warm in the oven.

Spoon chocolate ganache pastry cream into a pastry bag fitted with a plain tip and fill the beignets. Sprinkle the beignets heavily with confectioners' sugar and cocoa powder mixture. Serve warm.

special toolbox:

floured board

rolling pin

deep-fat frying thermometer

tongs

sifter

deep-fryer or large pot

platter

pastry bag fitted with a plain tip

1½ cups warm water

1 package active dry yeast (¼ ounce)

2 large eggs

1 cup evaporated milk

½ cup granulated sugar

1 teaspoon salt

7 cups all-purpose flour, divided

1 tablespoon unsweetened Dutch-processed cocoa powder

6 tablespoons Milk Chocolate Ganache (page 26), at room temperature

Peanut oil, for deep frying

3 cups Dark, Milk, or White Chocolate Ganache Pastry Cream (page 237)

Confectioners' sugar mixed with cocoa powder (4 to 1 ratio), to taste

Milk Chocolate
Ganache Muffins

STOP! I know it's easy to run to the store and grab a box of muffin mix, but don't. It's really not that hard to make these Milk Chocolate Ganache Muffins from scratch. This was my Grandmother Engoron's recipe, and, believe me: this apple didn't fall far from the tree. Grandma Bessie loved her milk chocolate as much as I do, and made the most amazing milk chocolate treats. This was one of them. It is simple, and the results are delicious. Sometimes you just can't beat an old-fashioned recipe.

Makes 18 muffins

Prep Time: 10 minutes
Baking Time: 15 to 17 minutes
Cooling Time: 10 minutes
Level: *

Preheat the oven to 400°F. Fill 18 muffin cups with paper or foil liners, or butter and lightly dust the muffin cups with cocoa powder.

In a large mixing bowl, whisk together the flour, sugar, ½ cup cocoa powder, baking powder, and salt. Stir in the half-and-half, butter, and eggs until barely mixed. Stir in the melted ganache. The batter may appear to be lumpy with streaks of flour.

Spoon the batter into the muffin cups, filling each about two-thirds full.

Bake for 15 to 17 minutes or until a cake tester comes out clean. Cool the muffins on a wire rack.

Option: Fold in ⅓ cup of milk chocolate chips for even more milk chocolate flavor—that's what Grandmother Bessie would have done.

special toolbox:

18 paper or foil muffin cup liners (2½ inches in diameter)

muffin tins for 18 muffins

cake tester

wire cooling rack

½ cup unsweetened natural cocoa powder, plus some for dusting

2½ cups all-purpose flour

1 cup granulated sugar

2 teaspoons baking powder

¼ teaspoon salt

1½ cups half-and-half

4 tablespoons unsalted butter, melted

2 large eggs, lightly beaten

½ cup Milk Chocolate Ganache (page 26), melted

Better-Than-Paradise Dark Chocolate Ganache Muffins

In Nora Ephron's movie, *Julie and Julia* with Meryl Streep and Amy Adams, I had to laugh at the scenes relating to the cooking discipline at Le Cordon Bleu, which were so reminiscent of my own experiences at that famed academy. During our baking semester, we had several classes on muffins. I found that the recipes produced heavy, paperweight-like scones, not at all like the lighter New England–style muffins I was accustomed to. I felt compelled to develop my own recipe, which is definitely better than Paris or Paradise. The instructor insisted that they were "très bon!"

Makes 18 muffins

Prep Time: 10 minutes
Baking Time: 15 to 17 minutes
Cooling Time: 10 minutes
Level: **

Preheat the oven to 400°F. Line 18 muffin cups with paper or foil liners, or butter and lightly flour the muffin cups.

In a large mixing bowl, whisk together the flour, sugar, cocoa powder, baking powder, and salt. Stir in the half-and-half, butter, and eggs until barely mixed. The batter may appear to be lumpy with streaks of flour.

Spoon the batter into the muffin cups, filling each about one third full. Top each with about ¾ tablespoon of the Hot Fudge Ganache and then top with additional batter to fill the cups two-thirds full.

Bake for 15 to 17 minutes or until a cake tester comes out clean. Cool the muffins on a wire rack.

ChefSecret: To have the lightest, fluffiest muffins, be very careful not to overmix the batter (which will make the muffins tough), and pop them into the oven as soon as they're mixed.

special toolbox:

18 paper or foil muffin cup liners (2½ inches in diameter)

muffin tins for 18 muffins

wooden spoon

cake tester

wire cooling rack

2½ cups all-purpose flour

1 cup granulated sugar

¼ cup unsweetened Dutch processed cocoa powder

2 teaspoons baking powder

¼ teaspoon salt

1½ cups half-and-half

6 tablespoons unsalted butter, melted

2 large eggs, lightly beaten

1 cup Hot Fudge Ganache (page 30)

Scan for Ed's ChefSecret

Chocolate Granola

Granola is the perfect breakfast food and energy snack for athletes and other champions. Because it is so lightweight, high in calories, and easy to store, it is often eaten by hikers, bikers, campers, and backpackers for a boost of energy. Our granola is made with rolled oats, nuts, honey, dried cranberries, brown sugar, and chocolate ganache. It is then baked until crunchy.

Try using this granola in combination with yogurt, honey, strawberries, bananas, and milk. Or sprinkle it over pastries and ice cream. Outstanding!

Makes 1 quart

Prep Time: 10 minutes
Baking Time: 40 minutes
Cooling Time: 20 minutes
Level: *

Preheat the oven to 250°F.

In a large bowl, mix together the oats, almonds, brown sugar, salt, and cinnamon.

In a small saucepan, warm the oil, Dark Chocolate Ganache, and honey over medium heat and stir until blended. Carefully pour over the oat mixture and stir gently with a wooden spoon. Finish mixing by hand.

Spread the granola onto a 13 x 9-inch baking pan in a thin layer. Bake for about 40 minutes, stirring carefully every 10 minutes.

Transfer the pan to a wire cooling rack. While still warm, stir in the dried cranberries and chocolate chips. Let the granola cool completely, about 20 minutes.

When completely cool, store the granola in an airtight container and keep at room temperature for up to four weeks or in the freezer for up to two months.

G gluten free

V vegan

D dairy free

special toolbox:
wooden spoon
13 x 9-inch baking pan
wire cooling rack
plastic container with tight-fitting lid

2 cups old-fashioned rolled oats
¾ cup sliced, blanched almonds
¼ cup packed light brown sugar
¼ teaspoon salt
¼ teaspoon ground cinnamon
¼ cup vegetable oil
¼ cup Dark Chocolate Ganache (page 28)
¼ cup honey
¼ cup dried cranberries
¼ cup mini semisweet chocolate chips

Chapter

14

ESSENTIALS

The recipes in this chapter are fundamental, indispensable formulas necessary for success with many of my recipes. They are also the basics that can be used with many other recipes and are as important as any of the other recipes in the book. They cover a variety of "essentials," including frostings, marshmallows, whipped creams, pastry creams, sauces, and topping. If you feel you want to use a Milk Chocolate Ganache Frosting instead of a White Chocolate Ganache Frosting, you'll find it's easy to mix and match. They are all basic, simple to make, and helpful for customizing recipes to your personal tastes or helping you create totally new ones, which you can include in your own cookbook!

Perfect Piecrust

The piecrust dilemma—do I buy a store-bought crust or do I make my own from scratch? Piecrusts are really quite simple to make. Here is the perfect seven-ingredient recipe that will give you home-baked results. While it is not fashionable to use animal fats, the combination of butter, vegetable shortening, and lard will give you both the perfect buttery flavor and flaky texture.

Makes 2 (9-inch) piecrusts

Prep Time: 40 minutes
Freezing Time: 30 minutes
Baking Time: 20 minutes
Level: *

special toolbox:

food processor fitted with a metal blade

2 sheets of parchment paper

9-inch pie pan

Rolling pin

2½ cups all-purpose flour

1 tablespoon granulated sugar

½ teaspoon salt

8 tablespoons (1 stick) cold unsalted butter, cut in ½-inch pieces

¼ cup cold vegetable shortening cut into ½-inch pieces (for an extra flaky crust, you can use lard)

2 tablespoons fresh lemon juice

¼ cup plus 2 tablespoons very cold water

In the bowl of a food processor fitted with a metal blade, briefly pulse the flour, sugar, and salt to mix. Add the butter and shortening and pulse for 30 seconds or until coarse crumbs form. Add the lemon juice and water. Pulse just until the dough just starts to come together. Do not over mix.

Turn the dough onto a work surface and gently shape it into two equal disks about 4 or 5 inches in diameter. Wrap in plastic and refrigerate for at least 1 hour or up to one day.

For a single-crust pie: Place one of the dough disks between two large pieces of lightly floured parchment and roll into a 14-inch-diameter round that's ⅛ inch thick. Remove the top sheet of parchment and gently roll the dough around the pin and position the pin over the pie pan. Unroll, gently easing the dough into the pan, gently but firmly pressing the dough against the sides and bottom, taking care not to pull or stretch. Trim the edge of the dough, leaving a ¾-inch margin from the outer edge of the pan. Tuck this dough under to shape a high edge crust that rests on top of the rim. Pinch, crimp, and poke with a fork to allow the steam to escape.

For blind baking: Freeze the crust for at least 30 minutes. Preheat the oven to 425°F.

Line the frozen crust with a large piece of foil, fill with pie weights (or dried beans or rice), and bake 12 minutes until set. Remove the foil and weights and continue baking the shell until golden, about 8 minutes longer, checking for bubbles (push them down gently with the back of a spoon).

For a double crust: Roll out the first disk of dough as noted above, lining a 9-inch pie pan, leaving the excess hanging over the side. Cover loosely with plastic film while you roll out the second disk between parchment paper. Place the filling into the shell. Brush the edge of the bottom crust with water. Roll the top crust around the pin and position it over the pie. Gently unroll, centering the dough over filling. Press the edges together and trim both crusts so they're ½ inch larger than the outer edge of the pie pan. Tuck this dough under to shape a high edge crust that rests on top of the rim. Pinch and crimp. With a paring knife, slash two or three vent holes in the top crust and bake following the recipe directions.

ChefSecret: If only making a single crust you can freeze the second dough disk for up to three months.

Chocolate Piecrust

special toolbox:

food processor fitted
with a metal blade

1⅔ cups all-purpose flour

½ cup unsweetened ultra
   Dutch-processed cocoa powder

4 tablespoons unsalted butter, chilled
   and cut into pieces

½ cup Hot Fudge Ganache (page
   30), chilled and cut into pieces

¼ cup granulated sugar

1 large egg, lightly beaten

Sometimes you can never have enough chocolate. When that's the case, I suggest you substitute my shortbread-style Chocolate Piecrust for another piecrust. It is perfect for pies, tarts, and even cheesecakes—very dark and very luscious.

Makes pastry for 1 (9-inch) pie

Prep Time: 20 minutes
Chilling Time: 20 minutes
Level: *

In the bowl of a food processor fitted with a metal blade, process the flour and cocoa powder just to mix. Add the butter, Hot Fudge Ganache, and sugar and pulse just until the pastry resembles fine crumbs. Add the egg and continue mixing until the dough comes together.

Turn the pastry out onto a lightly floured work surface and gently knead the dough to bring the pastry together. It is important not to overwork the pastry at this stage.

Roll the pastry into a ball, wrap in plastic, and refrigerate for about 20 minutes.

Malted Fudge Frosting

Once you make this, you will never use canned, store-bought frosting again. It's that easy to make from scratch, and tastes so much better. There is nothing more scrumptious than a freshly baked cake covered with this homemade malted, fudgy frosting.

Makes 5½ cups, enough for 1 (9-inch) two-layer cake or 12 jumbo cupcakes

Prep Time: 15 minutes
Level: *

In a microwave-safe bowl, heat the Hot Fudge Ganache and malted milk balls on 50% power for 2 minutes or until melted. Remove from the microwave and let cool slightly.

In the bowl of an electric mixer fitted with the whisk attachment, whip together the cream cheese, butter, and cream until light and fluffy, 4 to 5 minutes. Scrape down the sides of the bowl.

Reduce the speed to low. Very slowly, with mixer still running, add the melted ganache mixture. Whip until thick and fluffy. Scrape down the sides of the bowl and whisk again until smooth, light, and creamy, at least 5 minutes. If the frosting is too thick, add milk, as needed, to thin.

Cover the bowl with a clean dishtowel or plastic wrap and leave at room temperature until ready to use, or store in a tightly covered container and refrigerate for up to ten days. Remove from the refrigerator and bring to room temperature before using.

special toolbox:

microwave-safe bowl

electric stand mixer, bowl, and whisk

3 cups Hot Fudge Ganache (page 30), at room temperature

1 cup crushed malted milk balls (2 [5-ounce] boxes malted milk balls, such as Whoppers)

12 ounces cream cheese, at room temperature

6 tablespoons unsalted butter, at room temperature

4 tablespoons heavy cream

Milk, as needed

Dark Chocolate
Cream Cheese Frosting

special toolbox:

microwave-safe bowl

electric stand mixer, bowl, and whisk

3 cups Dark Chocolate Ganache (page 28), at room temperature

2 ounces unsweetened baking chocolate, coarsely chopped

12 ounces cream cheese, at room temperature

6 tablespoons unsalted butter, at room temperature

4 tablespoons heavy cream

1 tablespoon unsweetened ultra Dutch-processed cocoa powder or another high-quality cocoa powder

Milk, as needed

Cream cheese frostings are baking essentials. They are the perfect match for practically any cake, and leftovers are great dolloped onto some freshly cut fruit. This is a basic recipe; you can reduce the amount of butter if you want a bit more tang, and add some sugar to sweeten it more—all according to your taste. Dress it up with a shot of rum or brandy, a vanilla bean, or some coconut flakes.

Makes 5½ cups, enough for 1 (9-inch) two-layer cake or 12 jumbo cupcakes

Prep Time: 15 minutes
Level: *

In a microwave-safe bowl, heat the Dark Chocolate Ganache and baking chocolate on 50% power for 3 minutes or until melted. Remove from the microwave and let cool slightly.

In the bowl of an electric mixer fitted with the whisk attachment, whip together the cream cheese, butter, and cream until light and fluffy, 4 to 5 minutes. Scrape down the sides of the bowl. Turn the speed to low and beat in the cocoa powder.

Very slowly, with mixer still running, add the melted ganache mixture. Whip until thick and fluffy. Scrape down the sides and whip until smooth, light, and creamy, at least 5 minutes. If the frosting is too thick, add milk, as needed, to thin.

Cover the bowl with a clean dishtowel or plastic wrap and leave at room temperature until ready to use, or store in a tightly covered container and refrigerate for up to ten days. Remove from the refrigerator and bring to room temperature before using.

Milk Chocolate
Cream Cheese Frosting

This is a rich, whipped ganache and cream cheese frosting that has everyone asking if they can lick the bowl! It pipes very well, too.

Makes 5½ cups, enough for 1 (9-inch) two-layer cake or 12 jumbo cupcakes

Prep Time: 15 minutes
Level: *

In a microwave-safe bowl, heat the Milk Chocolate Ganache on 50% power for 2 minutes or until softened. Remove from the microwave, stir well, and let cool slightly.

In the bowl of an electric mixer fitted with the whisk attachment, whip together the cream cheese, butter, and cream until light and fluffy, 4 to 5 minutes. Scrape down the sides of the bowl. Turn the speed to low and beat in the cocoa powder.

Very slowly, with mixer still running, add the softened ganache. Whip until thick and fluffy. Scrape down the sides of the bowl and whip until smooth, light, and creamy, at least 5 minutes. If the frosting is too thick, add milk, as needed, to thin.

Cover the bowl with a clean dishtowel or plastic wrap and leave at room temperature until ready to use, or store in a lightly covered container and refrigerate for up to ten days. Remove from the refrigerator and bring to room temperature before using.

G gluten free

special toolbox:

microwave-safe bowl

electric stand mixer, bowl, and whisk

3 cups Milk Chocolate Ganache (page 26), at room temperature

12 ounces cream cheese, at room temperature

6 tablespoons unsalted butter, at room temperature

2 tablespoons heavy cream

1 tablespoon unsweetened Dutch-processed cocoa powder

White Chocolate
Cream Cheese Frosting

special toolbox:

microwave-safe bowl

electric stand mixer, bowl, and whisk

3 cups White Chocolate Ganache
  (page 29), at room temperature

12 ounces cream cheese,
  at room temperature

6 tablespoons unsalted butter,
  at room temperature

2 tablespoons heavy cream

1 teaspoon freshly grated lemon zest

Milk, as needed

Wow! This is so easy, and so tasty too. The perfect consistency for cakes, cupcakes, and cookies. It stores well, too, so if you don't use it all at once, no need to worry! You will find plenty of uses in the coming week.

Makes 5½ cups, enough for 1 (9-inch) two-layer cake or 12 jumbo cupcakes

Prep Time: 15 minutes
Level: *

In a microwave-safe bowl, heat the White Chocolate Ganache on 50% power until softened, about 2 minutes. Remove from the microwave, stir well, and let cool slightly.

In the bowl of an electric mixer fitted with the whisk attachment, whip together the cream cheese, butter, and cream until light and fluffy, 4 to 5 minutes. Scrape down the sides of the bowl. Turn the speed to low and beat in the lemon zest.

Very slowly, and with mixer still running, add the softened ganache. Whip until thick and fluffy. Scrape down the sides of the bowl and whip until smooth, light, and creamy, at least 5 minutes. If the frosting is too thick, add milk, as needed, to thin.

Cover the bowl with a clean dishtowel or plastic wrap and leave at room temperature until ready to use, or store in a tightly covered container and refrigerate for up to ten days. Remove from the refrigerator and bring to room temperature before using.

Azteca Milk Chocolate
Cream Cheese Frosting

A blending of cream cheese, Azteca Ganache, and Burnt Caramel Sauce, this frosting is a little tart, a little tangy, and all-around delicious. At the same time, when you taste it, you can't help but be reminded of a fluff of whipped cream.

Makes 5½ cups, enough for 1 (9-inch) two-layer cake or 12 jumbo cupcakes

Prep Time: 15 minutes
Level: *

In a microwave-safe bowl, heat the Azteca Chocolate Ganache on 50% power until softened, about 2 minutes. Remove from the microwave, stir well, and let the ganache cool slightly.

In the bowl of an electric mixer fitted with the whisk attachment, beat together the cream cheese, butter, and cream until light and fluffy, 4 to 5 minutes. Scrape down bowl. Turn the speed to low and beat in the cinnamon and Burnt Caramel Sauce.

Very slowly, and with mixer still running, add the softened ganache. Whip well until thick and fluffy. Scrape and whip again until smooth, light and creamy, for a total of at least 5 minutes. If the frosting is too thick, add a little milk, as needed, to thin it down.

Cover the bowl with a clean dishtowel or plastic wrap until ready to use, or spoon into a tightly covered container and refrigerate for up to ten days. Remove from the refrigerator and bring to room temperature before attempting to spread, frost, pipe, or decorate cakes.

 gluten free

special toolbox:
microwave-safe bowl
electric stand mixer, bowl, and whisk

3 cups Azteca Chocolate Ganache
  (page 33), at room temperature

12 ounces (1½ [8-ounce] packages)
  cream cheese, at room temperature

6 tablespoons unsalted butter,
  at room temperature

2 tablespoons heavy cream

1 teaspoon cinnamon

6 tablespoons Burnt Caramel Sauce
  (page 242), at room temperature

Milk, as needed

Homemade Marshmallows

When I was a kid in Boy Scouts, we used to sit around the campfire immolating puffed marshmallows on a stick. Everyone said they thought these smoldering lumps of puffy sugar were great—I didn't, and I don't believe anyone else really did either. I hated those overpuffed, sickeningly sweet, machine-made, sticky, white, commercial marshmallows. I like to make my own, they're so much better. These marshmallows will more closely resemble what would have been made in the early 1900s in America. And, that's a really good thing.

Makes 24 to 30 marshmallows

Prep Time: 15 minutes
Cooking Time: 15 minutes
Holding Time: overnight
Level: **

special toolbox:

12 x 8-inch or 13 x 9-inch pan

heavy 3-quart saucepan

candy thermometer

electric stand mixer, bowl, and whisk

parchment paper

thin-bladed knife

3 (¹⁄₄-ounce) envelopes
　unflavored gelatin

¹⁄₂ cup cold water

2 cups granulated sugar

³⁄₄ cup light corn syrup

Pinch of salt

2 large egg whites

1 teaspoon pure vanilla extract

1 cup cornstarch or
　confectioners' sugar

Lightly spray a 12 x 8-inch pan with vegetable oil spray.

In a small bowl, combine the gelatin and ¹⁄₂ cup cold water. Set aside to soften.

Lightly spray the candy thermometer with vegetable oil spray and set aside. This prevents the marshmallow mixture from sticking to the thermometer.

In a heavy 3-quart saucepan, cook the sugar, corn syrup, salt, and 1 tablespoon hot water over medium heat, stirring with a wooden spoon until the sugar dissolves. Once the syrup is clear, continue to cook without stirring until it reaches 240°F. Immediately remove from the heat and stir in the gelatin mixture.

In the bowl of an electric mixer fitted with the whisk attachment, whisk the egg whites on high speed until stiff peaks form. Add the hot syrup and the vanilla and continue whipping for 10 minutes. Using a rubber spatula, scrape the marshmallow mixture into the prepared pan, spreading evenly to the sides.

Spray a piece of parchment paper lightly with vegetable oil spray and place on top of the marshmallow, sprayed side down. Set aside at room temperature for at least 8 hours or overnight until set. Cut the marshmallows into 1-inch-squares.

Put the cornstarch in a large bowl and gently toss the marshmallows, a few at a time, to coat lightly, shaking off the excess.

ChefSecret: If stored in an airtight container, they will keep for up to two weeks. Before you cut the marshmallows into pieces, spread them with any flavor of whipped ganache that tickles your fancy for a special treat.

My Way Basic Pastry Cream

A classic pastry cream is used in bakeries and restaurants to fill cakes, pies, tarts, and pastries. Over the years, I have come to judge great pastry chefs on the quality of their pastry cream and have never found this criterion to let me down. What I like about this pastry cream is that when "as is," you can eat it like a pudding. I am always disappointed when I order dessert in a restaurant only to discover that the pastry chef uses some kind of plastic, gunky packaged mix. What's so hard about doing it my way?

Makes 2½ cups

Prep Time: 15 minutes
Cooking Time: 5 minutes
Cooling Time: 20 minutes
Level: *

In a medium mixing bowl, whisk together the egg yolks and egg.

In another bowl, whisk ⅓ cup of the sugar with the cornstarch. Stir into the eggs until smooth.

In a heavy saucepan, heat the milk and the remaining ¼ cup sugar over medium heat until boiling, stirring continuously. Drizzle the milk into the egg mixture in a slow, thin stream, whisking constantly, to temper the eggs so that they do not cook. Return the mixture to the saucepan and stir constantly over low heat until thickened, 3 to 4 minutes.

Remove the pan from the heat and whisk in the butter and vanilla until the pastry cream is smooth and blended. Lay a sheet of plastic wrap directly on top of the pastry cream to prevent a skin from forming. Let the pastry cream cool for about 20 minutes and then refrigerate until ready to use. The pastry cream will keep for up to one or two days. Whisk well before using.

Variations:

To make other flavors of pastry cream, beat ½ cup room temperature Dark Chocolate Ganache (page 28), Milk Chocolate Ganache (page 26), White Chocolate Ganache (page 29), Azteca Dark Chocolate Ganache (page 33), or Hot Fudge Ganache (page 30). Whisk the ganache into the pastry cream. You can also add ½ cup of Burnt Caramel Sauce (page 242) or Red Raspberry Sauce (page 243) to flavor up the pastry cream.

G gluten free

special toolbox:
heavy saucepan
wooden spoon
whisk

2 large egg yolks

1 large egg

⅓ cup plus ¼ cup granulated sugar, divided

¼ cup cornstarch

2 cups whole milk

2 tablespoons unsalted butter, softened

1 teaspoon pure vanilla extract

Vanilla Bean
Whipped Cream

Homemade, sweetened whipped cream is great by itself, but it's even better with added chocolate ganache for greater depth.

Makes 3 to 4 cups

Prep Time: 15 minutes
Level: *

In the bowl of an electric mixer fitted with the whisk attachment, beat the cream on high speed until soft peaks form, 6 to 8 minutes.

Add in the confectioners' sugar, vanilla extract, vanilla bean paste, and orange liqueur and beat on high speed until stiff peaks form.

The whipped cream may be used immediately as directed in a recipe or refrigerated in a rigid plastic or glass container with a tight-fitting lid for up to 24 hours.

Variations:

To make other flavors of whipped cream, beat ½ cup Dark Chocolate Ganache (page 28), Milk Chocolate Ganache (page 26), White Chocolate Ganache (page 29), Azteca Dark Chocolate Ganache (page 33), or Hot Fudge Ganache (page 30). Fold the ganache into the whipped cream with the confectioners' sugar. You can also add ⅓ cup of Burnt Caramel Sauce (page 242) or ¼ cup of Red Raspberry Sauce (page 243) to the whipped cream at the same time the confectioners' sugar is added.

ChefSecret: Vanilla bean paste is sold in many specialty stores, some supermarkets, and on the Internet. Many cooks find it easier to use than whole vanilla beans and yet it has the same intense flavor.

gluten free

special toolbox:

electric stand mixer, bowl, and whisk

2 cups heavy cream

¾ cup confectioners' sugar

1 teaspoon pure vanilla extract

½ teaspoon pure vanilla bean paste (see ChefSecret) or seeds from 1 vanilla bean

1 teaspoon orange liqueur, such as Grand Marnier or Cointreau

Scan for Ed's ChefSecret

Simple Syrup

Simple syrup is a basic mixture of sugar and water, used to moisten cake layers, among other things. It's made by stirring granulated sugar into boiling water until the sugar dissolves. You can flavor the syrup with a little vanilla, orange, or lemon extract, or a tiny bit of espresso or ground cinnamon. These additions add a layer of complexity to any dessert that calls for simple syrup.

Makes 2 cups

Prep Time: 5 minutes
Cooking Time: 10 minutes
Cooling Time: 10 to 15 minutes
Level: *

In a medium saucepan, bring the sugar and water to a boil over high heat. Whisk until the sugar dissolves. When the syrup is clear, remove the pan from the heat and let the syrup cool to room temperature.

Transfer to a rigid plastic or glass container with a tight-fitting lid and refrigerate for up to one month.

G gluten free

V vegan

D dairy free

1 cup granulated sugar
1 cup water

White Chocolate Ganache Marshmallow Sauce

One of America's most creative restaurants was the Nut Tree in Vacaville, California, located just outside of Sacramento. The Nut Tree Restaurant was an early pioneer of California cuisine, serving farm-fresh fruits and vegetables grown on the property and featured in its recipes. By 1978, it was identified by *Gourmet* magazine as "the region's most characteristic and influential restaurant." Small loaves of warm, freshly baked wheat and white breads and whipped honey butter were on every table, along with fresh-cut pineapple served with homemade marshmallow sauce. My secret to a really great marshmallow sauce is a healthy measure of White Chocolate Ganache.

Makes 1½ cups

Prep Time: 5 minutes
Resting Time: 5 to 10 minutes
Cooking Time: 15 minutes
Level: **

In a small bowl, sprinkle the gelatin over 2 tablespoons of cold water. Set aside for 5 to 10 minutes until softened.

In a heavy saucepan, combine the sugar, corn syrup, and ¼ cup of water. Attach a candy thermometer to the side of the pan. The tip should not touch the bottom of the pan. Bring the mixture to a boil over medium-high heat and cook to the soft-ball stage, or 235°F on the thermometer. Immediately remove the syrup from the heat and add the dissolved gelatin, swirling the pan to mix.

Meanwhile, in the bowl of an electric mixer fitted with the whisk attachment, whip the egg whites on high speed until soft peaks form, 8 to 10 minutes.

With the mixer running, slowly pour the hot syrup into the whipped egg whites. Add the White Chocolate Ganache and vanilla and continue whipping until the mixture thickens to soft peaks, 5 to 6 minutes. Set aside to cool. If the sauce is too thick to pour, thin with a small amount of hot water, if necessary, and whip it in. Use immediately.

ChefSecret: Don't have time to make homemade marshmallow sauce? In a microwave-safe bowl, mix together ¼ cup White Chocolate Ganache (page 29), 1 tablespoon water, and 2 cups store-bought Marshmallow Fluff. Microwave on low power until smooth and fluid.

G gluten free

special toolbox:

candy thermometer

electric stand mixer, bowl, and whisk

1 teaspoon unflavored gelatin

2 tablespoons cold water

½ cup granulated sugar

¼ cup light corn syrup

2 large egg whites

2 tablespoons White Chocolate Ganache (page 29), at room temperature

¼ teaspoon pure vanilla extract

Scan for Ed's ChefSecret

Milk Chocolate-Peanut Butter Sauce

Anyone who lives on the East Coast and frequents Friendly's Restaurants and Ice Cream Parlors surely knows about the deliciously decadent ice cream concoctions served there. Among the best are monstrous, sinfully big sundaes. My favorite always has been a colossal ice cream sundae drowned in whipped cream, hot fudge, and a peanut butter sauce sprinkled with whole, salted peanuts. This recipe will make it easy for you to have a similar experience because I have combined chocolate ganache with the peanut butter for a one-stop taste treat.

Makes 3 cups

Prep Time: 15 minutes
Level: *

In a microwave-safe bowl, microwave the peanut butter on high until pourable but still thick, about 20 seconds.

In the bowl of an electric mixer fitted with the paddle attachment, beat together the peanut butter, peanut oil, and Milk Chocolate Ganache on high speed until blended. Scrape down the sides of the bowl and continue to mix until thoroughly combined.

Use immediately or transfer to a rigid plastic or glass container with a tight-fitting lid and store at room temperature (do not refrigerate) for up to one month.

Variations:
For an old-fashioned ice cream parlor flavor, substitute Hot Fudge Ganache (page 30) for the Milk Chocolate Ganache.

 gluten free

special toolbox:
electric stand mixer, bowl, and paddle

1 (16.3-ounce) jar creamy
   peanut butter

1/4 cup peanut oil

1 cup Milk Chocolate Ganache
   (page 26), at room temperature

Burnt Caramel Sauce

I love the flavor of dark caramel more than the classic blond version. It is far less sweet, allowing the natural flavor of the chocolate to shine through. I also discovered that I much prefer the taste of burnt caramel sauce on my chocolate desserts, as do most of my guests. I can eat this wonderful sauce right out of the jar, but it is also great to accompany a pint of vanilla or coffee ice cream.

Makes 2½ cups

Cooking Time: 15 minutes
Cooling Time: 1 hour
Level: *

In a heavy, medium saucepan, bring the sugar and water to a boil over medium-high heat. Let the syrup boil, without stirring, until it begins to color around the edges, 2 to 3 minutes. Begin to whisk the syrup until it turns deep brown and just begins to smell burned, about 2 minutes longer. (The darker the syrup the deeper the flavor, so cook accordingly.)

Slowly and carefully add the cream to the syrup (it will froth vigorously to the top of the pan). Continue to whisk until the cream is completely incorporated and the sauce is smooth. Remove the pan from the heat and stir in the vanilla and salt. Set aside to cool to room temperature. Use immediately or transfer to a tightly covered container and refrigerate for up to one month.

ChefSecret: Vanilla extracts are volatile. Add the vanilla when the caramel starts to cool to prevent it from "flashing off" its flavor in the hot caramel.

G *gluten free*

special toolbox:
heavy, medium saucepan
wooden spoon
whisk

1½ cups granulated sugar
2 tablespoons water
2 cups heavy cream
2 teaspoons pure vanilla extract
½ teaspoon kosher salt

Red Raspberry Sauce

Raspberries rank near the top of all fruits for antioxidant strength, behind cranberries and wild blueberries and just ahead of apples. Maybe that's the reason they pair so well with dark chocolate, which boasts its own share of antioxidants. I don't think you can miss with a healthful combination of these ingredients. When we developed our decorative chocolate tablets and tapestries, I found that raspberries also combined well with white chocolate, and are featured in the swirl bars offered on the Choclatique Web site.

This flavorful raspberry sauce also works well as a quick finishing glaze on roasted or grilled chicken or any firm white-fleshed fish.

Makes 4 cups

Prep Time: 10 minutes
Cooking Time: 10 to 15 minutes
Cooling Time: 30 to 45 minutes
Level: *

G gluten free

V vegan

D dairy free

special toolbox:
heavy, medium saucepan
wooden spoon
immersion blender or standard blender
fine mesh sieve

4 pounds frozen raspberries, thawed
3 cups granulated sugar
1/3 cup freshly squeezed lemon juice
2 tablespoons grated lemon zest

In a medium saucepan, bring the raspberries and their juices, the sugar, lemon juice, and lemon zest to a simmer over low heat until thickened, 10 to 15 minutes, stirring often to prevent scorching.

Using an immersion blender, purée the sauce for about 1 minute until smooth. (Alternatively, purée the sauce in a blender or the bowl of a food processor fitted with a metal blade.)

Strain the sauce through a fine-mesh sieve into a bowl and let cool to room temperature. Use immediately or transfer to a tightly covered container and refrigerate for up to two weeks. The sauce will keep in the freezer for up to two months. Stir the sauce well before serving.

Variations:
You can easily make other berry sauces by substituting strawberries, blueberries, or blackberries for the raspberries. You can make a cherry or peach sauce by substituting the same amount of these fruits for the berries. For a tutti-frutti sauce, blend a variety of fresh summer fruits and berries.

Dark Chocolate Chip
Streusel Topping

special toolbox:

food processor fitted with a
metal blade

1 cup toasted pecans

1 cup all-purpose flour

½ cup granulated sugar

½ cup packed light brown sugar

2½ teaspoons ground cinnamon

2 teaspoons unsweetened cocoa
powder

¼ pound (1 stick) unsalted butter,
melted

½ cup mini semisweet chocolate
chips

This homemade streusel topping adds sweet crunch to baked goods such as muffins, coffee cakes, pies, and tarts.

Makes 2 cups

Prep Time: 10 minutes
Level: *

In the bowl of a food processor fitted with the metal blade, pulse the pecans, flour, sugars, cinnamon, and cocoa powder until the nuts are chopped. Add the melted butter and pulse lightly to combine. Add the chocolate chips and pulse just until combined. The streusel should be chunky and crumbly, not smooth.

Use immediately or transfer to a tightly covered container and refrigerate for up to two weeks.

DID YOU KNOW? The United States leads the world in the import of beans and production of chocolate candy.

Milk Chocolate-Burnt Caramel Whipped Butter

Two of my favorite chocolate bars are Milky Way and Snickers. Both have wonderful chocolate and caramel flavors that satisfy as only a good candy bar can. I used to melt them and blend them with butter for a waffle or pancake topping until I found an easier way to enrich butter with these flavors. It's as simple as using my Milk Chocolate Ganache and Burnt Caramel Sauce. You can add another level of flavor just by adding a tablespoon or two of smooth peanut butter to the recipe below.

Makes about ⅔ cup

Prep Time: 5 minutes
Level: *

In the bowl of an electric mixer fitted with the whisk attachment, whip the butter on medium-high speed until lightened, about 3 minutes. Add the Milk Chocolate Ganache, 1 tablespoon at a time, and beat until thoroughly combined.

Stop the mixer, scrape down the sides of the bowl, and drizzle in the Burnt Caramel Sauce and salt. Beat on medium speed until very light and fluffy, 6 to 8 minutes.

Use immediately or transfer to a tightly covered container and refrigerate for up to one month. Let the butter sit at room temperature for at least 1 hour before using to make it easier to spread.

G gluten free

special toolbox:

electric stand mixer, bowl, and whisk

¼ pound (1 stick) unsalted butter, at room temperature

2 tablespoons Milk Chocolate Ganache (page 26), at room temperature

2 tablespoons Burnt Caramel Sauce (page 242), at room temperature

Pinch of salt

Chocolate Whipped Butter

I love butter, but I love chocolate butter even more. At no time was this truer than when I prepared breakfast one day for an event at the Arid Club in Boise, Idaho. The croissants provided by the club's supplier were a little stale and flavorless, so I crisped them in the oven and slathered them with rich, whipped European-style butter. Oops! A little chocolate ganache found its way into the butter (how did that happen?), and the result was a treat the Boise residents gobbled up. Now, whether I am in Beverly Hills, Boise, Berlin, or Bangkok, chocolate butter is always on my breakfast table.

Makes about ⅔ cup

Prep Time: 5 minutes
Level: *

In the bowl of an electric mixer fitted with the whisk attachment, whip the butter on medium-high speed until lightened, about 3 minutes. Add the Hot Fudge Ganache, 1 tablespoon at a time, and beat until thoroughly combined.

Stop the mixer, scrape down the sides of the bowl, and add the cocoa powder and salt. Beat on medium speed until very light and fluffy, 6 to 8 minutes.

Use immediately or transfer to a tightly covered container and refrigerate for up to one month. Let the butter sit at room temperature for at least 1 hour before using to make it easier to spread.

Variations:

Milk Chocolate Whipped Butter: Substitute 3 tablespoons Milk Chocolate Ganache (page 26) for the Hot Fudge Ganache and 1 teaspoon confectioners' sugar for the cocoa powder.

White Chocolate Whipped Butter: Substitute 3 tablespoons White Chocolate Ganache (page 29) for the Hot Fudge Ganache and ½ teaspoon confectioners' sugar for the cocoa powder. Stir ½ teaspoon pure vanilla extract into the butter.

 gluten free

special toolbox:

electric stand mixer, bowl, and whisk

¼ pound (1 stick) unsalted butter, at room temperature

3 tablespoons Hot Fudge Ganache (page 30), at room temperature

1 teaspoon unsweetened Dutch-processed cocoa powder

Pinch of salt

Cinnamon-and-Spice Milk Chocolate Whipped Butter

Butter and spice and everything nice. I think this wonderful mélange of flavors works well with both sweet and savory dishes. I mistakenly brushed a freshly grilled steak with the butter and was thrilled by how well it went with the creamy mashed potatoes being served on the side. It is also a great topper for caramelized apples and bananas.

Makes about ⅔ cup

Prep Time: 5 minutes
Level: *

In the bowl of an electric mixer fitted with the whisk attachment, whip the butter on medium-high speed until lightened, about 3 minutes. Add the Milk Chocolate Ganache, 1 tablespoon at a time, and beat until thoroughly combined.

Stop the mixer, scrape down the sides of the bowl, and add the cocoa powder, cayenne pepper, vanilla, and salt. Beat on medium speed until very light and fluffy, 6 to 8 minutes.

Use immediately or transfer to a tightly covered container and refrigerate for up to one month. Let the butter sit at room temperature for at least 1 hour before using to make it easier to spread.

G gluten free

special toolbox:
electric stand mixer, bowl, and whisk

¼ pound (1 stick) unsalted butter, at room temperature

2 tablespoons Milk Chocolate Ganache (page 26), at room temperature

½ teaspoon unsweetened Dutch-processed cocoa powder

¼ teaspoon cayenne pepper

½ teaspoon pure vanilla extract

Pinch of salt

Mango-Pineapple Salsa
or Chutney

Makes 4 servings

Prep Time: 5 minutes
Chilling Time: 2 hours
Level: *

Cut the mangoes and the pineapple into ¼-inch cubes. Combine all the ingredients in a medium bowl. Cover and refrigerate for 2 hours before topping cheesecake.

Special Toolbox:

plastic sealable storage container

⅔ cup diced peeled ripe mango (1 medium)

⅔ cup diced fresh pineapple

½ teaspoon minced seeded fresh jalapeño pepper (just trust me)

1½ teaspoons chopped fresh mint

1½ teaspoons fresh lime juice

⅛ teaspoon salt

TIMELINE OF
CHOCOLATE INNOVATION

Choclatique Authentically American Chocolates from California wouldn't be the affordable, luscious candies we know today if it weren't for the technological ingenuity of those who traveled this road before us.

When the Industrial Revolution ushered in the age of production, new inventions and ingredients made it possible to produce solid, smooth chocolate quickly and affordably. Here is a chronological history of chocolate:

250–1521: Grinding Chocolate to Drink—Mesoamerican Origins

The Maya and Aztec peoples of ancient Mesoamerica first began grinding up cacao beans using stone manos and metates. Their chocolate was a chunky paste that could be dissolved in water to make a bitter, frothy beverage.

1519–early 1600: The Addition of Sugar

The Spanish sweetened the bitter brew by adding sugar. They established cacao plantations in Central and South America, grinding the beans in mills driven by wind or horses.

1732: The Steam-Driven Chocolate Mill

French inventor Monsieur Dubuisson created the steam-driven chocolate mill, which made it much easier to grind cacao beans and produce large amounts of chocolate.

1815: The "Dutching" Process

Coenraad van Houten invented a process called "Dutching," in which powdered chocolate is treated with alkaline salts to help it mix with water. This process also gives chocolate a darker color and a milder flavor.

1828: The Cocoa Press

Van Houten again revolutionized the chocolate industry with the invention of the cocoa press. It extracts cocoa butter from chocolate liquor, leaving behind the powder we call cocoa. This process made chocolate both more consistent and less expensive to produce.

1847: The First Chocolate Bar

Chocolate was primarily served as a drink or an ingredient in recipes until 1847. In that year, Fry & Sons Company of Bristol, England, introduced the first chocolate bar meant for eating as a snack.

To make their bar, the company first pressed some chocolate liquor to extract the cocoa butter. Then they blended this butter back into unpressed chocolate liquor to make a creamy, solid chocolate candy.

1875: The Addition of Condensed Milk

Swiss chocolate maker Daniel Peter decided to add milk to his candy recipe. He teamed up with countryman Henri Nestlé, who had developed a recipe for condensed milk. Adding condensed milk allowed chocolate makers to reduce the amount of chocolate liquor in their recipes, so chocolate became cheaper to make and buy—and people liked the smooth, creamy taste of "milk chocolate."

1879: The Conching Machine

Rodolphe Lindt, also from Switzerland, invented a machine that churned the paste squeezed from cacao nibs into a smooth blend. This process is called "conching" because the first machines resembled giant conch shells.

1900: The Hershey Bar

Milton Hershey, aware of the growing demand for chocolate in America, developed the perfect mix of ingredients for American tastes—milk, sugar, and chocolate—to make the first Hershey Bar and started the Hershey Chocolate Company.

1912: The First Combination Candy Bar

The Tennessee makers of GooGoo Clusters created the first combination chocolate candy bar. They mixed peanuts, caramels, and marshmallows together and coated the concoction with milk chocolate.

1924: The Liquid Center

H. S. Pain, a US government chemist, invented a new and ingenious method for making liquid center chocolate. He inserted special yeast into a solid center that could be easily coated in chocolate. After a two-month curing period, the yeast chemically broke down the center and turned it into a thick, creamy cherry liquid.

1880–1940: The End of Chocolate Molds

Nearly every corner candy shop sold chocolates fashioned in decorative molds by hand. By the mid-20th century, faster and less expensive ways to make mass-produced chocolates had largely replaced the handmade variety.

1930–1950: Comical Characters

The simple, animated style of Walt Disney characters inspired the design of candy during this era. Chocolates became more stylized and comical in nature, featuring famous cartoon characters such as Mickey Mouse. Candy cars, speedboats, and planes also reflected the public's fascination with seeing these relatively new modes of transportation in chocolate.

1950–1990: Plastic Production

The end of World War II saw the disappearance of many small chocolate makers and confectioners. Large companies began using a new revolutionary molding material called poly carbonate to sculpt their chocolates quickly and efficiently. A recent resurgence in small artisan chocolate makers, such as Choclatique, means more handmade and molded chocolates are available—and, with luck, are in your chocolate future!

1990–Present: Artisanal Chocolatiers Make a Comeback

Today, artisanal chocolatiers are making beautiful-looking, luscious chocolates on all continents. These dedicated professionals are creating new, contemporary flavors that reflect a variety of cultures and cuisines. Chocolate has never been hotter or more plentiful. Much of the world's population can enjoy it in all its forms, from baked to frozen to simply wonderful chocolate bars and truffles and America leads the way.

A Cook's Wares
211 37th Street
Beaver Falls, PA 15010
800-915-9788
www.cookswares.com
Since 1981 A Cook's Wares has been selling small kitchen appliances, bakeware, kitchen tools, cutlery, and ovenproof porcelain that have been selected by professionals for chefs and cooks.

American Chocolate Designs
11940 Alpharetta Highway
Suite 116
Alpharetta, GA 30009
877-442-3682
www.americanchocolatedesigns.com
American Chocolate Designs provides premium quality transfer sheets and chocolate dessert wafers from a large library of designs. They also produce custom designs and logos with excellent image clarity that offer greater durability. Their transfers are made with edible FDA-approved inks that become part of the chocolate, unlike other methods such as hand-screening or stamping. All designs are printed in Atlanta, Georgia, providing fast turn-around time. Minimum order of a single design is 25 sheets.

American Spoon Foods, Inc.
1668 Clarion Avenue
Petoskey, MI 49770
888-735-6700
www.spoon.com
The award-winning American Spoon Foods, Inc. carries a complete line of fruit-oriented pantry products, condiments, and a good variety of ingredients for use in chocolate-based sweets.

Amoretti Flavors
451 Lombard Street
Oxnard, CA 93030
800-266-7388
www.amoretti.com
Jack Barsoumian and his family have created an unparalleled line of flavors, colors, and ingredients for pastry, chocolate, ice cream, and beverages. With more than 1,800 choices, Amoretti has become one of the finest flavor houses in the country. They are the title sponsor of the National and World Pastry Team Championships and a major supplier to Choclatique.

Barry-Callebaut
www.barry-callebaut.com
Barry Callebaut is the world's leading supplier of quality cocoa and chocolate products with a comprehensive range of products from the bean to the shelf. They are actively engaged in initiatives and projects that contribute to a more sustainable cocoa supply chain. If you are interested in learning more about chocolate, sign up for their chocolate academy.

Boyajian
144 Will Drive
Canton, MA 02021
800-965-0665
www.boyajianinc.com
Boyajian sells some of the finest all-natural infused olive oils, vinegars, vinaigrettes, Asian oils, citrus oils, natural flavorings, and extracts. They offer free ground shipping on all orders of $50 or more in the continental United States. They also send along a free sample with every order.

Bridge Kitchenware

563 Eagle Rock Avenue

Roseland, NJ 07068

973-287-6163

www.bridgekitchenware.com

Bridge Kitchenware is a family-owned chef's haven for high-quality baking tools. They have received numerous awards from Zagat Surveyors as being the "best kitchenware store in the City [New York], providing anything and everything you could ever want for your kitchen."

Chef Rubber

6627 Schuster Street

Las Vegas, NV 89118

702-614-9350

www.chefrubber.com

Chef Rubber offers traditional, specialty, and hard-to-find items for artisan chefs, cake decorators, confectioners and mixologists. Located in Las Vegas, one of the more innovative food meccas on the "third rock," they supply come of the best "star chefs'" restaurants with innovative solutions. If you want to learn more about making chocolate confections, sign up for one of Chef Paul Edward's classes.

Choclatique

11030 Santa Monica Boulevard

Third Floor

Los Angeles, CA 90025

310-479-3849

www.choclatique.com

Choclatique is a privately owned, super-premium-quality chocolate company founded in California in 2003. By marrying classic French-style artisan techniques with old-fashioned American ingenuity, we have created the most beautiful, distinctive, luscious and Authentically American chocolates. Everything chocolate is available through the Internet, whether you are a baker or candy maker. Dark, Milk, and White chocolate couvertures and base chocolates; chocolate chips; cocoa powders; chocolate decoratifs; chocolate curls; and even a selection of ready-to-bake mixes made with crushed chocolate, not just cocoa. For those not wanting to go through the challenge, there are more than 200 flavors of truffles available for purchase in the Build-a-Box feature on the Choclatique Web site. Choclatique offers free ground shipping on all orders over $50 in California during warm-weather months and in the continental United States during the cooler months.

ChocoVision, Inc.

14 Catharine Street

Poughkeepsie, NY 12601

800-324-6252

www.chocovision.com

ChocoVision sells the small tempering machines that we use for decoration and color in our Chocolate Studio. They can be used as countertop tempering equipment for your homemade chocolate. ChocoVision is also an excellent source for other types of small equipment and both professional and hobby-grade molds. They sell a limited variety of Callebaut, Guittard, and Scharffen Berger couvertures for candy making.

The Container Store (locations in multiple cities)

500 Freeport Parkway

Coppell, TX 75019

972-538-6000

www.containerstore.com

With locations from coast to coast and over 10,000 products, The Container Store will supply all the packaging you need to create your own Tower of Chocolate. You'll find a wide assortment of holiday containers for truffles, baked goods, and even the proverbial Christmas fruitcake. If you can't find exactly what you looking for, there's always someone in a blue apron who's ready to help.

Cookin' Stuff

22217 Palos Verdes Boulevard

Torrance, CA 90505

(310) 371-2220

www.cookinstuff.com

"If we don't have it . . . you don't need it" is proven time and time again, as people come from all over the country to discover those "hard to find" cooking and bakeware items. Cookin' Stuff carries a complete line of products from the top cooking and baking product brands, such as All-Clad, Boston Warehouse, Chicago Metallic, Cuisinart, Culinary Institute of America, Harold Import, J.K. Adams, KitchenAid, Krups, Le Creuset, Messermeister, Norpro, Nordic Ware, Old Dutch, OXO Good Grips, RSVP International, and more.

Cooking.com

Los Angeles, CA

800-663-8810

www.cooking.com

One of our consulting clients from the 1990s, Cooking.com, stocks hard-to-find bakeware and cooking gadgets, including Silpats, molds, unusual chocolate tools, chocolate decoratifs (sprinkles), cake decorating supplies, and equipment at discount prices.

Cooking Enthusiast

242 Branford Road

North Branford, CT 06471

203-871-1000

www.cookingenthusiast.com

Cooking Enthusiast is a kitchen paradise filled with gourmet food and ingredients, kitchen decor and accessories, cookware, and cook's tools sourced worldwide. Every product is guaranteed to your complete satisfaction. They also carry a limited selection of Choclatique products.

Dean & Deluca (locations in multiple cities)

560 Broadway

New York, NY 10012

212-226-6800

Locations throughout the United States

www.deananddeluca.com

Dean & DeLuca is a purveyor of fine food, wine, and kitchenware and one of my favorite places to shop for unique foods and bakery items. In addition to some really great prepared savory foods, baked goods, and a full range of pantry items, produce, and seasonal surprises, Dean & DeLuca stocks a variety of baking staples, including hard-to-find flours, baking sugars, premium butters, bar and bulk chocolate, and a wide range of packaged candies.

Easy Leaf Products

6001 Santa Monica Boulevard

Los Angeles, CA 90038

323-769-4827

www.easyleafproducts.com

There's gold in them there chocolates, and it comes from Easy Leaf Products. They supply Choclatique and other like-minded luxury chocolatiers and cake decorators with the highest quality genuine Italian gold leaf and composition metal leaf products as well as related accessory items for your gilding needs.

E. Dehillerin

18-20, rue Coquilliere - 51

Paris, FR 75001

33 1 42 36 53 13

www.e-dehillerin.fr/en/index.php

It is definitely worth a trip to Paris just to shop at E. Dehillerin. Of course I'm always open for any excuse to go to Paris. Since 1820 they have kept alive the tradition of the French kitchen culture. It is a cook's paradise with a large selection of chocolate molds, copper pots, carbon and stainless steel knives, pastry molds, storage boxes, stainless steel pots and pans, and induction cooktop accessories that you would never find here in the States. You won't be intimidated with the language as many of their clerks will tell you, "Je parle anglais."

Fante's Kitchen Wares Shop

1006 S. Ninth Street
Philadelphia, PA 19147
800-443-2683
www.fantes.com

Established in the early 1900s and still family-owned, Fante's Kitchen Wares Shop is one of America's oldest and most distinguished resources for cookware. The Philadelphia store includes a full selection of cookware, cutlery, and many thousands of quality products. On their website, they narrow the focus to specialized utensils, many of which are not readily available elsewhere.

Fran's Cake & Candy Supplies

(Not to be confused with Fran's Chocolates in Seattle, Washington)
10927 Main Street
Fairfax, VA 22030
703-352-1471
www.franscakeandcandy.com

Fran Wheat's decorating and baking supply store offers a wealth of traditional cake pans as well as many hard-to-find decorative pans and molds, cake decorating equipment, plus an array of food colors, piping gels, sprinkles, nonpareils, and sanding sugars, decorative cupcake paper cups and picks, icing spatulas, offset spatulas, and pastry brushes.

Gloria's Cake & Candy Supplies

12453 Washington Boulevard
West Los Angeles, CA 90066
(310) 391-4557
www.gloriascakecandysuplys.com

I can't tell you how many times I have heard one of our chocolatiers tell me they're off to Gloria's. What would we do without our local cake and candy supplier? Gloria has come to our rescue when we needed a quick stock chocolate Santa mold or a Valentine's heart-shaped baking pan. She is always close by when we run out of lusters and colors, sprinkles, and decoratifs.

Gourmail

800-366-5900 - Ext. 96
www.gourmail.com

For more than 25 years, Gourmail has been a purveyor of fine imported and domestic chocolate for artisan bakers, five-star hotels, culinary schools, and caterers. They carry Barry Callebaut, Valrhona, El Rey, Noel, and Peter's Chocolates.

Guittard Chocolate Company

10 Guittard Road
Burlingame, CA 94010
800-468-2462
www.guittard.com

You know they've been around for a long time when the street they are on is named after the family. You can smell the chocolate aroma as you leave the Bayshore Freeway halfway between San Francisco and San Jose. Gary Guittard is the fifth generation to run this family-owned company established not long after the California Gold Rush. Their new E. Guittard line, which includes higher percentage cacao mass and single-bean varietals, is available on their site. They also sell hard to find cocoa nibs.

JB Prince Company

36 East 31st Street

New York, NY 10016

800-473-0577

www.jbprince.com

JB Prince offers a fine selection of cutlery, bakeware, tools, and smallwares, plus an array of specialty tools. They also carry reasonably priced chocolate molds and tempering machines.

Kerekes

6103 15th Avenue

Brooklyn, NY 11219

800-525-5556

www.bakedeco.com

For 50 years Kerekes has been synonymous with high-quality products, reasonable prices, and great service. Kerekes is a one-stop shop for the commercial kitchen and bakery. They also offer a good choice of chocolate molds and stock transfer sheets for home use.

Kitchen Arts & Letters

1435 Lexington Avenue

New York, NY 10128

212-876-5550

www.kitchenartsandletters.com

And we thought we had the biggest food library in America! Kitchen Arts & Letters has the most extensive inventory of books, with an impressive section on baking, desserts, and, of course, chocolate. Kitchen Arts & Letters will customize reading lists for individuals seeking information about specific areas of concentration.

Kitchen Krafts

P.O. Box 442

Waukon, Iowa 52172

800-776-0575

www.kitchenkrafts.com

Kitchen Krafts is a direct merchant for those hard-to-find kitchen tools and ingredients. They even sell invert sugar (Nulomoline) for candy making, which you find referenced in many cookbooks, but rarely find in your local supermarket.

The King Arthur Flour Company

The Baker's Catalogue

58 Billings Farm Road

White River Junction, VT 05001

800-827-6836

www.kingarthurflour.com

I love the wide selection of flours and sugars that are available at King Arthur Flour. When shopping here, stick to the basic commodity ingredients. (Now that you have this book, you won't need to buy mixes, because you can do it better for less money.) I am a repeat customer for their hard-to-find specialty bakeware, innovative gadgets, cake decorating supplies and equipment, flavored baking chips, oils and essences, ground nuts, and marzipan.

La Cuisine

323 Cameron Street

Alexandria, VA 22314

800-521-1176

www.lacuisineus.com

La Cuisine is an independently owned store in the historic district of Alexandria, Virginia. They source quality products, choosing to deal with smaller, independent suppliers and artisans who produce unusual and unique products. They stock fine bakeware, and a good selection of chocolate molds, transfer sheets, quality chocolates and cocoa powders—Michel Cluizel, Valrhona, and other chocolates—flavor extracts, nut pastes and nut flours, and decorations for pastries and cakes.

Linnea's Candy & Cake Supplies

975 Oak Street

San Bernardino, CA 92410

Phone: 909-383-7201

www.linneasinc.com

Linnea's Candy & Cake Supplies, Inc. is a supplier for the baking and confectionery industry. They offer a complete selection of professional bakery and confection equipment and supplies ranging from pans to parchment, fondant to buttercream, and colors to cake stands. They offer a large line of books, with titles covering candy and sugar art, cake decorating, candy making, and dessert creation.

Michaels Stores (locations in multiple cities)

8000 Bent Branch Drive

Irving, TX 75063

800-642-4235

www.michaels.com

Michaels is the nation's largest arts and crafts materials retailer. They sell a broad assortment of products, many for use in home chocolate making, including hobby-grade molds, lollipop sticks, and a limited range of packaging

National Peanut Board

2839 Paces Ferry Road

Suite 210

Atlanta, GA 30339

866-825-7946

www.nationalpeanutboard.org

While you can't purchase any nuts from this organization, it is the best source for information on this legume—you see, peanuts are technically not a nut. Founded in 2000, the National Peanut Board is a research and promotion board that works on behalf of U.S. peanut farmers. The National Peanut Board is funded by an assessment levied on all U.S. peanut farmers' crop values. The Board's annual funding supports development and implementation of domestic and export advertising and promotion programs. It also funds research to reduce production costs, improve quality and yield, improve shelf life and flavor, and explore nutrition research.

New York Cake

56 West 22nd Street

New York, NY 10021

212-675-2253

New York Cake West

10665 West Pico Boulevard

Los Angeles, CA 90064

310-481-0875

www.newyorkcake.com

New York Cake stocks bakeware and decorating supplies of all types and styles, including cake pans in a range of shapes and depths. They can be found on both coasts in New York and Los Angeles.

Nielsen-Massey Vanillas, Inc.

1550 Shields Drive

Waukegan, IL 60085

800-525-7873

www.nielsenmassey.com

They claim to make the finest pure vanillas in the world. We must agree, as this is the only vanilla we use at Choclatique. They have been producing pure vanilla products since 1907. Nielsen-Massey is a great source for vanilla beans, vanilla bean pastes, and pure vanilla extract, including our two favorites—Madagascar Bourbon and Tahitian vanillas.

NutsOnline

125 Moen Street

Cranford, NJ 07016

800-558-6887

www.nutsonline.com

At NutsOnline they roast your nuts the same day they're shipped, which means that when they reach you, they are as fresh as if you had bought them in an old-fashioned nut shop. They sell the highest-quality bulk nuts by the pound, as well as wholesale nuts by the case. They have seventeen varieties of almonds, six varieties of cashews, five varieties of walnuts, five varieties of macadamia nuts, nine varieties of pistachios, and six varieties of pecans. They are even well stocked with peanuts, even though they're technically a legume and not a nut.

Pastry Chef Central

561-999-9483

www.pastrychef.com

Aside from a great array of all kinds of bakery and confection supplies, Pastry Chef Central stocks a selection of rare and hard-to-find Belgian chocolate molds.

Penzey's Spices

(locations in multiple cities)

12001 West Capitol Drive

Wauwatosa, WI 53222

800-741-7787

www.penzeys.com

Both Joan (my business partner) and Penzeys were born in Wisconsin. And thanks to Joan, we discovered each other. The Chocolate Studio and test kitchens, as well as my home, are well stocked with a full range of spices and extracts. Compared to spices you'll get anywhere else, these are generally more volatile (stronger) and better priced than ingredients you can find at your local grocer or any other place online. There are custom mixed blends and a wide variety of all the regulars. They have an especially broad range of peppers, peppercorns, cinnamons, and salts. I love their decorticated cardamom.

Prévin, Inc.

2044 Rittenhouse Square

Philadelphia, PA 19103

888-285-9547

www.previninc.com

You can count on finding the newest and finest baking products available in this Philadelphia store. Prévin offers a prime assortment of spoons and tongs, pastry spatulas and cutters, dough scrapers, pastry bags and tips, rolling pins, baking sheets, and baking molds and Bundt pans, in addition to good selection of chocolate molds.

Qzina Specialty Foods

U.S. Headquarters

1726 West Atlantic Boulevard

Pompano Beach, FL 33069

800-532-5269

www.qzina.com

Qzina Specialty Foods provides the highest-quality and most innovative ingredients to North America's top chocolatiers and pastry chefs. Qzina is a direct importer, stocking a large selection of quality ingredients from the industry's leading premium suppliers, such as Barry Callebaut, Valrhona, Lindt, PCB, Boiron, Pidy, Cepalor, ChoCo'a, Bakels, Braun, El Rey, Dobla, IBC, Matisse, Lubeca, Perfect Puree, Hafner, Pruve, Neilsen-Massey, and many more.

Royal Oak Peanuts

13009 Cedar View Road

Drewryville, VA 23844

800-608-4590

www.royaloakpeanuts.com

The Pope family has been growing the finest Virginia peanuts since the late 1800s on their 3,000-acre farm in Southampton County, Virginia. They grow the world-famous Virginia jumbo peanut, prized by gourmets everywhere for its impressive size and even more incredible flavor. Each batch of peanuts is cooked, according to a time-honored family recipe, in pure peanut oil with no additives or preservatives. When you open a can of Royal Oak peanuts, you know you are getting a product that was shipped within a couple of days of being cooked and packed.

SaltWorks

15000 Wood-Red Road, NE, B-900

Woodinville, WA 98072

Phone: 425-885-7258

www.saltworks.us

SaltWorks is America's sea salt supplier, offering premium gourmet salts for the cook and confectioner. From *fleur de sel* and Bokek Dead Sea salt to Salish smoked salt and Himalayan salt, their products are the highest quality, suitable for both home and professional use. You can buy online in retail or wholesale quantities.

Simplers Botanical Company

P.O. Box 2534

Sebastopol, CA 95473

800-652-7646

www.simplers.com

Simplers Botanical produces essential oils, including rose, geranium, lavender, and lemon verbena. Their flavor library is made up of nearly 100 essential oils and more than 60 organic essential oils. Many of their products are also available at health food stores.

Sugarcraft, Inc.

3665 Dixie Highway

Hamilton, OH 45015

513-896-7089

www.sugarcraft.com

Once you start filling your basket on the Sugarcraft website, you'll find that you run up quite a bill. Not that their products

are so expensive, but you will see so many things that you can't live without you'll just keeping stacking them in your basket. We like the tiny decorations, like carrots and bunnies, for decorating some of our special and seasonal chocolate. They are also another source of invert sugar (Nulomoline).

Surfas

8777 West Washington Boulevard

Culver City, CA 90232

310-559-4770

www.surfasonline.com

Years ago, we discovered a warehouse stocked to the ceiling with thousands of professional items that transition into home use for food enthusiasts. Whether you are a chef or a home cook, you'll find ordinary to innovative imported and domestic food items, high-quality ingredients, commercial cookware, equipment, cutlery, specialty tools, china and glassware, packaging for food products, bakeware, confection equipment and supplies, and plenty of ideas for using all of these items.

Sur La Table (locations in multiple cities)

P.O. Box 840

Brownsburg, IN 46112

800-243-0852

www.surlatable.com

We shop at the Sur La Table in Santa Monica and the Los Angeles Farmers Market. They carry all kinds of kitchen tools, cake pans, molds, and a range of chocolate-specific materials for the baker. Sur La Table has a wide variety of bakeable paper pans that are great when you are baking for the holidays. All of their products are available on the Internet, by catalog, or in more than fifty retail stores in the United States. The stores also carry Scharffen Berger and Michel Cluizel chocolate.

The Vanilla Company

P.O. Box 3206

Santa Cruz, CA 95063

831-476-9111

www.vanilla.com

This is a source for all things vanilla. The best part is, anyone can buy vanilla in wholesale sizes for wholesale prices at the Vanilla Company. They sell premium pure Mexican, Tahitian, Madagascar Bourbon, Indonesian, double fold, and organic vanilla extracts, alcohol-free vanilla flavor, vanilla sugars, cinnamon sugar and chocolate sugar, vanilla paste, vanilla powder, vanilla cookbooks, and other books with interesting facts on vanilla. Stock up and buy in bulk.

Tomric Systems

85 River Rock Drive #202

Buffalo, NY 14207

(716) 854-6050

www.tomric.com

Tomric Systems designs, produces, stocks, and distributes high-quality candy molds, insert trays, accessories, equipment, and a limited amount of basic packaging for confectionery and food applications. They have a wide selection of polycarbonate European molds from both Belgium and Italy. They also make their own thermoformed plastic candy molds, which are a lot less expensive than the European molds but still very good.

Valley Fig Growers

2028 South Third Street

Fresno, CA 93702

559-237-3893

www.valleyfig.com

Figs are one of the earliest fruits cultivated by man. Figs and chocolate are one of the best examples of pairing the Old World foods of the Mediterranean with those of the New World of the Americas. Valley Fig Growers was established in 1959 and is the largest handler of figs in North America. Their retail products are sold under Valley Fig Growers' own brand names of Blue Ribbon Orchard Choice, Sun-Maid, and Old Orchard.

Whole Foods Markets

(locations in multiple cities)

www.wholefoodsmarket.com

Whole Foods is a natural and organic grocery supplier that maintains strict quality standards. They also have a commitment to sustainable agriculture. These upscale grocery stores have nearly 300 locations in the United States. Although stock in individual stores may vary, many stores carry Callebaut, El Rey, and Scharffen Berger chocolates cut from professional-sized bars and sold by the pound.

Williams-Sonoma

(locations in multiple cities)

151 Union Street

San Francisco, CA 94111

877-812-6235

www.williams-sonoma.com

With a full line of supplies available at two hundred retail stores, online, and through their catalog, this is a good source for cooks, candy makers and bakers. They carry cookie and cake decorating equipment and supplies, electric mixers, baking ingredients, and a selection of premium boxed cookies and candies.

Wilton Industries

2240 West 75th St.

Woodridge, IL 60517

800-794-5866

www.wilton.com

Wilton is the industry leader in cake decorating, quality bakeware, food crafting, and supplies. They are great resource for nationally located decorating classes, and each year they publish *Cake Decorating*, a yearbook packed with cake and dessert ideas, step-by-step instructions, a resource guide, a full product list, and more.

Zingerman's

422 Detroit Street

Ann Arbor, MI 48104

888-636-8162

www.zingermans.com

The proprietors, Mo Frechette, Toni Morell, and Tom Root, have stocked this Midwest specialty store with Valrhona, El Rey, Michel Cluizel, and Scharffen Berger chocolates in small bars that are handy for taste testing before buying larger quantities.

Local Stores Near You

If there isn't a great baking and candy-making supply store near you, and you can't wait for a mail-order delivery, many times you can find what you are looking for at a local art or hobby store that sells art and craft supplies.

CHOCOLATE GLOSSARY

Alkalized cocoa powder: I like the smooth, mild flavor of alkalized cocoa powder, which also is called Dutch processed. An alkali is added to natural (nonalkalized) cocoa powder to reduce the natural acidity of chocolate, resulting in alkalized cocoa. This cocoa is darker in color than nonalkalized, as well as milder in flavor.

Bittersweet chocolate: Bittersweet chocolate must have at least 35 percent chocolate liquor. Add sugar and cocoa butter, as well as lecithin and flavorings, such as vanilla (or vanillin), and you have bittersweet chocolate—similar to semisweet chocolate. For most recipes, either one will work. Bittersweet and semisweet chocolates are also called *dark chocolate* (not to be confused with unsweetened chocolate, which is used for baking).

Cacao: For Choclatique, everything begins with cacao. Cacao is a small evergreen tree native to the lower eastern slope of the Andes Mountains. Its fruit—a pod also called cacao—is the source of cocoa and, hence, chocolate. Choclatique cacao grows in partial shade at lower elevations than many cacao trees, where the average temperature is 75°F and the north and south latitudes are about 10 degrees. The tree thrives in this region, where the rainfall is between 40 and 120 inches a year.

Chocolate liquor: When the nibs of the cocoa bean are heated and ground into a paste, the result is called *chocolate liquor*. At its purest, chocolate liquor is more than 50 percent cocoa butter. Chocolate makers extract the butter and then return it to the liquor in varying amounts, and with other ingredients, to make all kinds of chocolate.

Cocoa butter: Cocoa butter is the fat naturally occurring in cocoa beans. This fat remains solid at room temperature.

Cocoa powder: Cocoa powder is made from the chocolate liquor after the cocoa butter is removed. The liquor is pressed and ground into unsweetened powder. For more on cocoa powder, turn to page 17.

Conching: Conching is a step in the chocolate-making process that further refines the chocolate mass and gives it its indescribable texture and richness. During conching, chocolate mass is kneaded in a machine with large, rotating blades, which reduces its moisture level and removes the volatile acids. At the same time, conching allows for the development of specific aromas and rounds out the flavor of the chocolate. Depending on the quality sought for the chocolate, it can be conched for a little as 12 hours and as long as 72 hours.

Confectionery coating: These are sometimes called *compound or summer coatings* and are not really chocolate. They are used for some candy-making purposes and are made from cocoa powder, sugar, vegetable fats, and dried milk.

Couverture chocolate: Couverture is high-quality chocolate, most often used for enrobing (covering) high-end truffles and similar candies, and for molding. It melts evenly and hardens into a smooth, shiny shell.

Dark Chocolate: Dark chocolate is another way to describe both bittersweet and semisweet chocolates. It must contain at least 43 percent cocoa mass to earn the designation of "dark," according to European norms. While a chocolate with

70 percent chocolate mass is considered quite dark, there are dark chocolates that boast 85 percent mass, and a few that are 88 percent. These very bitter chocolates have gained popularity with chocolate aficionados.

Dutch-processed cocoa: See *alkalized cocoa powder*. Also turn to page 17 for more on cocoa powder in general.

Fair Trade Chocolate: Fair trade chocolate has the same ingredients as any other chocolate. It also is subject to the same governmental and commercial regulations, but to earn the designation, the cocoa trees are grown on plantations where the wages for workers are fair and the working conditions are free of abusive practices. Trees grown on these plantations are also subject to environmentally sustainable agricultural methods.

Milk Chocolate: When milk solids and flavorings such as vanilla (or vanillin) are added to chocolate liquor along with sugar, the result is milk chocolate. The proteins in the milk are heat sensitive, so cooking with milk chocolate can be tricky. Milk chocolate cannot be substituted for dark chocolate in a recipe.

Nonalkalized cocoa powder: I go into some depth on page 17 to explain the differences between nonalkalized and alkalized cocoa powders. Nonalkalized cocoa powder is sometimes called *natural cocoa powder*. It has not been treated with an alkali, and therefore is a little lighter in color and bolder in flavor. Use the kind of cocoa powder called for in the specific recipe.

Semisweet chocolate: Semisweet chocolate contains at least 35 percent chocolate liquor and is very similar in composition to bittersweet chocolate. For most cooking needs, the two are interchangeable.

Temper: When chocolate is in temper, the cocoa butter crystals are stable. Heat the chocolate and it goes out of temper. Store chocolate improperly and it goes out of temper. When chocolate bars leave the manufacturer, they are in temper, and so is the chocolate you buy. Unless you plan to make high-end chocolate candies or truffles that require thin, glossy coatings with a good snap, knowing how to temper is not important for cooking and baking. None of the recipes in this book requires tempering.

Truffle: A truffle is a confection made of chocolate ganache and other flavorings that is shaped into balls. Truffles often are coated with cocoa powder or enrobed with tempered, couverture chocolate. Various exterior textures can be created by rolling the ganache center in cocoa powder, powdered sugar, or finely chopped nuts. Truffles got their name from the exotic mushroom of the same name, primarily because of a visual resemblance.

Unsweetened chocolate: Sometimes called *baking chocolate*, this is chocolate liquor that has no added sugar or other flavorings. It is used solely for cooking and baking.

White chocolate: As I have written elsewhere in the book, some people don't consider white chocolate "real chocolate" because it contains no chocolate liquor. I don't agree. White chocolate is chocolate in my book. It is made from sugar, cocoa butter, milk solids, and lecithin, and is smooth and sweet.

CONVERSION CHARTS

Volume Metric

US	Canadian		Australian	
¼ teaspoon	=	1 mL	=	1 ml
½ teaspoon	=	2 mL	=	2 ml
1 teaspoon	=	5 mL	=	5 ml
1 tablespoons	=	15 mL	=	20 ml
¼ cup	=	50 mL	=	60 ml
⅓ cup	=	75 mL	=	80 ml
½ cup	=	125 mL	=	125 ml
⅔ cup	=	150 mL	=	170 ml
¾ cup	=	175 mL	=	190 ml
1 cup	=	250 mL	–	250 ml
1 pint	=	475 ml	=	475 ml
1 quart	=	1 liter	=	1 liter
1 gallon	=	3.8 liters	=	3.8 liters

Volume Imperial

1 tablespoon	=	3 teaspoons	=	½ fluid ounce		
2 tablespoons	=	1/8 cup	=	1 fluid ounce		
4 tablespoons	=	¼ cup	=	2 fluid ounces		
5 tablespoons	=	⅓ cup	=	2⅔ fluid ounces + 1 teaspoon		
6 tablespoons	=	⅜ cup	=	3 fluid ounces		
8 tablespoons	=	½ cup	=	4 fluid ounces		
10 tablespoons	=	⅔ cup	=	5⅓ fluid ounces + 2 teaspoons		
12 tablespoons	=	¾ cup	=	6 fluid ounces		
14 tablespoons	=	⅞ cup	=	7 fluid ounces		
16 tablespoons	=	1 cup	=	8 fluid ounces		
1 cup	=	8 fluid ounces	=	½ pint		
2 cups	=	16 fluid ounces	=	1 pint		
3 cups	=	24 fluid ounces	=	1½ pints	=	¾ quart
4 cups	=	32 fluid ounces	=	2 pints	=	1 quart
6 cups	=	48 fluid ounces	=	3 pints	=	1½ quarts
8 cups	=	64 fluid ounces	=	2 quarts	=	½ gallon
16 cups	=	128 fluid ounces	=	4 quarts	=	1 gallon

Weight

1 ounce	=	30 grams	=	30 grams
2 ounces	=	55 grams	=	60 grams
3 ounces	=	85 grams	=	90 grams
4 ounces	=	115 grams	=	125 grams
8 ounces	=	225 grams	=	225 grams
16 ounces	=	455 grams	=	500 grams (½ kilogram)

Temperatures

Fahrenheit	Degrees Celsius		Fahrenheit	Degrees Celsius
32	0		375	190
212	100		400	200
250	120		425	220
275	140		450	230
300	150		475	240
325	160		500	260
350	180			

Various Conversions

(Pound, cups, tablespoon, and teaspoon conversions assume the base weight-volume of water.

Butter in the U.S. is sold in one-pound boxes, each box containing 4 sticks)

Decimals

0.25 = ¼	1 pound = 2 cups
0.33 = ⅓	1 ounce = 2 tablespoons
0.50 = ½	1 tablespoon = 3 teaspoons = 0.5 oz = 15 grams
0.66 = ⅔	1 teaspoon = 0.17 oz = 5 grams
0.75 = ¾	pinch =less than ⅛ teaspoon
	dl = deciliter = ¹⁄₁₀ of a liter = ½ cup

Weight-volume of:

Flour: 1 pound = 3½ cups

Sugar: 1 pound = 2¼ cups

Butter: 1 stick = ¼ pound = 110 grams

INDEX

Italicized numbers indicate
a photograph.

A

Abohr Farms Dairy, 195
Almonds and almond flour
  Chocolate-Almond Butter Toffee Crunch, 211
  Dark Chocolate Ganache Cheesecake, 86–87
  Milk Chocolate-Almond Bark Ice Cream, 196
  White Chocolate, Pine Nut, and Sesame
      Cookies, 105
  White Chocolate Raspberry Cheesecake, 91,
      96–97
Amazon River, 31–32, 103
Apple Pie, 131
Apricots
  Original Sacher Torte, 49, 58–59
Arid Club, 247
Aztec culture, 9–10, 31, 178, 250
Aztec inspired recipes
  Azteca Dark Chocolate Layer Cake with Milk
      Chocolate Frosting, 51
  Azteca Milk Chocolate Cream Cheese
      Frosting, 235
  Azteca Mini Chocolate Ganache Cheesecakes,
      92–93
  Azteca-Style Milk Chocolate Ganache, 26
  Spiced Azteca Chocolate Ganache, 15, 33
  Spiced Brazilian Chocolate on the "Rocks,"
      182

B

Bakeware, pots, and pans, 21–22
Bali, 138
Baratti & Milano, 188
Belgium, 6, 16
Berlin Wall, 57
Beverages. See Drinks
Bhumibol Adulyadej, King of Thailand, 39
Black Onyx cocoa powder, 17
Bloom, 12
Blueberries
  Chocolate Dumplings, 38
  Show-Stopping Chocolate Pasta, 39, 40
  Ultimate White Chocolate Cheesecake, 84–85
Boy Scout camp, 236
Brazil, 6, 31–32, 103, 182

Bread pudding
  White Chocolate Brioche Pudding, 170–71
Breakfast recipes, 215
  Aunt Waffle's Chocolate Waffles, 219
  Better-Than-Paradise Dark Chocolate
      Ganache Muffins, 222–23
  Chocolate-Filled Chocolate Beignets
      (New Orleans Doughnuts), 220
  Chocolate Granola, 224–25
  Milk Chocolate Ganache Muffins, 221
  3-D Chocolate-Filled Pancakes, 216–17
Brownies, 120
  Blushing White Chocolate Brownies, 128–29
  Christmas Morning Brownies, 126
  Double Chocolate Brownies, 121
  Ed's Best "Got Milk" Brownies, 120
  Peanutty Crispy Brownie Bars, 127
  Rocky Road Brownies, 122–23
Bundt cakes and pan, 61
  Triple Chocolate Glazed Mini-Bundt Cakes, 61
Butter, 19
  Chocolate Whipped Butter, 246–47
  Cinnamon-and-Spice Milk Chocolate
      Whipped Butter, 248
  Milk Chocolate-Burnt Caramel
      Whipped Butter, 245
  Milk Chocolate Whipped Butter, 247
  White Chocolate Whipped Butter, 247

C

Cacao beans
  chemical compounds in, 7
  cultivation of, 12, 13, 31–32
  currency use of, 10, 31
  history of, 9–10
  process to convert to chocolate, 10–11
  roasting, 10
Cakebread, Jack, 44
Cakes, 49
  Azteca Dark Chocolate Layer Cake with
      Milk Chocolate Frosting, 51
  Boston-Steamed Chocolate Cake, 69
  Chocolate Ganache Cake, 64
  Chocolate Gingerbread, 68
  Classic Chocolate Génoise, 52
  Classic White Chocolate Génoise, 52
  Coca-Cola Chocolate Cake, 49, 60
  Dark Chocolate Ganache Layer Cake, 50–51
  Milk Chocolate Ganache Layer Cake with
      Milk Chocolate Frosting, 51
  Never-Fail Molten Lava Cakes, 49, 62–63

  New York Sponge Cake, 90
  Old-Fashioned Six-Layer Devil's Food Cake,
      54–56
  Original Sacher Torte, 49, 58–59
  Sour Cream Chocolate Cake, 53
  Spicy Chocolate Swirl Cakes, 65
  Tres Leches Chocolate Cake, 66–67
  Triple Chocolate Glazed Mini-Bundt Cakes, 61
  White Chocolate Ganache Layer Cake with
      Dark Chocolate Frosting, 51
Candies, 203. See also Fudge
  Candy Bar Cheesecake, 98–99
  Chocolate-Almond Butter Toffee Crunch,
      211
  Chocolate Butter Finger Bars, 214
  Chocolate-Cherry Cordials, 206–07, 208–09
  Chocolate-Covered Peanut Brittle Bites,
      212–13
  Ed's Easy Soft Dark Chocolate Truffles, 210
  White Chocolate Toffee Pecan Ice Cream, 202
Caramel
  Burnt Caramel Sauce, 242
  Caramel Cheesecake Brûlée, 94–95
  Dark Chocolate French Crème Caramel,
      156–57
  Dark Chocolate Turtle Ice Cream, 194
  Milk Chocolate-Burnt Caramel Whipped
      Butter, 245
  Salted Caramel Chocolate Tart, 148–49
Cashews
  Dark Chocolate Rocky Road Ice Cream, 194
  Homemade Marshmallow Cashew Chocolate
      Cheesecake, 100–102
Central America, 9
Cheesecakes, 83
  Azteca Mini Chocolate Ganache Cheesecakes,
      92–93
  Candy Bar Cheesecake, 98–99
  Caramel Cheesecake Brûlée, 94–95
  Dark Chocolate Ganache Cheesecake, 86–87
  Homemade Marshmallow Cashew Chocolate
      Cheesecake, 100–102
  Marble Chocolate Cheesecake, 88–89
  New York Sponge Cake, 90
  Ultimate White Chocolate Cheesecake, 84–85
  White Chocolate Raspberry Cheesecake, 91,
      96–97
Cherrie, George, 31
Cherries
  Cherry Chocolate Pie, 150–51
  Chocolate-Cherry Cordials, 206–07, 208–09

Dark Chocolate Black Cherry Ice Cream, 194
Liqueur Cherries, 207
Chidester, Wayne, 96
Child, Julia, 169
Choclatique Chocolate Couverture, 16
Chocolate
    adventures related to, 6, 31–32, 103, 161
    bloom, 12
    care and welfare of, 11–12
    chemical compounds in, 7
    conching process, 11
    health and, 14
    history of, 9–10
    melting, 18–19
    passion about, 6–7
    as perfect food, 6
    pleasant effects of eating, 6–7, 14, 215
    process to make, 10–11
    quality and characteristics of, 16–17, 19, 25
    sexual function and desire and, 9, 14
    sources and supplies, 18, 252–61
    tasting process and samples, 12–14, 78
    tempering process, 11
    timeline of chocolate innovation, 250–52
    tips for beginners, 16–17
Chocolate liquor, 10–11
Christy, David, 64
Cinco de Mayo, 67, 92
Cinnamon. See also Spices and spicy recipes
    Cinnamon-and-Spice Milk Chocolate
        Whipped Butter, 248
    Cinnamon Water, 211
Coca-Cola Chocolate Cake, 49, 60
Cocoa butter
    extraction of, 10–11
    melting point, 29
    process to make chocolate with, 11
Cocoa powder
    baking with, 17–18
    Boston-Steamed Chocolate Cake, 69
    Chocolate Curl Meringue Kisses, 112–13
    Chocolate Marshmallows, 47
    Chocolate Piecrust, 230
    Christmas Morning Brownies, 126
    Coca-Cola Chocolate Cake, 49, 60
    Dark Chocolate Ganache Layer Cake, 50–51
    Deep, Dark Chocolate Ganache Cupcakes,
        70–71
    hot cocoa compared to hot chocolate, 177
    Old-Fashioned Six-Layer Devil's Food Cake,
        54–56

process to make, 11, 250
quality and characteristics of, 17–18, 19, 250
Spicy Chocolate Swirl Cakes, 65
substitution of different types, 18
types of, 17, 18
Coconut
    Orgasmic Chocolate Soup, 44
    White Chocolate Hawaiian Macadamia Nut
        Ice Cream, 202
Coffee and espresso
    Cappuccino Ciocolatta, 188
    Chocolate Espresso, 179
    Frozen Hot Cappuccino, 186
    Milk Chocolate Mocha Chip Ice Cream, 196
    Mocha Frosting, 115
Columbus, Christopher, 9–10
Complexity, 26
Conching process, 11
Conversion charts, 264–65
Cookies, 103
    Chocolate Chunkaholic Cookies, 118
    Chocolate Curl Meringue Kisses, 112–13
    Chocolate Ganache and Spice Cookies, 110
    Chocolate Madeleines, 111
    Chocolate Peanut Butter Ripples, 106–7
    Chocolate Spritz Cookies, 114
    Double Chocolate Chunk Cookies, 108
    Grandma Gray's Chocolate Cookies, 115
    Just-A-Great-Old-Fashioned Chocolate Chip
        Cookie, 104
    New York Deli-Style Black and White Cookies,
        116–17
    Peanut Butter Chocolate Cookies, 109
    White Chocolate, Pine Nut, and Sesame
        Cookies, 105
    White Chocolate and Macadamia Nut
        Cookies, 119
Le Cordon Bleu, 223
Couverture chocolate, 16, 17
Cream, whipped
    Azteca Chocolate Ganache Whipped Cream,
        238
    Dark Chocolate Ganache Whipped Cream,
        238
    Hot Fudge Ganache Whipped Cream, 238
    Milk Chocolate Ganache Whipped Cream,
        238
    Vanilla Bean Whipped Cream, 238
    White Chocolate Ganache Whipped Cream,
        238

Cream cheese
    Azteca Milk Chocolate Cream Cheese
        Frosting, 235
    Azteca Mini Chocolate Ganache Cheesecakes,
        92–93
    Candy Bar Cheesecake, 98–99
    Caramel Cheesecake Brûlée, 94–95
    Dark Chocolate Cream Cheese Frosting, 232
    Dark Chocolate Ganache Cheesecake, 86–87
    Homemade Marshmallow Cashew Chocolate
        Cheesecake, 100–102
    Malted Fudge Frosting, 231
    Marble Chocolate Cheesecake, 88–89
    Milk Chocolate Cream Cheese Frosting, 233
    Ultimate White Chocolate Cheesecake, 84–85
    White Chocolate Cream and Tropical
        Fruit Tart, 144–45
    White Chocolate Cream Cheese Frosting,
        234
    White Chocolate Raspberry Cheesecake, 91,
        96–97
Crème brûlée
    Chocolate Crème Brûlée, 166
    No-Bake—Quick and Easy—Chocolate
        Crème Brûlée, 167
    White-On-Black Chocolate Crème Brûlée,
        164–65
Crumb, 11
Cupcakes, 49, 71, 75
    in Berlin, 57
    Chocolate Bomb Cupcakes, 79–81, 80
    Chocolate-Pumped Cupcakes, 76–77
    Deep, Dark Chocolate Ganache Cupcakes,
        70–71
    Light and White Chocolate Ganache
        Chocolate Chip Cupcakes, 78
    Mile-High Meringue Chocolate Cupcakes,
        72–75, 73
Curls, chocolate, 35, 143
Curtiss Candy Company, 214
Custards. See Puddings and custards
Customs House Restaurants, 49, 121, 187

D
Dairy-free recipes, 7, 15
Dairy products, 19
Dardarian, Leo, 186
Dark chocolate
    appearance of, 13
    Authentically American Chocolate Pudding,
        154–55

Dark chocolate, cont'd

Azteca Chocolate Ganache Whipped Cream, 238

Azteca Dark Chocolate Layer Cake with Milk Chocolate Frosting, 51

Azteca Milk Chocolate Cream Cheese Frosting, 235

Azteca Mini Chocolate Ganache Cheesecakes, 92–93

Better-Than-Paradise Dark Chocolate Ganache Muffins, *222*–23

Bittersweet Chocolate Tart, 139–41, *140*

Blushing White Chocolate Brownies, 128–29

Cappuccino Ciocolatta, 188

Cherry Chocolate Pie, 150–51

Chocolate, Chocolate Pecan Pie, 132–33

Chocolate-Almond Butter Toffee Crunch, 211

Chocolate Bomb Cupcakes, 79–81, *80*

Chocolate Chunkaholic Cookies, 118

Chocolate Crème Brûlée, 166

Chocolate Curl Meringue Kisses, 112–*13*

Chocolate Ganache and Spice Cookies, 110

Chocolate Ganache Cake, 64

Chocolate Ganache Marshmallow Milkshake, 184–*85*

Chocolate Ganache Puddin' Pie, 142–43

Chocolate Gingerbread, 68

Chocolate Granola, 224–*25*

Chocolate Ice Blended Float, 183

Chocolate Madeleines, 111

Chocolate Peanut Butter Chip Glazed Fudge, 205

Chocolate Peanut Butter Ripples, 106–7

Chocolate Piecrust, 230

Chocolate-Pumped Cupcakes, 76–77

Chocolate Spritz Cookies, 114

Chocolate Whipped Butter, *246*–47

Classic Chocolate Génoise, 52

Coca-Cola Chocolate Cake, 49, 60

Cold-Processed Chocolate Custard Cups, 160

Creamy Dark Chocolate Fudge, 205

Dark Chocolate Black Cherry Ice Cream, 194

Dark Chocolate-Chip Ice Cream, 194

Dark Chocolate Chip Streusel Topping, 244

Dark Chocolate Cream Cheese Frosting, 232

Dark Chocolate French Crème Caramel, 156–57

Dark Chocolate Ganache, 15, *27*, 28

Dark Chocolate Ganache Cheesecake, 86–87

Dark Chocolate Ganache Ice Cream, 192–94

Dark Chocolate Ganache Layer Cake, 50–51

Dark Chocolate Ganache Whipped Cream, 238

Dark Chocolate-Raspberry Smoothie Float, 181

Dark Chocolate Raspberry Swirl Ice Cream, *193*, 194

Dark Chocolate Rocky Road Ice Cream, 194

Dark Chocolate Turtle Ice Cream, 194

Deep, Dark Chocolate Ganache Cupcakes, 70–71

Double Chocolate Brownies, 121

Double Chocolate Chunk Cookies, 108

Drunken Chocolate Cow, 189

Ed's Best "Got Milk" Brownies, 120

Ed's Easy Soft Dark Chocolate Truffles, 210

Fabulous Fudge, 204–5

Faultless Chocolate Soufflé, *162*–63

Go-for-the-Gold Chocolate Milk, 180

Grandma Gray's Chocolate Cookies, 115

Grand Marnier Dark Chocolate Crème, 159

health and, 14

Homemade Marshmallow Cashew Chocolate Cheesecake, *100*–102

Hot Dark Chocolate, 178

Hot Fudge Ganache Whipped Cream, 238

Hot Fudge Nut Trifle, 50, *172*–73

Hot Irish Chocolate, 190

Just-A-Great-Old-Fashioned Chocolate Chip Cookie, 104

Malted Fudge Frosting, 231

Marble Chocolate Cheesecake, 88–89

Mile-High Meringue Chocolate Cupcakes, 72–75, *73*

Mocha Frosting, 115

Never-Fail Molten Lava Cakes, 49, 62–*63*

New York Deli-Style Black and White Cookies, *116*–17

No Bake—Quick and Easy—Chocolate Crème Brûlée, 167

Old-Fashioned Hot Fudge Ganache, 15, 30

Old-Fashioned Six-Layer Devil's Food Cake, *54*–56

Original Sacher Torte, 49, 58–59

Peanut Butter and Jelly Milkshake, 187

Peanut Butter Chocolate Cookies, 109

Peanutty Crispy Brownie Bars, 127

process to make, 10–11

Rocky Road Brownies, *122*–23

Spiced Aztec Chocolate Ganache, 15

Spiced Brazilian Chocolate on the "Rocks," 182

3-D Chocolate-Filled Pancakes, 216–*17*

Traditional Chocolate Mousse, 169

Tres Leches Chocolate Cake, *66*–67

Triple Chocolate Glazed Mini-Bundt Cakes, 61

Upside-Down Chocolate-Pecan Meringue Pie, *134*–36

White-On-Black Chocolate Crème Brûlée, 164–65

De Neefe, Janet, 138

Denmark, 114, 216

Desserts

Chocolate Dumplings, 38

Chocolate Ganache Toas-Tites, *42*–43

Chocolate-Peanut Butter Wontons, 37

Chocolate Puffs, 36

Chocolate Salami, 41

Show-Stopping Chocolate Pasta, 39, 40

S'Mores Pizza, 46

Disneyland's Plaza Inn, 60

Doughnuts

Chocolate-Filled Chocolate Beignets (New Orleans Doughnuts), 220

Drinks, 177

Cappuccino Ciocolatta, 188

Chocolate Espresso, 179

Chocolate Ganache Marshmallow Milkshake, 184–*85*

Chocolate Ice Blended Float, 183

Dark Chocolate-Raspberry Smoothie Float, 181

Drunken Chocolate Cow, 189

Frozen Hot Cappuccino, 186

Go-for-the-Gold Chocolate Milk, 180

hot cocoa compared to hot chocolate, 177

Hot Dark Chocolate, 178

Hot Irish Chocolate, 190

Peanut Butter and Jelly Milkshake, 187

Spiced Brazilian Chocolate on the "Rocks," 182

xocolatl, 9

Dumplings

Chocolate Dumplings, 38

Dutch-processed cocoa powder, 17, 250

E

Edwards, Steve, 40

Eggs, 19

Authentically American Chocolate Pudding, 154–*55*

Chocolate Crème Brûlée, 166

Chocolate Curl Meringue Kisses, 112–*13*

Dark Chocolate French Crème Caramel, 156–57

Faultless Chocolate Soufflé, *162*–63

Frozen Chocolate Mousse Meringue Pot Pie, 146–47

Grand Marnier Dark Chocolate Crème, 159

Mousse Is Loose, 168

My Way Basic Pastry Cream, 237

No Bake—Quick and Easy—Chocolate Crème Brûlée, 167

tempering, 154

Traditional Chocolate Mousse, 169

Upside-Down Chocolate-Pecan Meringue Pie, 134–36

White Chocolate and Strawberry Creamy Custard, 158

White Chocolate Brioche Pudding, 170–71

White-On-Black Chocolate Crème Brûlée, 164–65

England, 177

Engoron, Bessie, 221

Engoron, Roy, 43

Ephron, Nora, 223

Espresso. See Coffee and espresso

F

Ferrare, Cristina, 40

Fields, Debbi, 119

Flour, 19

Fondue

Orgasmic Chocolate Soup, 44–45

The Food Show, 119, 124

France, 6, 10, 25, 111

Friendly's Restaurants and Ice Cream Parlors, 241

Frostings

Azteca Milk Chocolate Cream Cheese Frosting, 235

Dark Chocolate Cream Cheese Frosting, 232

Malted Fudge Frosting, 231

Milk Chocolate Cream Cheese Frosting, 233

Mocha Frosting, 115

White Chocolate Cream Cheese Frosting, 234

Frozen desserts. See also Ice cream and frozen yogurt

Frozen Chocolate Mousse Meringue Pot Pie, 146–47

Fruit

Orgasmic Chocolate Soup, 44–45

White Chocolate Cream and Tropical Fruit Tart, 144–45

Fry & Sons Company, 251

Fudge

Chocolate Peanut Butter Chip Glazed Fudge, 205

Creamy Dark Chocolate Fudge, 205

Fabulous Fudge, 204–5

Milk Chocolate Fudge, 205

G

Ganache

Azteca-Style Milk Chocolate Ganache, 26

balls, ganache, 36, 81

as basis for recipes, 7, 15, 16

characteristics of, 15–16, 25

Chocolate Peanut Butter Ganache, 26

Dark Chocolate Ganache, 15, 27, 28

making sauces from, 30

Old-Fashioned Hot Fudge Ganache, 15, 30

origins of, 25

Snowy White Chocolate Ganache, 15, 29

Spiced Azteca Chocolate Ganache, 15, 33

tips for beginners, 16–17

Velvety Smooth Milk Chocolate Ganache, 15, 26

Ganache soufflé, 25

Germany, 16, 57

Ginger, 68

Chocolate Ganache and Spice Cookies, 110

Chocolate Gingerbread, 68

Glossary, 262–63

Gluten-free recipes, 7

Graham crackers

Caramel Cheesecake Brûlée, 94–95

Cherry Chocolate Pie, 150–51

Marble Chocolate Cheesecake, 88–89

S'Mores Pizza, 46

White Chocolate Raspberry Cheesecake, 91, 96–97

Grand Marnier Dark Chocolate Crème, 159

Grubs, 103

H

Hershey, Milton, 26, 251

Hitchcock, Alfred, 33

Hit Man—We Deliver, 136

Home! 109

I

Ice cream and frozen yogurt, 191

Chocolate Ganache Marshmallow Milkshake, 184–85

Chocolate Ice Blended Float, 183

Dark Chocolate Black Cherry Ice Cream, 194

Dark Chocolate-Chip Ice Cream, 194

Dark Chocolate Ganache Ice Cream, 192–94

Dark Chocolate-Raspberry Smoothie Float, 181

Dark Chocolate Raspberry Swirl Ice Cream, 193, 194

Dark Chocolate Rocky Road Ice Cream, 194

Dark Chocolate Turtle Ice Cream, 194

Drunken Chocolate Cow, 189

Milk Chocolate-Almond Bark Ice Cream, 196

Milk Chocolate Birthday Cake Ice Cream, 197

Milk Chocolate Ganache Ice Cream, 195–97

Milk Chocolate Mocha Chip Ice Cream, 196

Milk Chocolate-Peanut Butter Ice Cream, 197

Peanut Butter and Jelly Milkshake, 187

Santa Fe "Hot" Milk Chocolate Ice Cream, 197

Spiced Brazilian Chocolate on the "Rocks," 182

tips for making ice cream, 191

White Chocolate Fresh Strawberry Ice Cream, 201, 202

White Chocolate Ganache Ice Cream, 200–202

White Chocolate Hawaiian Macadamia Nut Ice Cream, 202

White Chocolate Mixed Chip Ice Cream, 202

White Chocolate Toffee Pecan Ice Cream, 202

White Chocolate "White Out" Ice Cream, 202

Icons, 7

Indonesia, 138

Integrity, 141

Ireland, 190

Iron Curtain, 57

Italy, 188

J

Jensen, Birget, 114

Johnson, Suzie, 96

Julie and Julia, 223

K

Kells, Spencer, 106

Knives, 22

L

Land of Kings, 200

Lemon juice

Cold-Processed Chocolate Custard Cups, 160

Lindt, Rodolphe, 251

Linxe, M. Robert, 6

M

Macadamia nuts

White Chocolate and Macadamia Nut
Cookies, 119

White Chocolate Hawaiian Macadamia Nut
Ice Cream, 202

Malaysia, 6, 128

Mango-Pineapple Salsa or Chutney, 249

Mankind, 180

Marcos, Ferdinand, 91

Marcos, Imelda, 91

Marshmallows, 236

Chocolate Ganache Marshmallow Milkshake,
184–85

Chocolate Marshmallows, 47

Creamy Dark Chocolate Fudge, 205

Dark Chocolate Rocky Road Ice Cream, 194

Homemade Marshmallow Cashew Chocolate
Cheesecake, 100–102

Homemade Marshmallows, 236

Rocky Road Brownies, 122–23

Santa Fe "Hot" Milk Chocolate Ice Cream, 197

S'Mores Pizza, 46

White Chocolate Ganache
Marshmallow Sauce, 240

White Chocolate "White Out" Ice Cream, 202

Marzipan, 41

White Chocolate, Pine Nut, and Sesame
Cookies, 105

Mayan culture, 9–10, 31, 65, 177, 178, 250

Measurements and weights

conversion charts, 264–65

tools and gadgets, 20–21

Meese, Ed, 91

Metternich, Klemens Wenzel von, 58

Mexico, 6, 9, 67, 92, 177

Milk

Cappuccino Ciocolatta, 188

Chocolate Espresso, 179

Chocolate Ganache Marshmallow Milkshake,
184–85

Chocolate Ice Blended Float, 183

Dark Chocolate-Raspberry Smoothie Float,
181

Frozen Hot Cappuccino, 186

Go-for-the-Gold Chocolate Milk, 180

hot cocoa compared to hot chocolate, 177

Hot Dark Chocolate, 178

Hot Irish Chocolate, 190

Spiced Brazilian Chocolate on the "Rocks,"
182

Tres Leches Chocolate Cake, 66–67

Milk chocolate

Aunt Waffle's Chocolate Waffles, 219

Azteca-Style Milk Chocolate Ganache, 26

Candy Bar Cheesecake, 98–99

Cappuccino Ciocolatta, 188

Chocolate Butter Finger Bars, 214

Chocolate-Covered Peanut Brittle Bites,
212–13

Chocolate Espresso, 179

Chocolate-Filled Chocolate Beignets
(New Orleans Doughnuts), 220

Chocolate French Silk Pie, 137

Chocolate Ganache Marshmallow Milkshake,
184–85

Christmas Morning Brownies, 126

Cinnamon-and-Spice Milk Chocolate
Whipped Butter, 248

Double Chocolate Brownies, 121

Frozen Chocolate Mousse Meringue Pot Pie,
146–47

Frozen Hot Cappuccino, 186

Milk Chocolate-Almond Bark Ice Cream, 196

Milk Chocolate Birthday Cake Ice Cream, 197

Milk Chocolate-Burnt Caramel
Whipped Butter, 245

Milk Chocolate Cream Cheese Frosting, 233

Milk Chocolate Fudge, 205

Milk Chocolate Ganache Ice Cream, 195–97

Milk Chocolate Ganache Layer Cake with
Milk Chocolate Frosting, 51

Milk Chocolate Ganache Muffins, 221

Milk Chocolate Ganache Whipped Cream, 238

Milk Chocolate Mocha Chip Ice Cream, 196

Milk Chocolate-Peanut Butter Ice Cream, 197

Milk Chocolate-Peanut Butter Sauce, 241

Milk Chocolate Whipped Butter, 247

process to make, 10–11

Salted Caramel Chocolate Tart, 148–49

Santa Fe "Hot" Milk Chocolate Ice Cream, 197

Sour Cream Chocolate Cake, 53

Tres Leches Chocolate Cake, 66–67

Triple Chocolate Glazed Mini-Bundt Cakes, 61

Velvety Smooth Milk Chocolate Ganache,
15, 26

Mixers and mixing bowls, 22

Molasses

Chocolate Ganache and Spice Cookies, 110

Chocolate Gingerbread, 68

Mousse

Mousse Is Loose, 168

Traditional Chocolate Mousse, 169

Muffins

Better-Than-Paradise Dark Chocolate
Ganache Muffins, 222–23

Milk Chocolate Ganache Muffins, 221

Murphy, Dick, 91

N

Napa Valley Wine Chocolates, 44

National Peanut Board, 148, 257–58

Natura cocoa powder, 17

Negativity, 64

Nestlé, 125

Nestlé, Henri, 251

Nibs, 10

Nuts. See also specific kinds

Fabulous Fudge, 204–5

Nut Tree Restaurant, 240

O

Oats

Chocolate Granola, 224–25

Olmec culture, 65, 177

Olympic Games, 180, 188, 198–99

P

Pain, H. S., 251

Palm Grill, 131

Pancakes

3-D Chocolate-Filled Pancakes, 216–17

Pans, pots, and bakeware, 21–22

Parchment paper, 21, 107

Party menu, 35–38, 40–47

Pasta

Show-Stopping Chocolate Pasta, 39, 40

Pastry cream

My Way Basic Pastry Cream, 237

Pastry scrapers, brushes, and bags, 22–23

Peanut butter

Chocolate Butter Finger Bars, 214

Chocolate Peanut Butter Chip Glazed Fudge,
205

Chocolate Peanut Butter Ganache, 26

Chocolate Peanut Butter Ripples, 106–7

Chocolate-Peanut Butter Wontons, 37

Milk Chocolate-Peanut Butter Ice Cream, 197

Milk Chocolate-Peanut Butter Sauce, 241

Peanut Butter and Jelly Milkshake, 187
Peanut Butter Chocolate Cookies, 109
Peanutty Chocolate Milk, 180
Peanutty Crispy Brownie Bars, 127
Peanuts
  Chocolate-Covered Peanut Brittle Bites,
    212–13
  National Peanut Board recipe, 148
  Peanutty Crispy Brownie Bars, 127
Pecans
  Chocolate, Chocolate Pecan Pie, 132–33
  Dark Chocolate Chip Streusel Topping, 244
  Dark Chocolate Turtle Ice Cream, 194
  Ed's Best "Got Milk" Brownies, 120
  Hot Fudge Nut Trifle, 50, 172–73
  toasting, 133, 172
  Upside-Down Chocolate-Pecan Meringue Pie,
    134–36
  White Chocolate Toffee Pecan Ice Cream, 202
Peter, Daniel, 125, 251
Phelps, Michael, 180
Philippines, 91
Piecrusts
  Chocolate Piecrust, 230
  Perfect Piecrust, 228–29
Pies and tarts, 131, 136
  Bittersweet Chocolate Tart, 139–41, 140
  Cherry Chocolate Pie, 150–51
  Chocolate, Chocolate Pecan Pie, 132–33
  Chocolate French Silk Pie, 137
  Chocolate Ganache Puddin' Pie, 142–43
  Frozen Chocolate Mousse Meringue Pot Pie,
    146–47
  Salted Caramel Chocolate Tart, 148–49
  Upside-Down Chocolate-Pecan Meringue Pie,
    134–36
  White Chocolate Cream and Tropical Fruit
    Tart, 144–45
Pineapple
  Mango-Pineapple Salsa or Chutney, 249
  White Chocolate Hawaiian Macadamia Nut
    Ice Cream, 202
Pine nuts
  White Chocolate, Pine Nut, and Sesame
    Cookies, 105
Pingo Doce, 139
Pizza
  S'Mores Pizza, 46
Pots, pans, and bakeware, 21–22
Prestige Milk Chocolate, 16
Private Reserve Dark Chocolate, 16

Puddings and custards, 153.
    See also Crème brûlée
  Authentically American Chocolate Pudding,
    154–55
  Cold-Processed Chocolate Custard Cups, 160
  Dark Chocolate French Crème Caramel,
    156–57
  Grand Marnier Dark Chocolate Crème, 159
  White Chocolate and Strawberry Creamy
    Custard, 158
  White Chocolate Brioche Pudding, 170–71
Puff pastry
  Chocolate Puffs, 36

R
Raspberries
  Dark Chocolate Ganache Cheesecake, 86–87
  Dark Chocolate-Raspberry Smoothie Float,
    181
  Dark Chocolate Raspberry Swirl Ice Cream,
    193, 194
  Hot Fudge Nut Trifle, 50, 172–73
  Red Raspberry Sauce, 243
  Show Stopping Chocolate Pasta, 39, 40
  White Chocolate Raspberry Cheesecake, 91,
    96–97
Reagan, Ronald, 91
Red Rouge cocoa powder, 17
Rhymes, Gordon, 204
Rhymes, Peg, 204
Robuchon, Joël, 62
Rolling pin, 22
Rondon, Cândido, 31
Roosevelt, Theodore, 31, 32
Russia and Soviet Union, 198–99

S
Sacher, Franz, 58
Saint John, 146
Salami
  Chocolate Salami, 41
Salt, 19
Sauces and salsa
  Burnt Caramel Sauce, 242
  making sauces from ganache, 30
  Mango-Pineapple Salsa or Chutney, 249
  Milk Chocolate-Peanut Butter Sauce, 241
  Red Raspberry Sauce, 243
  White Chocolate Ganache Marshmallow
    Sauce, 240

  White Chocolate Sauce, 170–71
Serengeti Plain, 31, 64, 161
Sesame seeds
  White Chocolate, Pine Nut, and Sesame
    Cookies, 105
Simple Syrup, 239
Simplicity, 167
S'Mores Pizza, 46
Snowy White Chocolate, 11, 16, 78
Soufflés
  Faultless Chocolate Soufflé, 162–63
Soup
  Orgasmic Chocolate Soup, 44–45
Sources and supplies, 18, 252–61
Sour cream
  Dark Chocolate Ganache Cheesecake, 86–87
  recipe to make, 53
  Sour Cream Chocolate Cake, 53
  Ultimate White Chocolate Cheesecake, 84–85
Soviet Union and Russia, 198–99
Spain, 16, 144, 177, 250
Spices and spicy recipes
  Azteca Dark Chocolate Layer Cake with
    Milk Chocolate Frosting, 51
  Azteca Milk Chocolate Cream Cheese
    Frosting, 235
  Azteca Mini Chocolate Ganache Cheesecakes,
    92–93
  Azteca Style Milk Chocolate Ganache, 26
  Chocolate Ganache and Spice Cookies, 110
  Cinnamon-and-Spice Milk Chocolate
    Whipped Butter, 248
  Cinnamon Water, 211
  Santa Fe "Hot" Milk Chocolate Ice Cream, 197
  Spiced Azteca Chocolate Ganache, 15, 33
  Spiced Brazilian Chocolate on the "Rocks,"
    182
Sprinkles and the "Sprinkles
    Phenomenon," 49
Stories
  Chocolate on the Amazon, 31–32
  Discovering the Serengeti, 161
  Give Me Chocolate or Give Me Death, 218
  The King and I, 39
  "Mr. Engoron, this is the White House calling,"
    91
  My Prayers were Answered in Switzerland,
    124–25
  The Pleasures of Bali Ha'i, 138
  The Spy Who Came in from the Cold, 198–99
  The Wall Came Tumbling Down, 57

Strawberries
Show-Stopping Chocolate Pasta, 39, 40
White Chocolate and Strawberry Cream Trifle, *174–75*
White Chocolate and Strawberry Creamy Custard, 158
White Chocolate Fresh Strawberry Ice Cream, *201*, 202
Submarines, 218
Sugar
Burnt Caramel Sauce, 242
Simple Syrup, 239
Switzerland, 16, 25, 124–25, 251

T
Tempering process, 11
Thailand, 6, 39
Thompson, David, 39
Timeline of chocolate innovation, 250–52
Tonio's Restaurant, 186
Tools and gadgets, 20
measuring and weighing tools, 20–21
mixing tools, 22
pots, pans, and bakeware, 21–22
preparation tools, 21
small jobs and hand tools, 22–23
thermometers, 21
Toppings
Dark Chocolate Chip Streusel Topping, 244
Trifles, 171
Hot Fudge Nut Trifle, 50, 172–*73*
White Chocolate and Strawberry Cream Trifle, *174*–75
T.R.'s Restaurants, 137

V
van Houten, Coenraad, 250
Vegan recipes, 7, 15

W
Waffles
Aunt Waffle's Chocolate Waffles, 219
Chocolate Ganache Toas-Tites, *42*–43

Walnuts
Grandma Gray's Chocolate Cookies, 115
Rocky Road Brownies, 122–*23*
Weights. *See* Measurements and weights
White, Allan, 35
White chocolate
Blushing White Chocolate Brownies, 128–29
Cappuccino Ciocolatta, 188
Caramel Cheesecake Brûlée, 94–*95*
Chocolate, Chocolate Pecan Pie, 132–33
Chocolate Bomb Cupcakes, 79–81, *80*
Chocolate-Cherry Cordials, 206–07, *208-09*
Chocolate French Silk Pie, 137
Chocolate Ganache Puddin' Pie, 142–43
Christmas Morning Brownies, 126
Classic White Chocolate Génoise, 52
Drunken Chocolate Cow, 189
Go-for-the-Gold Chocolate Milk, 180
Hot Fudge Nut Trifle, 50, 172–*73*
Just-A-Great-Old-Fashioned Chocolate Chip Cookie, 104
Light and White Chocolate Ganache Chocolate Chip Cupcakes, 78
Marble Chocolate Cheesecake, 88–89
Mousse Is Loose, 168
New York Deli-Style Black and White Cookies, *116*–17
New York Sponge Cake, 90
Peanutty Crispy Brownie Bars, 127
process to make, 10–11
Snowy White Chocolate Ganache, 15, 29
Traditional Chocolate Mousse, 169
Tres Leches Chocolate Cake, *66*–67
Ultimate White Chocolate Cheesecake, 84–85
Upside-Down Chocolate-Pecan Meringue Pie, *134*–36
White Chocolate, Pine Nut, and Sesame Cookies, 105
White Chocolate and Macadamia Nut Cookies, 119
White Chocolate and Strawberry Cream Trifle, *174*–75
White Chocolate and Strawberry Creamy Custard, 158

White Chocolate Brioche Pudding, 170–71
White Chocolate Cream and Tropical Fruit Tart, 144–*45*
White Chocolate Cream Cheese Frosting, 234
White Chocolate Fresh Strawberry Ice Cream, *201*, 202
White Chocolate Ganache Ice Cream, 200–202
White Chocolate Ganache Layer Cake with Dark Chocolate Frosting, 51
White Chocolate Ganache Marshmallow Sauce, 240
White Chocolate Ganache Whipped Cream, 238
White Chocolate Hawaiian Macadamia Nut Ice Cream, 202
White Chocolate Mixed Chip Ice Cream, 202
White Chocolate Raspberry Cheesecake, 91, 96–97
White Chocolate Sauce, 170–71
White Chocolate Toffee Pecan Ice Cream, 202
White Chocolate Whipped Butter, 247
White Chocolate "White Out" Ice Cream, 202
White-On-Black Chocolate Crème Brûlée, 164–65
Wonton wrappers
Chocolate-Peanut Butter Wontons, 37

X
Xocolatl, 9

Y
Yanomami tribe, 31–32
Yogurt
Cold-Processed Chocolate Custard Cups, 160
Yorty, Sam, 136

Z
Zallie, George, 105